Reading in Library Science

Reading in Library Science

Dr. Satya Prakash

RANDOM PUBLICATIONS
NEW DELHI (INDIA)

Reading in Library Science

ISBN 978-93-5111-948-7

Published in 2016 in India by

RANDOM PUBLICATIONS

4376-A/4B, Gali Murari Lal, Ansari Road
New Delhi-110 002
Phone : +9111-43580356, 011-23289044, 011-43142548
e-mail: sales@randompublications.com,
info@randompublications.com, randomexports@gmail.com

Reprinted 2025

Type Setting by : Friends Media, Delhi-110089
Digitally Printed at : Replika Press Pvt. Ltd.

Preface

Library science is an interdisciplinary field that applies the practices, perspectives, tools of management, information technology, and education to libraries. This also includes the preservation, organization, dissemination and collection of information resources, and the political economy of information. The first and most fundamental document activity is reading. "Reading" encompasses a broad range of complex and poorly understood practices involving documents, including skimming, searching, browsing, speed-reading, surfing, reviewing, and rereading. Although we often take it for granted, reading can be hard work. We use the term active reading to distinguish this rich collection of activities from simply looking at words on a page.

Library and Information Science (LIS) is the academic and professional study of how information and information carriers are produced, disseminated, discovered, evaluated, selected, acquired, used, organized, maintained, and managed. This book intends to introduce the reader to fundamental concerns and emerging conversations in the field of library and information science. Readers often move paper documents to avoid glare, to speed up handwriting, or to adjust their perspective of a text. In contrast, most computer displays are stationary while in use, so that readers must move themselves— their heads, their bodies, and their arms— rather than their display. XLibris supports paper document-like tangibility by running on tablet displays. Although XLibris has not been deployed for real use, people say that holding a page-sized display in their lap and being able to easily reposition it changes their online reading experience. The tangibility of paper documents also supports navigation. Turning paper pages seems easy and natural, and the weight and thickness of a paper document convey length and location.

This unique work is a completed integrated presentation of library science. It will be highly informative to information scientists, programmers, librarians, students and laymen.

– Author

Contents

1

Reading and Digital Libraries

The first and most fundamental document activity is reading. "Reading" encompasses a broad range of complex and poorly understood practices involving documents, including skimming, searching, browsing, speed-reading, surfing, reviewing, and rereading. Although we often take it for granted, reading can be hard work. We use the term *active reading* to distinguish this rich collection of activities from simply looking at words on a page.

Desktop computers do not support active reading. Once expected to create a paperless office, computers have instead produced ever-increasing quantities of paper documents. Dataquest predicts printers and copiers will generate over 1012 pages in the U.S. in 1997.

This statistic suggests that people do not use computers to read. The reason for this is obvious: paper supports extended, focused, deep reading practices better. Current research on digital libraries does not address a broad range of reading activities. Instead, as David Levy points out, digital libraries support shallower, more fragmented, and less concentrated reading.

The research focus in this field is on tools for search, selection, and distillation, tools that promote identification and extraction of information fragments. Because digital library interfaces do not support active reading, people search online and then print documents to read them. This "search and print" reality contrasts with the "search and read" ideal held by researchers.

Although a dual online/paper system is not *a priori* undesirable, we will show the many advantages of an online system that enables a variety of reading practices. The XLibris active reading machine supports a broad class of reading activities by employing a "paper document metaphor" (as opposed to the desktop metaphor) that imitates the physical experience of reading and marking on paper. The paper document metaphor follows lessons learned from a number of studies comparing reading online to reading on paper, summarized below.

TANGIBILITY

Readers often move paper documents to avoid glare, to speed up handwriting, or to adjust their perspective of a text. In contrast, most computer displays are stationary while in use, so that readers must move themselves—their heads, their bodies, and their arms— rather than their display. XLibris supports paper document-like tangibility by running on tablet displays. Although XLibris has not been deployed for real use, people say that holding a page-sized display in their lap and being able to easily reposition it changes their online reading experience. The tangibility of paper documents also supports navigation. Turning paper pages seems easy and natural, and the weight and thickness of a paper document convey length and location.

In XLibris, pressure strips on the case of the device provide a tangible interface for page turning: pressing on one side of a sensor moves to the next or previous page, and holding down initiates riffling through pages. The harder you press, the faster you move. A quick animated transition indicates the direction of turning.

Beyond Paper: Supporting Active Reading with Free-form Digital Ink Annotations

Bill N. Schilit, Gene Golovchinsky, Morgan N. Price
FX Palo Alto Laboratory, Inc.
3400 Hillview Ave., Bldg. 4
Palo Alto, CA 94304
+1 650 813-7322
{schilit, gene, price}@pal.xerox.com

ABSTRACT

Reading frequently involves not just looking at words on a page, but also underlining, highlighting and commenting, either on the text or in a separate notebook. This combination of reading with critical thinking and learning is called *active reading* [1]. To explore the premise that computation can enhance active reading we have built the XLibris "active reading machine." XLibris uses a commercial high-resolution pen tablet display along with a paper-like user interface to support the key affordances of paper for active reading: the reader can hold a scanned image of a page in his lap and mark on it with digital ink. To go beyond paper, XLibris monitors the free-form ink annotations made while reading, and uses these to organize and to search for information. Readers can review, sort and filter clippings of their annotated text in a "Reader's Notebook." XLibris also searches for material related to the annotated text, and displays links to similar documents unobtrusively in the margin. XLibris demonstrates that computers can help active readers organize and find information while retaining many of the advantages of reading on paper.

Keywords

Paper-like user interface, reading online, affordances of paper, pen computing, dynamic hypertext, document metaphor, information retrieval

INTRODUCTION

Computers, once expected to create a paper-less office, have instead produced ever-increasing quantities of paper documents. Dataquest predicts that 1,344 billion pages will be generated by printers and copiers in the US in 1997 [13]. This statistic suggests that people are not using computers to read. Whereas paper is lightweight, inexpensive, and easy to annotate, interfaces for reading online typically involve clumsy interactions with bulky desktop monitors.

Although reading online presents a number of problems, we will show that integrating computation with reading also presents novel opportunities for improving the reading process. Thus there is a tension between the advantages provided by computation and the advantages provided by paper: the choice depends on the reader's goals. For reading a romance novel at the beach, low weight and portability are essential, and it is unlikely that computation could provide any real benefits. For other, more dynamic, types of reading, however, computation may be desirable.

Active reading is the combination of reading with critical thinking and learning, and is a fundamental part of education and knowledge work. Active reading involves not just reading *per se*, but also underlining, highlighting and commenting, either on the text or in a separate notebook [1]. Readers use these marks to organize information for later review and retrieval. In addition, active reading often requires readers to move from one text to another to satisfy their information needs.

We have built an "active reading machine," XLibris, to explore the premise that computation can enhance active reading. XLibris has three major features: the paper document metaphor, a "Reader's Notebook" for organizing annotated documents, and margin links for serendipitous discovery of related material.

XLibris emulates the physical experience of reading a document on paper. The metaphor of a paper document pervades the design: the hardware approximates the form factor of a stack of paper, and the software supports a paper-like interface. Readers hold a lightweight pen tablet that displays one page of a scanned or printed document at a time. As on paper, readers can use a pen to mark anywhere on the page.

To go beyond paper, XLibris monitors free-form ink annotations that readers make as part of their existing reading practice. These annotations, replete with meaning to the reader, can also be meaningful to the system. The system can use the extent of the annotations to determine

abc abc abc play audio record audio stop audio 1 previous view next view Documents Index Clippings further reading Show Links Skim

Finally, "location guides" of varying thickness drawn in the top cor- ners of each page provide feedback about the length of the document and the reader's current location.

Page Orientation and Fixed Layout

Paper documents are laid out on fixed-size pages. The page layout often communicates the type of the document (*e.g.*, business letter versus technical article) and where to find important information (*e.g.*, a return address). The fixed layout also supports spatial memory and helps readers find old information.

In these and other ways, paper pages give readers an excellent "sense of the document." This sense of the document is often lost online.

Most CRT monitors cannot display a full page of text legibly, leading to awkward scrolling and zooming. Word processors and Web browsers commonly re-flow the text on a "page." And hypertext versions of paper documents can lead to disorientation and a sense of being lost. XLibris respects pages by displaying the image of a single page at a time.

Because the LCD panels we use are designed for landscape viewing, XLibris rotates the image 90° to approximate the portrait orientation of a typical printed page. XLibris stores the image of each page and the underlying text; this "image + text" file format is compatible with printed and with scanned documents.

Multiple Displays

People often work with multiple pieces of paper simultaneously, either with several pages from one document or with several documents. Most of today's computers provide multiple virtual displays through use of a windowing system. Unfortunately, the effort of managing window layout and switching among windows can interfere with reading.

Therefore XLibris displays a single page image and does not support windows. Since limiting the digital library information appliance to a single page image is problematic, we have considered a number of ways to address the need for collateral displays.

Presenting two full-page images side by side, as in Book Emulator, makes text unreadable on current tablet displays, but may be feasible as LCD technology evolves. A form factor with multiple physical displays is another approach.

(Bush's vision of a Memex desk included multiple displays). In our case, to maintain mobility, a book (instead of a tablet or desk) with two opposable LCD panels may be appropriate. Weiser presents an enticing vision of ubiquitous computing with devices so cheap they can be scattered and used as paper.

In the near term, however, a small number of pen computers in conjunction with nearby desktop displays or even paper may provide the most practical solution to the problem of collateral document work. In summary, XLibris employs tangibility, page orientation, and fixed layout to provide an online reading experience comparable, in many ways, to reading from paper.

FREE FORM INK ANNOTATION

"Until we provide support for smooth integration of annotation with reading, it is likely that people will continue to annotate paper materials, even as they read materials in a digital library." – Cathy Marshall The second key document activity is annotation.

Knowledge work involves reading combined with categorizing, speculating, remembering, judging, or, more broadly, critical thinking.

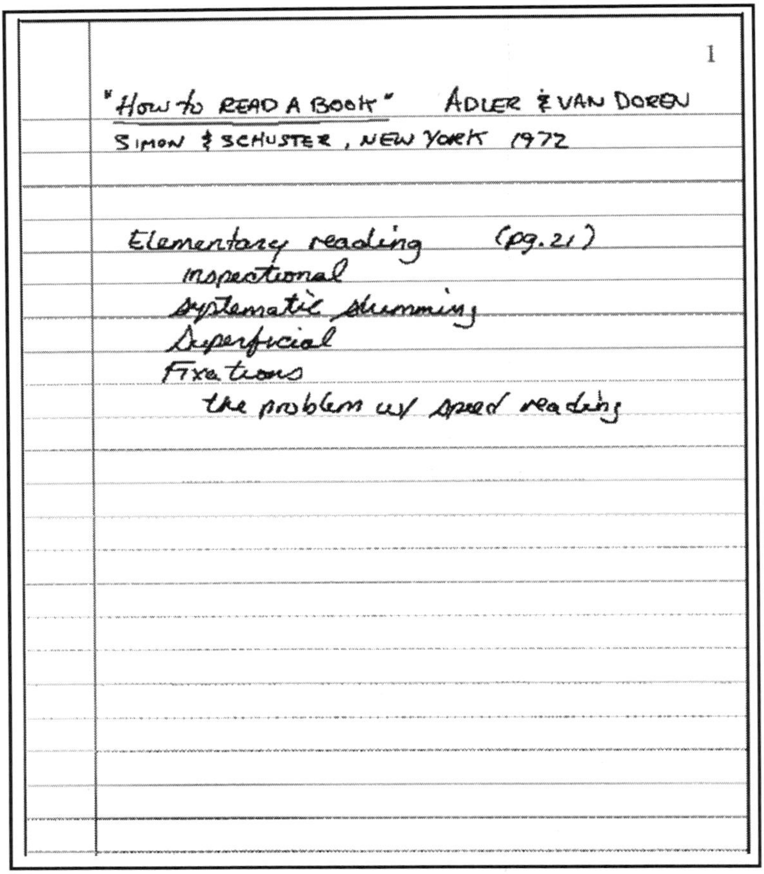

Fig. A Notebook page from XLibris.

This active reading process is facilitated by underlining, highlighting and making notes on the text or in a separate notebook. Marking on paper helps readers "make the text their own" and is a common practice associated with deep understanding of written information. In a nutshell, readers write. Unfortunately, annotation online is quite different from its paper-based cousin.

Interfaces for annotating often involve selecting a command, pointing with a mouse, and typing on a keyboard. They generally require much more effort than scribbling with a pen.

Text annotations are not as visually distinct as ink marks, and online annotations often cause changes in the layout of the document.

We believe that the ability to make unstructured, free-form, idiosyncratic ink marks is a crucial feature of any interface to digital libraries.

Although such marks may not have explicit meaning to the computer, they have rich semantic meaning, supporting visual and episodic memory. An essential aspect of ink on paper is its lack of modality: users can write anything they want, anywhere on the page.

In XLibris, we followed this principle by letting users scribble notes, draw figures, highlight, or annotate text, all without switching modes or applications. Readers highlight and mark-up document page images as they read or flip to a blank page in a lined notebook for more space. XLibris provides several colours of ink, several highlighter pens, and a stroke-based eraser.

STRUCTURE FOR BUILDING BENCH STRENGTH

SUCCESSION PLANNING AND DEVELOPMENT: WHAT IT TAKES TO SUCCEED

Succession planning and development happen only when the right ingredients are there at the start. They are

- Commitment from top management
- Ownership
- Vision of what the library needs
- Snapshot of present conditions
- Openness to non-traditional sources of talent
- Culture
- Training and development programmes
- Objectivity

COMMITMENT FROM TOP MANAGEMENT

Leadership has to see the planning and development programme as an important endeavor, one that requires focused attention and dedicated resources.

The development needed to improve a library's overall bench strength must come from *all* managers and leaders in the organization, not just a few who are exceptionally skilled at developing their staffs. In most organizations it is easy to spot the highly skilled leaders and managers; they are the people whose staffs step up to volunteer for stretch assignments, team leadership, and promotion.

They may also be the people to whose departments employees who "need a little work" are transferred, because senior leadership has confidence in their ability to help someone get on a good track and realize her potential. There will always be managers and leaders who have exceptional development skills, but an organization that depends on only a few people to develop its entire bench strength will fail. Managers and leaders must first understand the need to devote time, energy, and resources to developing staff; many of them must also strengthen their own skills and abilities in this area; and they must also encourage the managers they supervise in their long-term efforts.

Managers and leaders must understand that building bench strength is a key part of their job, not a set of new tasks that takes away from their "real work." That understanding sets in when senior leadership continues to set goals, provide resources, and hold themselves and others accountable for results.

Two library directors who have demonstrated their commitment to succession planning efforts are Charles Brown, director of libraries of the Public Library of Charlotte and Mecklenburg County (N.C.), and Patrick Losinski, executive director of the Columbus (Ohio) Metropolitan Library. They shared insights with us. When it comes to succession planning, Brown emphasizes three points. One is the importance of providing developmental opportunities so staffs are ready to move up when the time is right. The competencies he considers necessary for future leaders not only are technical but must reflect superb communications skills, a good attitude, the ability to deal effectively with change, the skill to get along with others, the vision to see beyond the four walls of the library, and a strong customer focus. A second imperative is for staff to be trained and groomed to be competitive with the best candidates from outside the library system and with each other. The Public Library of Charlotte and Mecklenburg County seeks a good, strong pool of candidates when a position opens and hopes to be able to say "a selection of one is difficult since we have four or five good candidates."

Brown embraces a big picture of staff development. Although he seeks to retain staff with high potential, he is proud of those who leave for senior positions at other library systems across the country. "Even if we lose some high potentials, it still speaks well of this library. Staff are being trained so well that other libraries want our staff." Brown's third point provides the foundation of his views on succession planning: the significance of having bench strength when a leader leaves the library system. He believes that there must be some one or preferably several internal candidates in a position to compete with the best and ready to take on any leadership position should someone retire, move on, or get hit by the metaphorical bus.

"If a leader doesn't leave a bench, I'm not sure he's been successful as a leader. That is one of the most important jobs of a leader." Columbus Metropolitan Library's evolving philosophy of succession management focuses on attracting, mentoring, and empowering people so they can compete for senior-level positions in leadership. Like Brown, Losinski wants to develop staff so they can compete for, not be awarded, positions. These library directors are looking for the best, wish to cast a wide net, and would like to see their staff strongly competing against the top people nationwide in and outside the library world. If staff members leave to join other libraries, that too is all right. Many of the directors, deputy directors, and others we spoke with are also comfortable knowing that they may lose some strong incumbents to other library systems. Losinski brought out an interesting point: "If five positions become vacant and if we fill them with outsiders, that means we don't really have a succession management plan, do we?... Clearly," he continued, "we have been inadequately preparing our people for the next level."

OWNERSHIP

The HR department may develop succession planning; it may administer it. But it *must* be sponsored and owned by management. The HR unit, as a business partner to library leadership, is vested in the continuity of the organization, but management has the vision, talent, and skills to identify the attributes of future leadership and provide development opportunities and the feedback necessary for high-potential employees to morph into leaders.

We spoke with libraries from coast to coast, and each one that considered its succession planning programme successful had one thing in common: the library director was an enthusiastic sponsor. In smaller libraries without HR departments or personnel specialists, the library director probably already takes the lead in thinking about these issues. In such circumstances, do not hesitate to ask your city or county HR staff for support. One of our clients, Patty Wong, director of Yolo County (Calif.)

Library, has created such a partnership with the Yolo County HR department, resulting in help and support with workforce and succession planning, organization design, and classification issues—all at no cost to the library.

VISION OF WHAT THE LIBRARY NEEDS

To achieve strategic alignment of your staffing with your library's needs, you must work from your library's strategic plan. You set important targets, goals, and questions during your strategic planning process. You studied the changing demographics of the library service area, how they will directly affect the library, and over what time period the changes will hit. The question now is, do you have the human capital to support your goals and make them happen?

For example, if your strategic plan calls for teaching students and seniors alike how to use social networking tools, you need to ask if you have staff with the technical, training, and interpersonal skills to do this. If not, will you train?

Develop? Hire externally? Who are your internal candidates? Why did you select them? What knowledge, skills, abilities, and competencies (characteristics that describe successful performance) have they demonstrated to enable them to undertake this training?

SNAPSHOT OF PRESENT CONDITIONS

Do whatever is necessary to get a frank, objective, and accurate understanding of the current workforce. You need a solid sense of which talents currently are found in the organization and which are currently lacking. You need a good understanding of how the skill sets will change over the planning horizon and ideas of how the library will recruit or develop these skills.

Ask the following questions:

- What is your workforce situation? What shortages will you face? Involving which skills? Where? When?
- Where and when will retirements hit you the hardest? What key skills and experience must you retain and pass along?
- What motivates staff at your library? What are their passions? Why do employees join, stay, and leave your library?
- Which skill sets and talent will move your library forward? Which will help fulfill your strategic plan and meet the needs of your customers, patrons, and taxpayers?
- From where do you recruit? What are your feeder programmes? Will this continue? Some library schools are closing; fewer people are attending library school and, given the changes in the economy, we are seeing a reluctance to move clear across the country for a job.
- What do the employees who are eligible for retirement want to do? Retire? Work at something else? Come back to the library on a part-time or substitute basis? Mentor?
- Review the "Checklist of Trends to Count On". How will you prepare for them? Record your ideas in a worksheet.

DEVELOPMENT OF TOMORROW'S DIGITAL LIBRARY

The development of tomorrow's digital library information appliances is an iterative process. Our current cycle, however, is not complete until we evaluate the ideas presented in this paper. Towards this end, we have begun a series of laboratory user interface experiments and are in the planning stage for a real-world deployment. One experiment suggests that free-form ink marks made while reading are better for query formulation than traditional relevance feedback.

People who have tried XLibris agree that our approach of taking a work practice and augmenting it— rather than redefining it— makes the system immediately accessible. Information *appliances* must be accessible. The digital library community must decide whether digital libraries should, as we propose, support users throughout the process of turning information into knowledge. If so, there are many issues that must be addressed. One reviewer of this paper asked: "Where is the digital library?" We purposely avoided describing protocols, services, and architectures because we believe infrastructure should *support* the vision of working with a digital library information appliance, not *define* it. The next step is to understand how users of digital library information appliances should interact with external repositories. For example, should users pay authors to cache documents on their devices, even when they do not read them? How should users search repositories that are not always accessible?

How should searches be distributed between local and remote databases? These and other issues require further investigation. We have shown how information appliances based on the paper document metaphor can support active reading. Because these systems allow people to work on digital documents much as they would on paper, this provides an alternative to the standard "search and print" model of digital libraries.

Furthermore, by integrating a wide variety of document activities, and by allowing fluid movement among them, disruptive transitions between paper and digital media can be eliminated. The combination of the paper-like and the digital allows us to augment these activities without redefining them. Finally, the mobility of a digital library information appliance supports work away from the desk. With all these benefits, digital library information appliances can create a rich, universally accessible, digital library experience that improves the way we work. Clearly there is an exciting future for digital library information appliances in the digital library.

DIGITAL LIBRARIANS: PRESERVING THE PAST, LOOKING FORWARD

Throughout the same eras of upheaval and change, librarians faced similarly daunting challenges. Researcher calls heralding the imminent demise of a proud profession crowded the professional literature of every specialised sector of librarianship for decades. In response, various innovators have explored a mulitiplicity of strategies. Nancy Lemon argues that rethinking traditional roles enables librarians to climb organisational "value chains;" Researchers review the plight of news media libraries and see a history of cyclical renewal, in which existing jobs give way to new opportunities in new locations. Among corporate libraries, a wide variety of bareknuckle strategies have been put forward, urging librarians to find a competitive edge by offering services that can be demonstrated to boost profits.

In the public libary sphere, despite straitened civic budgets and the shock of new media, libraries have achieved a degree of success in staying relevant. Circulation, library card membership and on-site use of services are at an all-time high, countering the idea that community libraries are outdated during the digital era. On the contrary, they are more popular than ever.

Therefore even as pessimism about the future became a standard feature in the professional literature, a parallel stream of daring and innovative thinking has run concurrently among a wide spectrum of library specialists. The resulting intellectual ferment has produced new paradigms and new energy for rethinking library goals in light of the emergence of digital technology. Rather than wait to see what would happen, librarians repeatedly took initiative with new media. They staked an early claim on the crucial issue of intellectual property and copyright, working both with and against publishers as needed to preserve the library's public service mission. As part of this process, librarians became more deeply aware of the publishing industry's travails with digital media. This awareness led to greater strategic knowledge about the marketplace.

Spanning "Online" Eras

Librarians were shaken by the rapid emergence of Web-based information resources, because they had been important players in the previous "online" economy that was dominated by firms like LEXIS/NEXIS and Dialog Information Services. This first "online" era gave librarians the opportunity to cast themselves as experts who conducted mediated searches on behalf of users such as attorneys, scientists and business leaders. As the initial "online" era faded and the Internet exploded into growth, librarians joined the first wave of Internet e-mail "conversationalists", Web content users, Web site producers, and aggregators of high quality information.

They also grasped the importance of creating stable and robust Web portals, which organised and "branded" library-hosted aggregations of databases; such activist strategies stretched scarce budgets while formalising a Web-based library presence. Similarly, the economic upheaval caused by the skyrocketing price of scholarly journals generated energetic responses on the part of research libraries, including formation of the Scholarly Publishing and Academic Resources Coalition (SPARC), as well as active congressional lobbying to protect copyright and "fair use" principles from a runaway marketplace.

The same upheaval also sparked a sustained outreach to faculty, in search of much stronger partnerships with the academy's principle content creators. In general, digital librarians have been agents for innovation over the past 15 years, and have participated in the sweeping process of rethinking scholarly communications.

This lengthy process of trial and error has transformed digital librarians' self-perception. Rather than viewing digital media as a force of dislocation that would bring ruin to the profession, digital librarians have instead embraced it. Likewise, constant downward pressure on budgets forced innovative survival plans to the forefront, emphasising new technologies.

From Online Repository to Publishing Platform

The turmoil of the Internet's early years also produced solid initiatives to understand the digital library as a publisher in its own right. Thomas provides an early and comprehensive road map that offers large research libraries a template for launching high quality publishing services. She also describes the early emergence of online repositories as a new form of curated information resources. Online repositories grew quickly throughout the early years of the twenty-first century, taking much inspiration from the digital archiving efforts of the computer science and engineering fields.

Librarymanaged repositories also grew up with a strong bias for interoperability, which has led to more dialogue about the need for large-scale "federations" of digital libraries, even at the international level. As these repositories became more accepted, use skyrocted. The University of California's eScholarship repository experienced more than one million downloads in its first two years of operation. "Post prints" and research reports are now also collected in online repositories, and are frequently overseen by digital librarians, or at least coordinated by them.

In late 2009, eScholarship recast itself as a full-scale "publishing platform," which drew strength from the reputation of its source - the University of California system. Although this is not the only example of a library-sponsored publishing service with university imprimatur, it is certainly one of the most high profile experiments. The evolution of library-based online repositories and their current transformation into fullscale publishing platforms is a prime example of how contributors can expand their role and move into new "zones of progressive release". Digital librarians' publishing solutions are guided by two objectives: first, to empower authors, and second, to create robust, collaborative blocs of institutions that share expertise and improve access. These are new "treatments" that address the changing needs of academic publishing. Publishers are rushing to reinvigourate their relationships with authors, but to some degree they are playing a game of catch-up.

Metadata as Enhanced Competency

Perhaps the most significant advance on the part of digital librarians has been the profession's embrace of structured metadata and taxonomy as a reinvigourated core competency. Even as they faced the twin challenges of integrating new technologies and shrinking budgets, digital librarians participated in the formation of international metadata standards such as the Dublin Core.

Libraries became key institutional members of new groups such as the Coalition for Networked Information and the National Digital Library Federation. Academic librarians experimented with diverse forms of preservation, including digital repositories, e-journals, and increasingly, full-scale publishing initiatives that originate within the library. Many metadata platforms and languages have been explored, but Extensible Markup Language (XML) has become a dominant tool for managing digital assets.

XML is a "meta-language of languages," enabling developers to create taxonomies and metadata schema that are customisable, portable and attached to the "digital objects" they describe. The emergence of national and international standards for metadata, the ascendance of digital objects which are transferrable among collections, and a strong focus on systems interoperability have elevated the library profession to a technical status considerably higher than it enjoyed before the advent of the digital era. Although digital librarians are not the only XML developers - many computing firms and other academics are heavily involved—they have left an imprint on the development stream of XML.

XML-based systems have become accepted across many industries beyond the academy, and now play a crucial role in information management and data warehousing by large corporate firms. XML-based information architectures are essential tools for managing text, images and other artifacts, creating new workflows that are based on the principle of "one text, multiple outputs".This kind of workflow would transfer very effectively to the publishing world, yet the publishing industry has been slower to adopt XML workflows at a universal level. The opportunity to manage digital assets using XML is an important leap forward that publishers have not yet fully embraced, and forward-looking commentators have recognised this shortfall.

PERSPECTIVE OF THE DIGITAL LIBRARY FUNDERS

The primary funders of digital library research in the U.S. were the NSF, within the Directorate for Computer and Information Science (CISE), DARPA, NASA, and NIH, with lesser contributions from NEH, IMLS (Institute of Museum and Library Services), and the Library of Congress. The notable characteristic of all the primary funders is their focus on technology-oriented science, in contrast to social science, humanities, or arts.

This focus is reflected in a research programme that funded mainly core computer science and its applications to networked information, with very little attention to network information as a sociotechnical phenomenon. In fact, the first phase of Digital Library Initiative (DLI) funding was exclusively technical.

This was moderated somewhat in the second phase. Influenced by the results of a 1996 NSF workshop that called for increased research on the social aspects of digital libraries, the NSF included social science research in the DLI-2 solicitation. An examination of documents published early in the digital library effort reveals the underlying assumptions and biases of the lead agencies that shaped the nature of the funding programmes and their vision of the digital libraries that would emerge from it.

Although it appeared in a visionary 1988 document from Kahn and Cerf, the term "digital libraries" was introduced into the national research agenda in February 1994 in a report from a task force on Information Infrastructure Technologies and Applications (IITA). This report was commissioned by the newly funded High Performance Computing and Communications programme, which was formed to leverage advances in computing and networking for the general social benefit.

The report defines digital libraries as follows:

- "[Digital libraries are] both technologies and applications which will lead to significant advances in the generation, storage, and use of digital information of different kinds across high speed networks. A digital library is a knowledge center without walls, open 24 hours a day and accessible by way of a network. Research areas range from advanced mass storage, online capture of multimedia data, intelligent filtering, knowledge navigation, effective user interfaces, system integration, to prototyping and technology demonstration".

The list of research areas enumerated in this statement is notable for its omission of the implications of eliminating the "walls", or a being open "24 hours a day." Clearly, the impression of the task force, or at least the only concern, was that the transfer of information to an online form raised only technical issues and that the larger social issues raised by this transfer were either inconsequential, unforeseen, or not worthy of study.

Another report from the same era, authored by Gladney and Fox, demonstrates prevailing thinking of the time that perhaps underlies this decision by the funders to focus only on technical issues:

- "The concept "library" has been refined over several centuries. It would be injudicious to depart from what people expect merely because a digital service is replacing a material one. Except where explicit reasons suggest an improvement that is easily explained to ordinary users (*e.g.*, in query services), library services should implement a familiar model".

Implicit in this text is the assumption that the nature of the institution and the information model it entails should remain as a stable overlay on a changed technical foundation. A digital library should, by nature, imply the same notions of integrity, trust, and quality, historically associated with libraries.

Books might turn into bits, the catalogue might become an online database, and shelves might turn into repositories, but the values, structures, and practices of the "institution" should be based on a "familiar model." Even as the web continue to grow in importance and scale, the notion that digital libraries were the focus for "serious" information-oriented activities persisted.

The web was relegated to a more lowbrow status–an unfiltered mishmash of questionable and frequently objection-able content. For example, a 2001 (U.S.)

President's Information Technology Advisory Committee report called the web a "rudimentary" information environment that "only hint[s] at the future of digital libraries".

Even if the funding agencies had decided that the broader implications of the transfer of information to the online environment deserved investigation, it is doubtful whether they were structurally configured to handle such investigations.

In a retrospective on the Digital Libraries Initiatives, Griffin takes note of the problem that agencies such as the NSF have with research that is by nature long-term: "The programme funding models did not work optimally, particularly for the mid-size, longer-term, interdisciplinary research and test bed projects."

PERSPECTIVE OF THE COMPUTER SCIENCE RESEARCH COMMUNITY

The computer science research community had every incentive to follow the funding agencies in this selective interpretation of digital library research. The DL initiatives were a new and relatively large stream of funding for extending their pre-existing database and information retrieval research into a new application area.

As stated by researchers: "The computer scientists] could see, or at least imagine, *how current library functions would be moved forward by an injection of computing insight*".

The computer scientists who dominated DL research had little interest in examining the nature of "current library functions" or in understanding how the "injection of computing insight" might affect the foundations of these functions. The library was really only a convenient platform for technically focused work.

Indeed as researchers noted the computer science researchers had little patience for the less technically manageable aspects, and "nagging downsides" of digital library research. For example, issues related to copyright and intellectual property were perceived as an annoyance that interfered with work on more interesting technical problems.

Furthermore, the work often required collaboration with librarians who seemed overly focused on metadata "that the computer scientists felt would be replaceable by just another clever search algorithm improvement".

In hindsight, the attraction of the computer science research community to the field of digital libraries was really not based on special allegiance to the library notion, but was just a case of following the funding. When the funding disappeared and it became obvious that the web was a more attractive, and less restrictive environment for studying and exercising emerging computer science techniques such as machine learning, many of the former prominent members of the digital library community disappeared.

PERSPECTIVE OF THE LIBRARY COMMUNITY

The "real" librarians, those with over a century-long tradition collecting, curating, and preserving books and other materials, entered the realm of digital libraries with a consider-ably more institutionally-focused definition of the library and vision of what the digital library would look like.

From their perspective the library, as an institution, had successfully managed previous transitions to new media (the transition of the printed form from scrolls to the codex book to the printed book, the inclusion of recordings, etc.) and had a track record of incorporating new technology into established practices, such as the computer-based catalogue.

The "digital" library would be just another library and through all, the venerable institution would prevail:

- The functions of the librarian have always been to select the material that his constituents will require. to catalogue it so that those who would use it can know what is available and where it is. and to preserve it so that both contemporary readers and those who will follow will be able to use it...none of these tasks will disappear with the emergence of the electronic library. Somebody will have to perform them: if not the librarian, then his replacement. The anarchy of the Internet may be daunting for the neo-phyte, but it differs little from the bibliographic chaos that is the result of five and a half centuries of the printing press.

Because of this allegiance to the institutional basis of the library and the belief that it was a necessary component of a useful information environment, librarians vigourously resisted the encroachment of the web on the domain formally dominated by the library. For librarians the intrusion of the web into the work on digital libraries was much more difficult to integrate.

Initially, they were largely dismissive and disdainful of the web as a serious information space, declaring that the "web is not a library" and likening it to a bookstore in which "the entire stock is just piled up in the middle of the floor". As the amount of valuable content increased on the web, they responded with efforts to fold the web into standard operations, such as cataloguing.

While these efforts to catalogue the web were ultimately abandoned, they demonstrate how persistent traditional practices can be even in the face of a rapidly changing technical landscape. In summary, the application of the library concept to the uncharted and unruly context of networked information reveals the distinctly narrow and flawed assumptions of the three parties responsible for its origin and use.

The funding agencies mistakenly assumed that they could fund (and shape) the development of a new information infrastructure as a mainly technical endeavour. The computer scientists followed suit by framing digital libraries by-and-large as applications of familiar distributed database problems in which "predictable, repeatable ... access and retrieval is a prime value." In fact, the unpredictability of the web and its seemingly autonomous dynamism has not only affected our perceptions of information use and management, but it has had a far-reaching effect on computer science shifting it from its deterministic, algorithmic foundations to a more probabilistic and socially-oriented focus.

Finally, the librarians assumed that they could safely wrap radically new technology and traditional organizational values and structures in the same embrace. In combination, these flawed assumptions lead to a research area that by and large treads the middle ground.

At a fine granular level, it produced a number of interesting research results and applications of those results. But, at the higher level, it failed to explore the more far-reaching questions of how putting information online and giving people power over their information might change the nature of the information and the way people use it.

It is useful in closing this part to quote Agre who, "Information and institutional change", spoke of the dangers of naively mixing historical forms with innovations:

- A concept of "library" that is too fully rooted in past historical forms will make innovation impossible, but a superficial concept of "library" that draws out only a few aspects of those past historical forms (for example, a library as a big container of documents) will pass over phenomena whose absence in a newly designed system may be fatal. The middle ground between the maximal and simplistic conceptions of "library" is enormous and is not easily mapped.

OPENNESS TO NON-TRADITIONAL SOURCES OF TALENT

If library leaders continue to look for employees in traditional labour markets, they may fail. More likely, leadership will have to redefine the ideal worker, who may be part-time, multilingual, young, telecommuting, or not a librarian. Alternatives to traditional working hours and locations will facilitate staffing. This is increasingly true as family patterns change and gas prices continue to rise and fall. Rethink the work as well as the worker. When do you need an MLS-prepared librarian and when are you filling the vacancy with a candidate with an MLS just because you always have? Maybe you could consider a teacher instead of a children's librarian, maybe a library associate with supervisory experience to supervise circulation or a party planner to run your events.

CULTURE

Managers and leaders must be, or must learn to be, comfortable identifying and discussing high, medium, and low performers as well as high, medium, and low potential for increased responsibilities and promotional opportunities. It is also helpful if there is an effective performance management system in place and supervisors are able to coach and provide feedback.

We cannot say enough about this. So often, employees do not get a clear and specific message about what their performance goals are, and what specifically they are doing that is on- or off-track. It is impossible for someone to learn what to start, stop, or continue doing unless a manager provides feedback that is clear, honest, and direct. A wonderful example of managers handling staff members' questions and concerns comes from Pat Olafson, the HR director of Sno-Isle Libraries.

We asked her if there is any jealousy among staff not given the opportunities afforded to those who have been tapped for additional development in the library's succession planning programme. Olafson did not hesitate in her answer. She did not equivocate, fall into the fairness and equity rap, or indicate any defensive posture or avoidance with employees. She said simply that when that occurs she responds, and encourages managers to respond, as follows:

- I understand that you are concerned that you are not given development opportunities. Let's talk about your performance. Are there any issues with your performance? If so, how can you correct them? If not, have you let your supervisor know that you are interested in these opportunities? What opportunities do think you are ready to tackle? Why? Let's look at your résumé. Let's talk about your talents vis-à-vis the library's leadership competencies. Let's talk about what you can do so that you are someone senior staff seeks out for development.

Your programme will be supported even further if managers and leaders are held accountable through their own performance review process for staff development. This will take time and becomes a critical competency for this process. It also takes commitment and honesty—and practice.

TRAINING AND DEVELOPMENT PROGRAMMES

Succession planning works best when the library already has a culture of learning and development. If yours does not have one, this is the time to begin to institute it. Whether or not you go forward with a succession planning and development process, the type and pace of change we all live in requires continuous learning, and learning how to learn. "Just in time" learning and development, though important for technical and other skills, is insufficient to cultivate new leadership over a period of years. It takes foresight and patience to get there.

Leadership development is a key activity of many libraries across the county. Leadership skills are needed across the library of today and in the library today's leaders will leave behind.

OBJECTIVITY

Leaders must be able to put aside their biases about employees and positions and keep an open mind about both. As hard as it is, this is the time to let go of the preconceptions we have about a staff member and focus on her performance and potential and not on poor performance ten years ago that has improved measurably over the years. This is also the time to keep an open mind about hidden talents in employees that to date have not even been considered.

You may find yourself being very surprised. Likewise, you may be so accustomed to hiring someone with a particular credential to fill a position that you do not stop to question what the position requires today—and will require in the next few years. "The way we've always done it" might not be the best way to do it now.

BUILDING LIBRARY RESOURCES AND SERVICES

The libraries in adult education set ups are, by design, small budget libraries, confined to one room space, and adult education staff manages them manually on part time basis. Such members of adult educators who do not have any formal education and training in library and information science would find it easy and simple to learn library skills and apply them for building library collections and rendering library services.

They can take the following step-by-step approach:

- *Step 1:* Acquisition Procedures
- *Step 2*: Classification and Cataloguing Procedures
- *Step 3:* Library Services

STEP 1: ACQUISITION PROCEDURES

Library acquisition is about procedures for selection of published material for library acquisition, procedures for placing orders for purchase books and other reading material, their accessioning as well as of material received as gratis. It also about procedures for payment of bills, and about upkeep and maintenance of records as required for the purpose.

Procedure for Book Selection

The first step in book selection operations is to invite recommendations from users for purchase of new books and other reading material. For this, the library could take initiative by inviting books on approval from booksellers, or give users publisher catalogues for selection, or send them to visit book exhibitions. Based on this exercise, a tentative listing of useful books is complied.

The second step is to get the compiled list of books approved by the Library Advisory Committee. The Committee might approve it in total or shortlist it as per their judgement. While finalizing books and other reading materials for purchase, the Committee should pay special attention to the usefulness of the selected material, currency of information given in the books, their cost and availability of funds. The book selection exercise should be undertaken on regular basis through out the year, and not towards the end of the financial year once, just to exhaust book budget.

Procedure for Book Purchase

The second step in book acquisitions is to initiate action for placing orders with the approved vendors or booksellers for selected books. In this regard, the Library needs to obtain first the financial sanction of the competent authority in the organisation. It could be either head of the organisation, or its deputy or any other designated person for the purpose. For operational performance, it will be useful if the In-Charge Library is given financial authority to sanction expenditure, say, up to ₹5000/-only in respect of such books and other reading material as recomm-ended by the Library Advisory Committee.

The library should by default purchase only latest edition of a book, unless desired otherwise specifically. Sometimes cheap editions of foreign books are printed. In such cases, it is advisable to go for cheaper editions only. However, if one of the roles of the library is to archive books for future, in such a case the library should purchase books printed on good quality paper. The Library may draw up a panel of vendors/booksellers as per following criteria.

It may purchase books from booksellers on the panel:

- Bookseller must have membership of the Delhi State Booksellers Association/Federation of Indian Publishers;
- Bookseller must have experience in the line for at least two years;
- Must have PAN Number from the Income Tax;
- The panel may be reviewed every year for performance on the parameters of relevance, quality and compre-hensiveness of the books displayed for approval or on the parameter of efficiency and effectiveness with which the bookseller supplied books against order.

The next step is to place formal orders with approved for purchase of books. There is no need for inviting quotations since as per financial rules of the Government of India books are not store items. Purchase orders can be placed on the catalogue price of the book. As per standard practice, booksellers offer discount on the catalogue price of books, ranging from 10 to 15 per cent.

Books priced in foreign currencies are to be paid in Rupee currency. The foreign currency conversion is done as per bank's TT selling rate as prevalent on the day of the supply of books. Information about bank conversion rate can be had from newspapers such as The Economic Times, and The Financial Times. The booksellers are required to supply books along the bill in triplicate. One copy of bill is to be returned to the bookseller duly signed as a token of receipt of books supplied. The library should insist on price proof of the book and bank conversion rate from the booksellers before accepting the supply of books.

Accession of Books

Libraries need to maintain records of the books acquired in accession register. This register constitutes a permanent record of the library. Figure below shows a sample outline of columns of an accession registers. Printed accession registers are also available in the market. Before accessioning, the library needs to physically check the books supplied against order in terms of latest edition, year of publication, and price. The next step in book acquisition is accession of books by making record entries in the accession register, wherein each book is assigned an accession number.

This number is reproduced later on several different pages in the book accessioned such as:

- Back of the title page–bottom portion,
- Secret page in a book. (This is a discrete page in a book which invariably carries its accession number. The secret page number is known only to the library staff and hence it is known as a secret page); and
- On the last page of the book; and on all the copies of the bill/cash memo.

Date	Accession Number	Author	Title	Ed	Place and Publisher	Year of Publi-cation	Vol	Pages	Cost	Vendor	Bill No and Date	Remarks

Fig. A Sample Outline of Columns of Accession Register

Printed accession registers are available in multiple of 1000 entries per register with a minimum of 5000 entries. Accession register starts from accession number 1 and goes up to 5000. Additional accession register, if required, should begin in continuation of the last accession number in the previous register. Avoid overwriting and cuttings of any kind in the Accession register.

The competent authority in the Library must affix a certificate in the beginning pages of the Accession Register certifying that 'This register contains...(so many) pages in which accession number run from...to....." While making entry in the Accession register it is advisable to use ink of lasting quality so that its colour doesn't fade away with the passage of time. The Accession register is a valuable document and must be kept under lock and key when not in use. After accessioning, books stamped bearing the name of the library. Book tag, book plate, book card pockets and due date slip are to be pasted at the appropriate places in the book as decided upon by the library.

STEP 2: CLASSIFICATION AND CATALOGUING PROCEDURES

Each accessioned book is classified, for assigning it a unique (numeric or alphanumeric) call number and catalogued to facilitate its access and retrieval from the card catalogue by author, title, subject and call number. The call number of the book is reproduced on the back of the title page, book plate and on the book card. The book card records necessary information about the book such as its accession number, author, and title. After verifying all these details, the book is released for circulation.

Classification

One of the major management tasks of the librarian is to organise the reading material for browsing, searching and retrieval by subject and language. The job of classifier involves giving each book in the library a unique numeric or alphanumeric number called 'Call Number'—as per library parlance. This number defines placement/shelving position of the book in the stacks. The other objective of call number is to bring books on the same subject together for browsing and retrieval.

According to Ranganathan a classified arrangement should be such that the library staff is able to:

- Locate a book demanded by a reader immediately even if the library has miles of shelves of books;
- Replace the book at its correct place on the shelf;
- Find out a proper place for a newly purchased book among other books on the same subject;
- Find a place for a new book on a new subject among the already existing books on related subjects.

Choice of the Scheme of Classification

Quite a few schemes of classification have been in use in libraries. These include Colon Classification, Dewey Decimal Classification, Universal Decimal Classification, and Library of Classification, etc. Some of the small libraries design and develop their local scheme of classification. Applying an established and widely used scheme of classification is always better than designing and developing a local one. This gives the library the benefit of continuity in experience in classifying documents and to build thereby the foundation for the future.

Most libraries use *Dewey Decimal Classification* (DDC). It is now running into 22nd edition. This speaks volumes about its popularity amongst libraries throughout the world. One of the advantages of using DDC is that it can be adapted to the needs of any large or small library. Its abridged editions are designed to meet the special requirements of small libraries. This schedule alone may not be found adequate to represent all the facets of a subject.

Therefore, the use of the Standard Subdivisions of 1000 classes at times may be found necessary to separate a book from other books having the same ultimate class. These standard subdivisions are not in themselves class number and hence can't be used in isolation, but may be suffixed/and added to any number from the schedule.

Cataloguing

A library catalogue is a vital link between the reader and the book. It serves as the key to ascertain the availability of wanted book in a library and its physical location in the stacks. Conventionally, cataloguing of books in libraries is done by using standard cataloguing codes such as *Anglo-American Cataloguing Rules* (AACR), Classified Cataloguing Code.

According to these cataloguing codes, the levels of catalo-guing differ from library to library. For example, a major library may apply for highest level of cataloguing, in which information that goes into the cataloguing entry is very extensive and detailed. However, a small library set up—like the one in adult education organisations—could consider going in for lowest level of cataloguing, in which the elements that go into the cataloguing entry are minimal to ensure access and retrieval of a book by author, title, and subject. A sample catalogue entry using AACR2 code is given below for illustration. This entry is made on a model on 5"x3" cataloguing card.

Main Entry and Added Entry Cards

The cataloguing can be done by using cataloguing software or manually. If a library plans to go in for manual cataloguing, cataloguing entries are to be made on 5"x3" card catalogues. For every book, main entry as per sample given above is made. Additional entries are made in case the book has more than one author. Additional entries are also made for access by title and subject. For making added entry cards, main entry card is made in duplicate, and search element such as second author, title, or subject heading is imposed on the top of each duplicated card. For example, if there are two authors then there would one added entry card for the second author, the first author has already been given access point in the main entry card.

Catalogues are of different types such as author catalogue, title catalogue, or subject catalogue. Each catalogue type has catalogue entry cards arranged alphabetically. These different types of catalogue entries can also be merged together and filed in a single sequence. Such a catalogue is known as dictionary catalogue.

For convenience in searching information from the cataloguing tray, for every bunch of 100 cards, guide cards is inserted. Appropriate starting letters in the alphabetical sequence are inscribed on the guide cards. The cataloguing tray can hold 1000-1500 catalogue cards.

STEP 3: LIBRARY SERVICES

The services offered by libraries can be grouped as conventional library services and the services for promoting library use:

- Conventional Library Services
  - Library Rules
  - Circulation: Issue and Return of Books
  - Inter-Library Loan Service
- Service Promoting Library Use
  - Initiation/Orientation Service
  - Reference Service
  - Current Awareness Service
  - New Books Display
  - Thematic Display
  - Press Clipping Service

Let us first discuss conventional library rules and then deal with service promoting library use.

Conventional Library Services

Library Rules

Every library frames a set of rules for regulating its services to members. Rules are framed keeping in mind the library objectives and members interests. As far as possible rules should be explicit, free from any ambiguity.

The basic issues addressed in framing library rules are the following:

- Who can use the library?
- Opening and closing hours of the library
- How many books can a member borrow at a time?
- For how long can the member retain borrowed books?
- Conditions of loan, find for the late return of books, loss or damage of books during the loaned period
- Reservation of books
- Recall of issued books
- Renewal of loans
- Suspension of membership privileges
- Personal books/property counter, etc.

Circulation: Issue and Return of Books

Circulation means issuing books to valid members on loan, and canceling loans them from issue records upon return of books by members. It is one of the most important activities of a library from users' perspective. For managing circulation, the library needs a proper circulation system designed and developed for the effective control of circulation operations in terms of time per transactions, manpower deployment requirement, and accuracy in record keeping.

The manual systems currently in use are:

- 'Newark' system,
- 'Browne' system,
- 'Passbook' system.

Of all these systems, Browne system of issue and return is most popular for its efficiency in time per transaction. It is therefore important that a library in the adult education set up may apply Browne system for managing its circulation operations.

Browne System

In Browne system, the members are given Reader's Ticket(s) to enable them to borrow books from the library. The design of the reader ticket is such that it has a pouch on its front side. The pouch is used to hold Book card when a book is issued to a member. For every library book, a Book card is made. It is kept inside the 'Book Pocket' provided in the book. While issuing a book the Circulation-in-Charge simply removes the Book Card from the Book Pocket and inserts it in the Reader's Ticket pouch, puts in due date stamp on the date slip provided in the book.

The 'Book Card' coupled with the 'Reader's Ticket' is arranged behind date guides in the charging tray. This is the simplest of all the methods for issue and return of books. It reduces paper work in managing circulation transactions to the bare minimum. At the time of receiving books from the borrowers, Book card is separated from the Reader's Ticket and it is inserted back in the Book Pocket of the book received. At the close of the day, the issue record is got rearranged and filed behind Due Date guides. For books not received by due date, it is a good practice to send reminders to the borrowers for returning the overdue books. Secondly, the library may consider giving grace period to members before issuing such reminders.

Late Fine

Though it may be unfair to impose fines for the late return of borrowed books, yet it is essential in a library to enforce discipline amongst members. This is done mainly as a deterrent since the amount collected as fine is always very trivial. Formal receipt is, however, issued after realizing late fee money from defaulters in cash. As far as possible, a library in an adult education set up may not resort to this system unless it is warranted by circumstances.

Conscience Box

An alternative to fine system for late return of books is Conscience Box. This concept was designed and developed by Dr S R Ranganathan. In this method no formal receipt is issued to the borrower, instead money as overdue charges is dropped in the Consciences Box. The key to this Box always remains with the authority in the organisation. The Conscience Box is opened at a convenient time in the presence of several officials. The distinct advantage of this method is that it saves time and develops in members a feeling of civic sense and responsibility.

Reservation of Books

Books in heavy demand usually remain in circulation. Members in the waiting list could reserve such books so that they could get the priority in borrowing them upon their receipt in the library. The library informs the member in the waiting list about the availability of the reserved book.

Loss of Books

Books reported as lost by borrowers are required to be dealt as per library rules. Usually, the borrower is advised to replace the book with a new copy. If, however, the book is out of stock in the market, he may be asked to pay the current price of the book after getting it verified from the Publisher's catalogue or from trade bibliographies. The price may also be got ascertained from the Accession Register and formal receipt issued to the borrower. Necessary postings may be done in the Accession Register indicating in the Remarks Column about the 'Lost and cost realised vide receipt no...dated....'

Inter-Library Loan Service

Every library has a liaison with other libraries in the vicinity. In case of urgent requirements, the resource of such nearby libraries could be harnessed for borrowing books on inter-library loan, or get a photocopy made of the wanted material. The library in the adult education set up could consider building such type of cooperative networks for the purpose.

Service Promoting Library Use

You can use the following devices to promote the use of library by adult members of a community.

Initiation/Orientation Service

For most of users, a visit to the library is the first encounter with the world of books. The users have to be made aware of the privileges they are entitled to as also the rules they are to follow to derive full benefits from the library. There are certain 'do's and don'ts which need to be explained to users at the time of their first formal visit to the library. This information is given to new members upon registration during initiation/orientation service. This service is also important for inculcating reading habits in neo-literates.

Reference Service

Reference service is a reactive service given to members on demand. In an adult education set up, the emphasis in reference service should be on giving knowledge and not just information or documents.

Current Awareness Service

For promoting library services, the library needs to offer proactive services such as current awareness service, selective dissemination of information service, etc.

Display

All the books added into the library stock must be put on display for limited period so as to bring them to the notice of all library users. On special occasions, such as birth day of an important author or leader, festivals, sport events, relevant books may be separated from the general sequence and put on a display to bring them to the notice of users.

Press Clipping Service

Newspapers are the most important sources of latest information. It would be most appropriate if the relevant cuttings of write-ups, editorials letters, statements, news items, events etc. are organised in some logical order for future reference and use.

DIGITAL ARCHIVING: INDIAN SCENARIO

Before the advent of digital video storage analog recordings on films and video tapes were placed on the shelves with a card catalogue. Whenever the library has to make room for the inclusion of new material, some of the old materials were removed and stored off-site, which is properly viewed as an archive. These analog and physical archives had limited shelf life depending on the medium on which the content is stored. In the digital age archiving is in the digital form-that is migrating the content electronically to new media for the purpose of preservation.

The classic meaning of archiving is:

- To place the documents in a secure place for presentation.
- To remove the data or documents from common use and conserve for future use.

The word *'Archive'* derives from the Greek word *Arkheia* meaning "Public records". The word denotes local, regional and national government collections of documents and other records kept for consultation and research purposes. One of the earliest digital-archives was a use-net news group called Talkorigins, which was devoted to mainstream theories in geology, biology, cosmology, theology etc. Contributions arguing the Darwinian evolutionary line were posed and often sent to bear all the hallmarks of serious research arguments and bibliographic referencing.

DIGITAL ARCHIVING

Digitization is sometimes recommended as a preservation strategy for materials that are in fragile formats and which are not in frequent use. Images and audio-visual materials are being stored in digital formats more than ever before, for example, digitizing pages of delicate manuscripts, preserving images of texts which are important for scholars. The primary goal of digital archiving is the storage, retrieval and access of rare documents with the aid of electronic technology for image capturing and reproducing.

The aim is to create conditions, whereby the researcher can consult the manuscripts without physically handling the individual items and at the same time the artistic quality of the calligraphy and decoration of the manuscripts could be preserved for future generation. In each and every country of the world the *National Archives department* is responsible for the preservation of important documents of that particular nation. Digital Archives can be defined as Repositories of digital information, that are collectively responsible for ensuring through the exercise of various migration strategies, that the integrity and long term accessibility of the nation's social, economic, cultural and intellectual heritage is preserved in digital form.

ADVANTAGES OF DIGITIZATION

The most promising strategy for saving the intellectual and artistic content of endangered volumes is to transform or convert it to a different medium by copying it to a film or digital form. Digital archiving is a recent work of digital libraries and ensures long term storage and access. By digitizing the documents, lots of space can be saved-a stack of CD's will take much lesser space compared to the space occupied if the same information was to be stored as hard copies. In addition, Electronic-files can be accessed from any where, at any time and at a cheaper price.

MIGRATION OF DIGITAL INFORMATION

Refreshing digital information by copying it from medium to medium and the possibility of maintaining a complex set of emulators describe two distinct points on a continuum of approaches to preserving digital information. It is a periodic transfer of digital material from one hardware and software configuration to another or from one generation of computer technology to a subsequent generation.

CREATION OF INFORMATION IN DIGITAL FORM

Information objects in digital form have to be created, edited described and indexed, annotated, revised, re-created, modified, disseminated and retained for future use, by a complex interwoven community of creators and other owners, value-added services and institutional and individual users. The process of preserving digital information will vary with different kinds of objects like textual, numeric, image, video, sound, multimedia simulation etc.

ORGANIZATION OF DATA

Before scanning the documents for digitization, one has to organize the data, that is to be archived, so that the process will go on in a smooth way and the scanned data can be retrieved properly.

The most important steps which are to be followed are given below:

- Organize the data that is to be archived in to files.
- Decide how to organize the scanned file, for example-by subject, by code number, by chrono-logical order, by keyword, by author, by title etc.
- File names should be clearly identified, so that one can easily recognize the contents of the file.
- All the files or documents which are to be scanned should be kept in order.
- All the staples and paper pins, if present, should be removed.
- The paper folds and creases in the paper should be smoothened out.

Scanners

Different scanners are available for scanning the docu-ments but one has to select the scanner on the basis of materials, like

- Vacuum-fed belt scanners–can be used for fragile and odd shaped material.
- Plane-protected wide-angle scanners–can be used for book scanning.
- High-volume scanners can be used for–architectural drawings and other oversize materials.
- Flat-bed scanners can be used for–delicate and fragile materials.

METHOD OF SCANNING

After deciding the type of scanner and type of material to be used, one has to decide whether to scan the documents as images or with OCR (Optical Character Recognition).If the document is scanned with OCR, the files need to be saved in the form of application for easy editing. The benefit of OCR is that the documents are converted to an editable format. If the document is to be archived to maintain the integrity of the records for preserving, they should be scanned as images. The documents should be scanned at a minimum resolution of 150 ppi, through 300 ppi, for future use or print.

The choices available for saving the documents as images are:-

- *BMP:* Bit Map is the native image format for the windows operating system and will provide high quality images.

- *TIFF:* Tagged Image File Format is very detailed and it is supported by many operating systems.
- *JPEG:* Joint Photographic Experts Group format comprises the data, but it is enough for normal use.

STORAGE METHOD

When all the documents are scanned, they should be saved on CD zip disks or floppy disks or tape drives. For storing the files on the disks, labeled folders should be created, the disks as well as the disk cases should be labeled. In digital archives there may be many levels of storage on the basis of expected use for the retrieval. Seldom-used material may be stored offline, usually in tape media, which is less expensive. The data which is in high demand and where retrieval time is at a premium, online storage in magnetic media may serve best.

An intermediate solution is near-line storage, where the data can be stored on optical or tape media and loaded in jute box, which is more responsive to users demand than offline storage. The most promising strategy for saving the intellectual and artistic content of endangered volumes is to transform or convert it to a different medium by copying it to a film or digital form. Paper documents can be transferred to microfilms, DVD's (Digital Video Data) and CD-ROM's (Compact Disk Read Only Memory).This process is known as Archiving. Digital archives can use any of the three methods.

RETRIEVING DIGITAL ARCHIVES

Digital archives must maintain the information in a form, so that the users can access the information over the net through search engines, print, audio etc. If the archives are saved on CD's, floppies or tape mediums they should be checked periodically for content redundancy. If the digital archives need to be accessed in a distributed network environment, the digitized data should be connected to networks using proper protocols and bandwidth suitable for retrieving the information.

ARCHIVING IN INDIA

Preservation of Indian culture and literature is one of the oldest traditions of India. Thousands of years ago, Indian philosophers, scholars and poets have expounded their knowledge through treatises, sacred songs, commentaries on scriptures etc. which were recorded on specially treated palm leaves and birch barks, in the form of engravings on brass and copper plates etc. for future use. Before the invention of the printing press, the texts were handwritten by the craftsmen so that the universal knowledge can be preserved for future use. This proves our theory that Archiving has existed since long in India.

Indian National Archives

Indian National Archives department, which is located in Delhi is making efforts through various conservation methods and photo duplication processes to preserve the important documents of Indian cultural art, political and economical and literature. Department of Indian National Archives is using a unique method of rejuvenating and repairing the old documents with the help of "Cellulose acetate foil and tissue paper", which is known as "Solvent of Hand lamination".

The Conservation Research Laboratory is a department of Indian National Archives has been successful in retrieving palm leaves that have gone dry since the last three decades. The National Archives is trying to ensure the longevity of documents by microfilming and reprographing.

Preservation of Indian Art

C-DAC–Center For Development of Advanced Compu-ting is trying to digitally preserve and disseminate Indian Art in the form of paintings. By using HP (Hewlett Packard) equipment to capture, store and make available via internet to the researchers and art lovers.

In this project, using comprehensive suite of H.P. Technologies, the scientists capture images in extraordinary details using digital cameras to store and process the images on workstations and to develop new colour pallets and drivers to make the individual works and print realistic reproductions on large prints. By digitizing Indian art in this way not only the art is preserved but is also made available to a larger audience.

Muktabodha Institute-Archiving of Indian Manuscripts

Muktabodha institute is working in collaboration with libraries and institutions around India to make digital images of specific, rare manuscripts and texts. The institute recognizes the importance of saving the spiritual knowledge and preserved around 871 works in microfilm format. Around 262 of these works were converted to digital image format. The institute is launching the "On-line digital library" web site with 74 volumes of the Kashmir series of texts and studies. These volumes were originally published in Sanskrit language.

The main contribution of this institute is in the preser-vation and accessibility of photographic images of rare manuscripts and religious scriptures, so that the valuable information is more easily available to scholars around the world. At present Muktabodha discontinued the practice of microfilming the manuscripts and started producing digital images directly from the manuscripts. Since the main objective of the institute is in the dissemination of old religious literature by digitizing and preserving them, the institute decided not to face the hassels of microfilming and adopted the process of digital imagery.

COMMERCIAL ARCHIVING ORGANIZATIONS

Many commercial organizations have come up and made it easy to have any time anywhere, to access to information. These organizations provide electronic publicizing, content management, digital archiving etc. for the E-Publishers, individual purposes and institutions like libraries etc. Some of the organizations of India are the following.

DPS (Digital Publishing Solutions)

The Digital Publishing Solutions (DPS) is a Pune based organization, which has digitized so far 3.5 million pages and made digital archiving a reality. It scans the data from paper, photographs, negatives, microfilm, microfiche, transparencies and then the data digitized using the OCR and stored the digitized data in E-book format. Now the data is sold online using DX Reader, online XML reader. This organization is a approaching the libraries interested in preserving the rare books, manuscripts etc. In India DPS is working for 15 libraries, National research Institute, Indian national science academy etc.

JALVA

Mumbai based Jalva Media provides solutions for media management, indexing, content archiving data distribution, with partnership of other companies like mediasite, Ibeam Broadcasting, Madge.web, microsoft, Real and Apple. Jalva and SGI are offering better technologies like MPEG2 (moving picture experts group 2) which allows archiving data in DVD (digital versatile disk) by providing longer storage like and cross-platform compatibility.

Sampradaya

SAMPRADAYA Which means *handling down of tradition*. It serves as a resource centre by documenting the various aspects of the South Indian (Karnatic) music. It was founded in 1980, by two students of South Indian music Michael, Nixon of Veena and Ludwig, Pesch of Flute, under the guidence of late Savitri Rajan with the purpose of documenting Sampradaya Sangeetam. The main contribution of this organization is to bring to light and preserve this music tradition by documen-tation, archiving of recordings, music books, journals, manuscripts etc. This organization is conducting in-depth taped interviews of eminent Carnatic musicians, and organizing seminars and workshops on important topics of South Indian Music. Sampradaya Audio listening library is only one of its kind in South India, where the public has free access to music recordings and archival collections. It has 8 separate music listening stations.

2

Growth and Development of Oriental Libraries in India

GROWTH OF LIBRARIES IN INDIA

Libraries have always had a pivotal role in the storage, processing, and dissemination of information. Some may serve general needs, but special libraries serve the needs of a particular community of users. Among special libraries, Oriental libraries hold an important place because they preserve the cultural heritage of a nation or a civilization.

ORIENTAL LIBRARIES

"Oriental Libraries" are those libraries that have literature pertaining to Oriental studies and languages. "Oriental" in this context refers to the ancient Near East, including India, Persia, and ancient Arabia, among other places, and the languages and literatures of those places and peoples.

Growth and Development

India is a vast repository of different cultures, both because it was invaded by a number of foreign countries and peoples, and because of its contacts with people from the East. The languages from those Eastern countries are part of Indian literature. The literature in those Eastern languages created India's Oriental libraries.

Their history can be traced back to the Vedic period, when the written literature was kept in Ashrams or Gurukuls. Gurukuls were mostly located peaceful forest environments. With the passage of time, Gurukuls were also established in cities.

Jain and Buddhist Era

Taxila was one of the famous educational centres where students came from different parts of the country. Varanasi also distinguished itself by having a large number of Gurukulas. During this period, the literature was preserved in the Sutra style of composition. Buddhist and Jain Monastries acted as repositories of knowledge, for religious literature as well as other types. Monastic Oriental Libraries were also called Viharas. Over time, these Viharas developed into institutions of higher learning. A federation of Viharas constituted a Mahavihara, which was a larger educational institutional institution.

Nalanda Mahavihara is the best example. Fa-Hien, a Chinese traveller, also found a number of monastaries in India. Kanyakubja, Sravasti, Kusunagara, Vaisali, and Patliputra were centres of Oriental literature according to Fa-Hien. Hiuen-Tsang, another Chinese traveller, visited India during A.D. 629-645. He left a detailed account of his visit, which gives us significant information about Buddhist educational institutions possessing a rich variety of Eastern literature. Taxila was a center of learning in Ancient India and a large number of people from all over the world and the subcontinent itself visited this place to gain knowledge.

Literature related to medicine and archery enriched the library at Taxila. Rahula Sankrityayana, Angiris set up a seminary with a Granthakuti attached to it at Taxila, which later flourished in to an academy or university. Nalanda University is the best known of ancient India's universities. It has been called the treasure house of information by European archeologists. The information there helped locate Buddhist shrines in India.

It is believed that King Kumara Gupta built the first monastery at Nalanda to train Buddhist monks. Nalanda University was an expansion of this seminary. King Buddha Gupta, Jagatha Gupta, Baladitya, and Vijra made additions and expansions to the building.

There were three large libraries with vast amount of literature in Oriental languages on subjects such as science, medicine, astrology, fine arts, literature. The University of Valabhi was built by the Maitraka Kings during the years A.D 475-775. Its library had a variety of Eastern literature. This great university and its library lasted until the 12th century, when they were completely destroyed by Arab invaders.

Odantapuri University was founded by King Gopala and was a well-known center of learning. It had a library that was rich in Brahmanical and Buddhist works. Mohammad Bakhtiyar Khilji destroyed this monastic university along with its library. Somapuri also possessed a wealth of Oriental literature, but it was destroyed by fire in the middle of the 11th century.

Vikramasila monastery, built by King Dharmapala, had a variety of literature on metaphysics, tantras, grammar, ritualism, and logic. The library fulfilled the demands of outsiders, especially those from Tibet, by providing them copies of manuscripts in a most liberal way. Another University with a significant Oriental collection, especially in Tantric Buddhism, was Jagaddala, founded by King Ramapala. Another monastery with a rich wealth on different aspects of Oriental literature was Kanheri University, built during the reign of Amoghavarsha. By the 10th century, the corpus of Jain literature had increased many times, and Jain monks had contributed substantially to nearly all branches of knowledge known at that time. The Jayendra monastery of Kashmir had a good library where the Chinese traveller Hiuen–Tsang spent two years copying manuscripts.

Similarly, he spent fourteen months at the Chinapati monastery. Several Hindu kings and their ministers, who flourished between 10th and 12th centuries AD, are credited with establishing libraries and supporting the library movement. Among them was King Bhoja of Dhara, who flourished in the 11th century, and was a distinguished scholar with a rich library. King Kumarapaladeva of the Chaulakyas is said to have established 21 Jain Libraries. He kept a copy of Kalpasutra written in golden ink in each one of them.

Mughal Empire

When the Muslims established their rule in India at the beginning of the 13th century, Muslim emperors paid special attention to libraries, taking care to establish libraries in educational institutions. They constructed no separate library buildings; rather, books were deposited and preserved in educational institutions, mosques, and Khangahs.

Many Muslim rulers were from the East, and they helped enrich libraries with Oriental literature. Paper began be used as a writing material in the 12th century, and this helped book production in this periods. Mughal sovereigns and their courtiers were educated and accomplished, and some maintained personal libraries.

The Muslim sovereigns collected and preserve the Vedas, the *Ramayana*, and other Hindu religious books. They also translated a variety of books in Hindi in to Persian and Arabic, and helped disseminate Hindu art and culture. After the establishment of Sultans of Delhi in 1202, a new period in the history of Oriental libraries came in to existence. These minor Muslim rulers and nobles encouraged Islamic learning and established *maktabs* (primary schools), *madrasas* (schools of higher learning), libraries, and mosques.

They encouraged Arabic and Persian literatures in all branches of learning, and enriched Oriental literature in the libraries. They gave shelter and protection to scholars, who brought literature from other parts of the world to India. The Library of Khwajah Nizam-ud-din Auliya was an important Oriental library.

It was the property of the *Waqf* (religious board) and was open to every man of letters. During the reign of the Khilji dynasty the number of Oriental libraries increased. Jala-ud-din Khiljee established the Imperial Library at Delhi and appointed Amir Khusru as its librarian.

The Tughluq Dynasty opened a new chapter in the history of Oriental libraries in India. Mohammad Tughluq built one thousand madrasas, each with a library with collections in Arabic and Persian. Humayun ascended the throne in 1530 and a library known as Khan-i-Tilism. Humayun's library played a significant role in Mughal history. Akbar, the greatest of Mughal emperors maintained a very rich library. He added a sizable number of books, obtained from his conquest, from libraries in Gujarat, Jaunpur, Kashmir, Bihar, Bengal, and the Deccan.

His library was unique in its collection of rare books, among which was the Persian *Divan of Human Shah.* By the time of Akbar's grandson, Shah Jahan, the library was a complex organization with a large staff, and headed by Nazim, a noble of the court. In Kashmir, a picture of the first library is found in the Shrine of Hazrat Bulbul Shah, which was established by Muslims.

A magnificient monastery and mosque were constructed by the emperor of Kashmir, Sultan Sadruddin, for Hazrat Bulbul Shah. A library was attached to this mosque. Amir Kabir Syed Hamdani, a theologian and scholar had a well established personal library that contained Oriental literature. He established a number of libraries in Kashmir which added to the wealth of the Indian Oriental libraries.

The Sultans of Kashmir had given funds to establish madrasas and libraries. Each madrasa had a library. Sultan Zain-ul-Abedin-ul constructed a library which historians tell was one of the best in the world. Among the other libraries built by Budshah, Darul-ul-Uloom Nausherah was the best.

Another library, by the name of Madrasa-i-Sher, was built by Budshah near modern Islamabad. During the Chak Sultanate many libraries thrived and brought Oriental literature to the limelight. Akbar conquered Kashmir in 1587 and established many madrasas and libraries there. In Gujrat and Malwa, a number of libraries were introduced by Ahmad Shah I and Dilawar Khan.

Shah Jahan, like his predecessors, patronized learning and education and built a library with a rich collection of Arabic and Persian manuscripts. Dara Shikkoh, Aurangzeb, and Bahadur Shah Zafar also contributed to the development of Oriental libraries. Mughal rule was a period of literary excellence. Most of the emperors were themselves scholars, and also extended their patronage to scholarship and learning.

Other Kingdoms

There were kingdoms in other parts of India that also had libraries enriched by Oriental literature. The kingdoms of Bahmani and Deccan had independent kings who reigned for 340 years, and who were patrons of learning, as were the Bahmani kings, who continued their rule up to AD 1526 and had an empire that stretched from coast to coast.

They founded many colleges and libraries. Ahmad Shah built a magnificient college near Gulbarga. Muhammad Shah Bahmani II built another imposing college at Bidar that is one of the many beautiful remains of the grandeur of the Bahmanis. All these colleges had libraries that possessed an enormous amount of Oriental literature. Arabian and Iranian literature brought by visitors and travellers were added to the libraries of Bahmanis. The Urdu language was at its zenith during the reign of Firoz Shah Bahmani, and a vast amount of Urdu literature enriched the Bahmani Libraries.

The library of Gesudaraj was distinguished among the libraries of Deccan. Books on Sufism and religion were available in this library. The emperors of Qutub Shahi also established a good number of libraries during their reign, and a vast amount of literature in Persian was included. Tipu Sultan, son of Haider Ali and emperor of Mysore established a number of libraries.

"Zaimul-Umoor" was the great university of Seringa Patnam in his reign. He collected books from many countries including Europe. The library had a copy of the Holy Quran which was written by the hand of Aurangzeb Alamgir. It is estimated that the library had nearly 2,000 volumes of Persian, Arabic, and Hindi manuscripts from all branches of Islamic literature.

After the downfall of the Mughals, and with the invasion of Ahmad Shah Abdali, the literary wealth of the Indian libraries was looted away. In 1857, after the Sepoy mutiny, thousands of books were destroyed and thousands of important, valuable, and rare books were siphoned to England.

British and other Europeans

The growth and development of Oriental libraries was regenerated again during European and British rule. The interest shown by the British and European scholars in Oriental Learning and Indology, along with the social, cultural and religious movements spearheaded by eminent Indians, resulted in new Oriental libraries. These institutions established libraries for Oriental scholarship. The result of this renaissance is a number of special libraries devoted to Oriental and Indological collections in various parts of the country.

Rampur Raza Library, very rich in Indo-Islamic studies and arts, was created by Nawab Faizullah Khan in 1794, and has tremendous manuscript wealth. One can find manuscripts in Arabic, Persian, Urdu, Sanskrit, Sinhali, Tamil, Kannada, and other Oriental languages.

The Asiatic Society Library, Kolkata, a premier and leading oriental institutions of the country was established in 1784 by Sir William Jones. Colonel Mackenzie, an Englishman and an engineer by profession established an Oriental Library by the name of " *Government Oriental Manuscript Library* (GOML) " in Chennai.

Contemporary Libraries

Khuda Baksh Oriental Library was founded in 1842 by Maulvi Khuda Baksh Khan, who donated his entire personal collection. Since 1977 it has been issuing regularly a multi-lingual research quarterly *Khuda Baksh Library Journal.* The library has been recognized as a research center by seven Indian universities. The collection has a rich repository of Persian and Arabic manuscripts. Maulana Azad Library, Aligarh Muslim University was initially founded as "Anglo Oriental College (MAOC) at Aligarh in 1875 and raised to the status of a university in 1920.

The personal collection of Maulana Azad also enriches the library. The library has a total collection of over 1 million volumes and 14,571 manuscripts. The Maulana Azad Library has the largest collection of Urdu books in the Indian subcontinent, which is perhaps largest in the world as well.

The collection includes:

- Urdu
- Arabic
- Persian
- Sanskrit
- Hindi
- Sir Syed Collection
- Gandhian Collection
- Aligarh Collection
- Thesis Collection
- Archives
- Microfiche
- Manuscripts

Hakim Mohammad Syed Library, Jamia Hamdard, New Delhi is a leading university founded in 1906.

It has a well known Oriental library, which has a number of special collections:

- Nazaria Collection
- Abdul Sattar Siddiqui Collection
- Maulana Abdul Salam Niazi Collection
- Jaffri Collection
- Shafi Ahmad Collection
- Dr Tanveer Alvi Collection

The library has 4,500 rare manuscripts. Osmania University Library was established in 1918 and is considered seventh oldest in India, the third oldest in South India, and the first to be established in state of Hyderabad.

The library has a collection of rare books and manuscripts including Palm Leaf manuscripts. The National Library of India, which came in to existence in 1948, is the largest library in India. Previously it was known as the Imperial Library which was formed in 1891 by combining a number of Secretariat libraries.

It has a wide range of collections in a variety of national and international languages. A good number of Arabic and Persian documents are also available here. The Oriental library initiative that took place in ancient India reached its zenith in the period when the British and other Europeans came to India. The Mughals also contributed a great deal to the development of Oriental libraries. Eventually, their extravagant ways caused the libraries to deteriorate, but social and political conditions eventually led to better libraries with larger collections.

DEVELOPMENT OF PUBLIC LIBRARIES IN INDIA

Public libraries arose worldwide along with growth in education, literacy, and publications. Every country has its own public library history with influential leaders. Monarchs, wealthy people, and philanthropists have all made a contribution to society in the form of public library development. India is no exception. Libraries were established in ancient India mainly by the patronage extended by emperors, major capitalists, and scholars. Indian emperors and kings were supported scholars and scholarship. There is evidence of well-developed libraries even in the sixth century A.D. The famous Nalanda University in Bihar had its own magnificent library with a massive collection of manuscripts covering the universe of knowledge. Admission to library was restricted to scholars.

Other ancient universities, such as Taxila and Vikramashila, also had valuable libraries. Muslim influence in India during the 13th century A.D. marked the dawn of another era of learning and scholarship. The Mughal period gave a further stimulus to the growth of libraries. Mughal rulers attached considerable importance to libraries and appointed scholars as librarians. The Mughal emperors were patrons of art and literature. In the period of Emperor Babur, Humayun, and Akbar many new libraries were established and existing ones further developed. Mughal libraries featured magnificent buildings, rare manuscripts, and scholar librarians.

The names of Maharaja Sawai Man Singh of Jaipur and Maharaja Ranjit Singh of Punjab will be remembered with appreciation in the history of library services in India. The Maharaja of Tanjuar started the famous Saraswati Mahal Library in 17th century A.D. It remains a unique institution in its nature of collection and services Libraries established by the kings and capitalists functioned like private institutions and the admission was limited. Service to the general public had to wait for the British. Unfortunately, the arrival of the British and resulting political disorder also brought chaos to the Indian way of life.

This was a severe blow to the cultural heritage of India, which had arisen from the Indus valley civilization. When libraries began developing in India during the early nineteenth century, they were a western product. In 1808, the Government of Bombay proposed to register libraries, which were to be given copies of books published from the "funds for the encouragement of literature".

According to the "Sinha Committee", this was the beginning of the first phase of public library development in India. During the first half of the 19th century, the three presidency towns of Bombay, Calcutta, and Madras had public libraries. These libraries were mostly financed by Europeans residing in these towns.

Of these, the establishment of the public library at Calcutta in 1835 was the most significant. This was the library which later developed into the National Library of India. Almost simultaneous, subscription libraries were started in many Indian cities. These were, of course, not public libraries in the true sense of the term, and did not provide free books for all. Founded in imitation of their western counterparts, the use of these libraries was confined to small, affluent portion of society. The first three decades of the 20th century can be looked on as the golden age of the Indian library system. On January 31, 1902, the Imperial Library Act was passed and Lord Curzon transformed the Calcutta Public Library into the Imperial Library in 1906. Developments in Baroda were also notable. Espranza sums them up:

- The development of public libraries in Baroda was unique. Baroda developed a network of public libraries to serve the entire Princely State. Maharaja Sayaji Rao Gaekwad III of Baroda who traveled all over the world was deeply impressed by the role played by public libraries in the promotion of education in the United States and thought of extending such benefits to his own subjects. In 1910 he invited an American expert, William Alson Borden to organize the public library system for his state. The public library movement that flourished in Baroda was a glorious one. But that was not a general trend of that period because in no other part of India, a parallel development occurred.

Yet another development during the period was the organisation of a host of conferences such as:

- The first conference of library workers and persons interested in the library movement was held at Beswada, Andhra in 1914.
- The first All India Library Conference of Librarians was held in 1918 at Lahore.
- The first All India Library Conference was held at Calcutta in 1933.
- The first All India Public Library Conference was held at Madras in 1934.

With the existence of democratic governments in several provinces beginning in 1937, another phase of the library movement began. Between 1937 and 1942, a number of village libraries and travelling libraries sprang up in Assam, Bihar, Punjab, and Travancore. It was estimated that there were about 13,000 village libraries in India in 1942. Another remarkable development was the appointment of the 'Library Development Committee' by the Government of Bombay, with A.A.A. Fyzee as its chairman. The Committee ambitiously recommended a comprehensive library system to be implemented in three successive stages. Because of financial constraints, the government could only implement part of the recommendations.

AFTER INDEPENDENCE

After independence, the growth of libraries in general has been remarkable, although not as remarkable as that of academic and special libraries. At the time of independence, India was facing a host of challenges. Those in the rural population, 88 per cent of the total, were nearly all illiterate. Transportation was poor and mass media merely nominal. Nevertheless, the public library scene in India improved considerably during the post independence period, though it is still lacking on several fronts. Verma and Agrawal argue that to compare our public libraries with those of the developed nations on equal footing, we have to go a long way. The 1951 census, the first conducted after independence, found 2,843 local governments in the urban and rural areas in India, of which 320 were rural district boards.

Only about one third of local governments maintained public libraries, about 950. In addition, there were about 1,500 subscription libraries. So-called public libraries were primarily reading rooms with a few hundred books for reading on the premises. The Delhi public library deserves special mention. It was founded in 1951 as the first UNESCO Public Library Pilot Project under the joint auspices of UNESCO and Government of India. The purpose of the library was to adapt "modern techniques to Indian conditions" and to serve as a model public library for Asia. The establishment of Delhi Public Library, the involvement of union government in the public library movement, and the enactment of public library legislation in some states are the main factors which contributed to the improvement of public libraries after independence. Although the government of India allotted funds for public library development in its five-year plans, this funding was not connected to effective planning.

ADVISORY COMMITTEE FOR LIBRARIES

The Government of India appointed a committee in 1957 to report on the status of public library development in the country. It is also called the Sinha Committee, after its chair, the late Dr. A.P. Sinha, who was at that time Director of Public Instruction in Bihar. The Sinha Committee's charge included:

- Determining present reading needs, how they are met, and what part existing library systems play in meeting the needs;
- Determining reading tastes, what agencies provide suitable literature, and how reading taste can be improved;
- Recommending future library structure in India;
- Recommending areas of cooperation between libraries and education systems;
- Considering the training of librarians and the conditions of their service;

- Recommending the administrative and financial measures necessary to support public libraries in India.

The committee submitted its report to Dr. K.L. Shrimali, who was Minister for Education, on the 12th of November, 1958. The Committee described the situation as dismal and called libraries in most cases, "a stagnant pool of books," because new books were not added regularly. The committee at the same time observed that wherever large collections did exist, they were not fully used because of rigid rules. Library users were not trusted and were required to deposit large sums of money as a kind of insurance, which lower income people could not afford. As of March 1954 there were 32,000 libraries in India, with a little more than 7,100,000 books and a total circulation of about 37,700,000. The report observed that genuine public library service was rarity, and that public library service throughout the country was unsatisfactory. The committee recommended creating state library networks based on uniform library legislation. The chief recommendations of the report were:

- Library service should be made free to every citizen of India;
- The hierarchy of public library service in the country should begin with National Library, and proceed to State Central Library, District Library, Block Library, and Panchayat Library;
- An independent Director of Social Education and Libraries should be set up in every state, with a fulltime senior class-1 officer of the rank of Deputy Director of Education to plan, organize, and administer library services;
- An All India Library Advisory Council should be constituted as a central agency to review and assess the work done at the state level;
- Library Associations should actively assist the development of libraries in the country;
- University libraries should cooperate with public library systems by allowing selected public readers to use their collection;
- State governments should accept responsibility for public library services in their states;
- Librarians and social education workers should cooperate to promote literacy;
- A library cess of six paisa for each rupee of property tax should be levied with the permission of local bodies.
- The Government of India should match the amount collected in the states. State governments should also give matching grants to local bodies over the succeeding 25 years, their contribution should be raised to three times the cess collected.
- State and national governments should enact comprehensive state library laws incorporating the right of every citizen to have free access to libraries. The Government of India should provide necessary financial assistance to the state governments for this purpose.

RAJA RAM MOHAN ROY LIBRARY FOUNDATION

Another positive step taken by the Central Government was the establishment of the *Raja Ram Mohan Roy Library Foundation* (RRRLF) at Calcutta on May 22, 1972, as a part of the bicentenary celebrations of the birth of Raja Ram Mohan Roy, a social reformer of the early 19th century. Its objectives are library development in general and rural library development in particular. It provides financial assistance to public libraries in the form of matching grants. It assists State Central Libraries and District Central Libraries, which has helped many states and Union Territories develop rural public library services.

MAIN OBJECTIVES OF RRRLF

The main objectives of RRRLF are:

- Promotion of the library movement in India;
- The adoption of a national library policy by the central and state governments;
- Development of a National Library System by integrating the services of National Libraries, State Central Libraries, District Libraries, and other types of libraries through an interlibrary lending system;
- Propagation and adoption of library legislation in the country;
- Provision of financial and technical assistance to libraries;
- Provision of financial assistance to voluntary organizations and library associations for the promotion of library development;
- Periodic publication of reports on library development;
- To act as a clearing house for ideas and information on library development in India and abroad;
- To advise the Government of India library development;
- Promotion of research in problems of library development

The primary objective of RRRLF is the promotion of the library movement. The rest are subsidiary objectives. RRRLF is the first government-sponsored body specifically created for this purpose. The foundation also has a programme of assistance to libraries for workshops, conferences, and exhibits. The foundation has taken the major initiative for the formulation of a national policy on library and information systems by the Government of India. The current programmes of assistance are:

- Collection building;
- Rural libraries and mobile library service for rural areas;
- Seminars, workshops, conferences, training courses, and exhibits;
- Facilities and equipment for storage and display of materials;
- Public library buildings;
- Television and VCR equipment for educational purposes;
- Assistance to voluntary organisations providing public library services;

- Assistance to children's libraries or children's sections of general public libraries

During the last three decades, the foundation has assisted more than 500 libraries, including many in rural areas

NATIONAL POLICY ON LIBRARY AND INFORMATION SYSTEM (NAPLIS)

In 1985, a committee was set up under the chairmanship of Prof. D.P. Chattopadhyay to formulate a *National Policy on Library and Information System* (NAPLIS). The Committee submitted its report in May 1986. Following that, another committee looked at implications of the report and created an action plan for its implementation.

The Empowerment Committee submitted its report in April 1988 and an Implementation Cell was formed to implement its recommendations within a period of six months. Yet another Working Group, under the Joint Secretary to the Government of India in the Department of Culture, was constituted to examine its recommendations for implementation. The Working Group submitted its report in July 1993 and suggested implementing only 29 of 60 recommendations made by the NAPLIS. The following are some of the recommendations of NAPLIS related to public libraries:

- Proposals for maintenance and development of public libraries should preferably come from State Legislative Enactment. The Central Government may revise the Model Public Library Bill. Funds for library development should come from each state, either from general revenue or from local taxation. Central Government agencies may provide funds under Plan Expenditure.
- Efforts should emphasize rural public libraries. A village or a cluster of villages with an adequate population should have a community library/rural community centre, which will also serve as an information centre. Resources from various agencies engaged in the public health, adult education, State and central government, etc., should be used to build up and maintain this centre.
- The central government increase its assistance to state governments in the development of public libraries. The RRRLF, as the national agency for coordinating and assisting the development of public libraries, should be suitably strengthened in order to do this.
- Standards and guidelines for library service should be created.
- There should be a system of national libraries consisting of National Library, Calcutta as the National Library of India, National Depository libraries in Delhi, Bombay, Madras, National Subject Libraries, and others. These national libraries should form part of one integrated system.

- A National Commission on Libraries and Information System or National Commission on Informatics and Documentation may be constituted by an Act of Parliament to serve under the Ministry of Human Resource Development. The Commission will have representation from appropriate central and state agencies and could provide guidance and coordinate library development programmes in all sectors. This body will have the primary responsibility for the implementation of NAPLIS programmes.
- National Depository libraries; Connemara Public library, Chennai; Central Library, Bombay; and Delhi Public Library, Delhi should concentrate on development of collections and preservation of Indian culture produced in the languages of their regions, supplementing and complementing the efforts of the Indian National Library.
- The Indian National Bibliography should have a comprehensive coverage of the national output of documents and should be updated regularly. This responsibility should be vested in the National Library.
- Government should create a national awareness of the need to preserve the nation's cultural heritage. National libraries should be responsible, with preservation facilities created there. Links between libraries, archives, and museums should be established for the purpose of national preservation.
- The Ministry of Rural Development has a plan for one community centre in every Panchayat Centre. The Department of Culture and the Ministry of Rural Development have agreed to provide library services at each of these Rural Community Centres.
- An important link should be established between community centre library and primary schools. If the schools do not have libraries of their own, the community centre library should provide children with adequate services.
- A community centre library should have an important role in adult education programmes.
- A district library should provide facilities and recreation for the disabled and low-income people, *e.g.*, literature in Braille.
- Libraries should be built in areas of tribal concentration and in minority communities to help in developing and sustaining their distinctive cultures.
- Libraries should be equipped with relevant resources, such as publications covering Open University and vocational educational courses, for their role in support of distance education.
- All public libraries within a state should form a part of a network extending from village library through community centre library, district library, and state network, and should be linked to the national information grid.

1951-1956

- The first five-year plan for educational development included a proposal for "Improvement of Library Service." This proposal envisioned a network of libraries throughout the country, coordinated by National Central Library at New Delhi
- During the first five-year plan, nine state governments, *i.e.*, Assam, Madhya Pradesh, West Bengal, Punjab, PEPSU, Rajasthan, Savarashtra, Bhopal, and Vindhya Pradesh, decided to set up State Central Libraries.

1956-1961

- At this time, the government allocated funds to set up a national network of libraries in its 320 districts. As a result, most states established State Central Libraries and District Libraries as the main distributing centres

1961-1966

During this period, the system of central government assistance to the states was changed, and funding for libraries was kept to a minimum. It was up to the individual states to take initiative and develop their public libraries. The programme to assist state governments in establishing state central libraries, district central libraries, and block development libraries was abandoned.

The decision was a major setback to the development of public libraries. During this period four national libraries were established at Delhi, Calcutta, Bombay, and Madras. A Working Group on libraries was appointed by the Planning Commission in 1964 to take a stock of library development. The working group submitted its report on 7th September 1965 with following recommendations:

- The central and state governments should share responsibility for providing adequate public library service. New government agencies in the central government under the Minister of Education, a directorate of libraries and a state library advisory council in each state should be set up to execute the programmes effectively.
- State central libraries should be established in four states: Madhya Pradesh, Mysore, Nagaland, and Orissa.
- States which do not possess adequate functional buildings for their state central libraries should be provided with library buildings.
- The state central library must have a children's section.
- There should be 335 District Libraries for the 327 districts in the country, *i.e.*, in large and populous districts, two district libraries may be provided.

- New buildings should be constructed for the existing 100 district libraries.
- Block libraries are the chief feeding centre for the rural reading public, and therefore, 2,500 new block libraries, covering 75 per cent of blocks in the country should be constructed.
- A sum of 10 million rupees shall be provided for distribution of grant in aid to such libraries of urban and rural areas which depend on subscription and donations.
- Three public libraries on model of Delhi Public Library should be set up
- The Institute of Library Science established by the Ministry of Education at Delhi University in 1958-59, and then closed in 1962, should be reopened. Such institutes should be established at the state levels also to train graduate and undergraduate librarians to meet future requirements.
- A sum of ₹.10,000 shall be allocated as financial assistance to all national level and state level library associations to create library consciousness in the country by organizing seminars, conducting surveys, and producing library literature.
- A programme of book production should be undertaken.
- A draft of the Library Act should be produced

1969-1974

This plan proposed a substantial sum for the social education programme. A much lower sum was allocated. Of this, only a very small amount was available for the development of libraries in the country.

1974-1979

This plan included measures to strengthen the buildings, collections, and staff of the central and state libraries, as well as strengthening the district, block, and village libraries. During this period, attempts were made to develop a district-level library system, so that district library could act as a leader for the smaller libraries in the district. The adult education programme was the hallmark of this plan. The programme was to be supported by a network of libraries at the village and block levels and various community centres. Thus steps were taken to strengthen not only the village and block libraries, but also the central, state libraries and the district libraries

1980-85

This plan emphasized establishing a network of rural public libraries to sustain literacy and disseminate information to rural areas. It discussed the necessity of integrating school and college libraries with the system of public libraries. During this period, 26 states or union territories out of 31 had established state central libraries and 291 district libraries.

1985-90

During this period, the Commission's objective was to address the needs of 90 million people in the Adult Education Programme. The network of libraries was to play a role in the development of literature for neo-literates. Library systems were to be strengthened, with specific attention given to improvement of facilities at national level institutions. An important development was the 1986 adoption of National Literacy Mission, which emphasised the education of women and the establishment of rural libraries. In addition, the RRRLF set up an Integrated Research Cell-cum-Computer Unit for promoting research in librarianship and database of public libraries in the country There were two annual plans for the years 1990-91 and 1991-92.

1992-97

During this period it was proposed to reorganize the Central Reference Library into the National Bibliographical and Documentation Centre, which would also have a computer centre. The Delhi Public Library set up two new libraries in its service area. RRRLF created programmes to help state central libraries purchase reprographic equipment, to help libraries process rare books, and to give special assistance to networks of public libraries that were at least 100 years old.

1997-2002

During the 9th five year plan, the National Library, Kolkatta, undertook several major initiatives to upgrade and modernize its collection building programme, reader services, and conservation of library material. The major activities completed during the period were automation of the circulation system in the lending section, setting up of a local area network, improved reader services, and more efficient collection management. The conservation activities in the library got a major advance with the purchase of modern equipment to preserve rare books and other materials. The Central Reference Library, Kolkatta computerised various functions during the Ninth Plan. As a result, the publication of the *Indian National Bibliography* is now up to date, with records available online.

Funds were provided to the Delhi Public Library and Central Secretariat Library, Delhi, for acquisition of new material in different languages and media as well as for modernizing their infrastructure. The benefits of these efforts can be seen in improved reader services, networking, and resource sharing. The Central Secretariat Library organized a number of computer training programmes for resource sharing, standardization of cataloguing formats, and co-operative acquisition. Funds for modernizing and computerization were also provided from central grants to the Connemara Library, Chennai, Thanjavur Maharaja Serovji Sarasvati Mahal Library, Thanjavur and the State Central Library, Mumbai. Besides these, the RRRLF provided assistance to public libraries across the country for collections and storage, construction, and seminars and workshops.

Tenth Five-Year Plan (Action Plan)

The Planning Commission proposed further modernization of central and public libraries during the Tenth Plan. A national bibliographic database would be developed to encourage resource sharing, networking, and to improve reader services. The Commission resolved to strengthen public library infrastructure through the RRRLF. The Tenth Plan focused on upgrading existing libraries, including private collections, and widening the programme for bibliographic control and documentation. To make readers services more comprehensive and effective, the National Library is expected to act as the ultimate referral centre for various subjects. To keep pace with the latest developments in information technology in public libraries, the upgrading and networking of central and state libraries was also planned.

ACADEMIC LIBRARIES IN INDIA: A HISTORICAL STUDY

Research in library history in India has remained largely neglected area which has resulted into availability of very limited and scanty literature. Commenting on the status of library history in India, Donald G. Davis, Jr. of the University of Texas at Austin, writes that "although a core literature on Indian library history exists, it has many imbalances and gaps. The scholars are very dispersed in their interests and their geographical location. With one person rarely contributing more than one work. There is little pattern to existing research efforts."

In this context, the role of historian happens to be much more crucial and significant to make an assessment of the growth and development of libraries in India, the factors responsible for their development and the impact of those factors on the library progress. Rajgopalan, in his 1987 presidential address to the Indian Library Association rightly said, "it is generally acknowledged that our libraries are underutilized in relation to investments being made in them.

Non-use and low-use of libraries amount to wastage of facilities being made available. Maybe the literacy rate, lack of reading habits, etc., are the causes for low use from the side of patrons... User education programmes must be organized by libraries in a way that libraries are fully utilized." He further remarked that, "if library historians would address the roots and trends of library issues, they would provide a valuable service to the profession and society."

The Father of Library and Information Science in India,Padmashri Dr. S.R. Ranganathan while giving a radio talk in April 1956 said: "an account of the libraries in the first four periods must necessarily depend upon the historical research. This has not yet been done. The library profession is too small in India to spare a person to fill up this antiquarian gap. Those trained in the scientific method of tracing history are too preoccupied with dynastic and political history to spare sufficient time for cultural history in general and library history in particular."

Thus, an historical study of the growth and development of academic libraries in India, is a desideratum, the fulfilment of which should go a long way in removing the imbalances and gaps. Such a study becomes significant not only in view of the tremendous activity concerning the growth and development of libraries in India, but also because their growth has been shaped in the first phase by the phenomena that have shaped the historical course of this period and, secondly, the rise of library as an important instrument in the advancement of knowledge and socio-economic transformation.

Source Material for Writing History of Libraries

For the purpose of scientific writing of history of libraries, an understanding of the nature of existing source material and knowing the art of using it is essential. The sources for writing the history are available in Pali, Sanskrit, Chinese, Arabic, Persian and European Languages and most of them have been translated into English. These exist in various formats, such as Manuscripts, inscriptions, copper plates etc.

They are either indigenous or foreign. The contribution of foreign travelogues such as Tibetan, Chinese, Muslim, Portuguese, English and other Europeans is highly useful. Some noteworthy foreign travelogues are Itsing, Fahien, Hieun Tsang, Alberuni, Ibn Batuta, Minhaj, Firishta, Badauni, Afif, bernier, mandelso, Manrique de Lara, Martin, Count Noer.

In addition to the contribution of the travelogues, the contribution of historians like Henry M. Eliot, John Dawson, Stanley Lane-Pool, Ishwari Prasad, R.C. Majumdar, Jadunath Sarkar, V.D. Mahajan, Mohammed Muhammed Zubair, J.S. Sarma and N.N. Law etc. is also significant.

Though scanty, yet there are articles written by the library professionals on history of libraries. A few efforts have also been made for conduct of research in the area of history of libraries and such like works have been consulted for the purpose of writing this paper.

University Libraries in Ancient India

In the Vedic age instructions were imparted "orally, without the medium of books." Taxila from 700 B.C. to AD 300 was considered to be the most respected seat of higher learning and education in India but still there is no evidence found so far in the archaeological excavations at Taxila that there had been a good library system in the Taxila University.

Fa-Hien noticed such libraries at Jetavana monastery at Sravasti. In A.D. 400, there came into being one of the biggest known universities, the Nalanda University, which by A.D 450. became a renowned seat of learning, its fame spreading beyond the boundaries of India. Nalanda near Patna grew to be the foremost Buddhist monastery and an educational centre. Most of what we know of the Nalanda University during the 6th and the 7th centuries A.D. is due to the accounts left by Hiuen-tsang, who lived in the institution for three years in the first half of the 7th century, and I-tsing who also stayed there for ten years towards the latter part of the same century.

Information on the Nalanda University Library is also found in the Tibetan accounts, from which we understand that the library was situated in a special area known by the poetical name the Dharmaganja, which comprised three huge buildings, called the Ratnasagara, the Ratnodadhi and the Ratnaranjaka of which the Ratnasagara was a ninestoried building and housed the collection of manuscripts and rare sacred works like Prajnaparamita Sutra etc.

The library at Nalanda had a rich stock of manuscripts on philosophy and religion and contained texts relating to grammar, logic, literature, the Vedas, the Vedanta, and the Samkhya philosophy, the Dharmasastras, the Puranas, Astronomy, Astrology and Medicine. The University of Nalanda and its library flourished down to the 12th century A.D. until Bakhtiyar Khalji sacked it in A.D. 1197-1203. and set fire to the establish-ment of Nalanda.

The world famous universities, such as, the Vikramasila, the Vallabhi and the Kanchi were coming up in other parts of the country during the period from the 5th century A.D. to the 8th century A.D. All these universities possessed rich libraries and in the hall containing such books there used to be an image of the goddess Saraswati with a book in her hand.

The Nalanda and the Vikramshila universities were under the control of the king Dharmapala. He founded the Vikramshila monastery in the 8th century A.D. It had a rich collection of texts in the Sanskrit, the Prakrit and the Tibetan languages.

Regarding the library of the university, the *Tabaqat-i-Nasiri* informs us that there were great number of books on the religion of Hindus there; and when all these books came under the observation of the Mussalamans, they summoned, a number of Hindus that they might give them information regarding the import of these books; but the whole of the Hindu community was killed in the war.

Muslim vandalism caused the disappearance of the excellent collection at Vikramashila. The Jaggadal Vihara in Varendra-bhumi was also an important centre of learning with considerable collection of the reading material. It was established by the king Kampala, who ruled from A.D. 1084 to 1130.

The provision of facilities for reading, writing, editing and translating manuscripts shows that this library was in no way less than its contemporary libraries in importance. Though not as large as the library of Nalanda, it abounded in private collection of texts.

Likewise Mithila had been famous for its scholars since the days of Rajrishi Janaka and had a rich collection of various commentaries on the different branches of the Hindu *Shastras*. The library of its university played an important role in teaching and learning. A needle *(Shalaka)* was pierced through the manuscript on the subject of the student's specialization and he was expected to explain the last page pierced.

In this way the student's all-round mastery of the subject was tested. Mithila continued to enjoy its all India importance in the field of learning till the end of the 15th century AD. The university at Sompuri, like that of Vikramshila, occupied a significant position since the days of Dharampala.

Like Nalanda, this university also had its own library. Atisa Dipankar, a noted scholar, lived there. He with the help of other scholars, translated into the Tibetan the *Madhyamkaratnapradipa* of Bhavaviveka. This university was destroyed by fire in the middle of the 11th century A.D. Efforts were made by the monk Vipulsrimitra to renovate the university but it could not regain its past glory.

At a time when Nalanda was famous for its *Mahayana* courses of study, the Maitrakakings provided their patronage to the Mahavihara of Vallabhi. This university was famous for its *Hinayana* studies. The fact that this university had a good library is supported by a reference in a grant of Guhasena, dated A.D. 559, wherein a provision was made out of the royal grant for the purchase of books for the library.

This important seat of learning at Kanheri, on the West Coast, flourished during the reign of Amoghavarsha in the 9th century A.D. The library occupied a significant position within the establishment, and the donors provided money to buy books for the library.

The last of the famous seats of learning in Eastern India was Navadwipa in Bengal. It reached its height of glory from 1083 to A.D. 1106 as a centre of intellectual excellence as well as its rich library facilities, when Lakshman Sen, a king of Gauda, made it his capital. However, this library was also destroyed along with the centre by Bakhtiyar Khalji.

Situated in South India at Amaravati, on the banks of the Krishna, the Nagarjuna Vidyapeeth flourished in about 7th century A.D. Its library housed in the top floor of the five storyed building of the university had an enormous collection on the Buddhist philosophy, particularly of the *Mahayana* school that Nagarjuna had founded, science and medicine.

There is enough archaeological evidence that supports the existence of this 7th century university and its library. The enormity of the collection in this library is borne out by the fact that it not only had works on the Buddhist literature and the *Tripitakas,* but also works on several branches of scientific knowledge, such as, Botany, Geography, Mineralogy and Medicine. It was a great attraction for scholars from the different parts of India and from countries, like, China, Burma and Ceylon.

University Libraries in Medieval India

The existence of academic libraries during the medieval period of Indian history is not known, though the Muslim rulers did patronize libraries in their own palaces. A lone exception, however, was a library attached to a college at Bidar, having a collection of 3000 books on different subjects. Aurangzeb got this Library transferred to Delhi to merge it with his palace library. During the medieval period, due to Muslim invasions and political troubles, the powerful empires and kingdoms of Indian rulers fell one by one. This affected higher education and the development of academic libraries as well.

LIBRARIES IN MODERN INDIA

During the British rule in India, number of academic institutions were established by the East India Company, and by the Christan missionaries. Some of the worth mentioning events which led to the growth and development of higher education in India during this period were the establishment of the Calcutta College in 1781, Jonathan Duncan, then a British agent, founded the Benaras Sanskrit College in 1792. The Calcutta Fort William College was founded in 1800. All these colleges were having their own libraries.

The Charter Act of 1813, the foundation of Fort William and Serampore Colleges, Calcutta, Madras and Bombay universities and their libraries, Hunter, Raleigh and Calcutta University Commissions, library training programmes, the establishment of Inter University Board, Sargent Report and appointment of the University Grants Committee, the establishment of Madras University, University of Bombay, University of Calcutta and their libraries, the constitution of Inter-University Board, the appointment of Hartog Committee, the Montague-Chelmsford reforms of 1919, the Government of India Act of 1935, and the Sargent Committee Report etc. laid foundation for establishment of libraries in various parts of the country.

The Fort William College was founded in Calcutta on 18th August 1800 by the Marquis of Welleselay, the Governor-General of India during 1798-1805. Reverend David Brown, Provost of the college was instrumental in setting up the library which had a well rounded collection of Eastern manuscripts.

In the absence of adequate financial support, the library could not survive for long and in 1835 it was decided to close the library and its valuable collection was transferred to the Asiatic Society Library in Calcutta between 1835-39. The Charter Act of 1813 passed by the British Parliament gave the East India

Company complete responsibility for educating Indians. The establishment of C.M.S. College in Kottayam, Hindu College in Calcutta in 1816 and Raven Shaw College in Cuttack in 1816 was the immediate result of the Charter Act 1813. These and other colleges came into existence thereafter had their own libraries the day they were established. Serampore College during this period was founded by the Danes in 1818 and the King of Denmark in 1927 agreed to give this college an academic status by providing equivalence to the Danish Universities with power to confer degrees.

The library of this college too was established along with its foundation and at a later stage the college was given affiliation to the University of Burdwan for the purpose of conferring degrees. The 7th March 1835 decision of the British Indian Government to promote English literature and sciences in India was resulted into the spread of number of colleges in India and by 1839 there were over forty colleges with attached libraries in the British territory in India.

For their establishment, lots of money was made available by the Indians in the form of donations. In 1840 Presidency College was founded in Madras, followed by a medical college in Bombay in 1845. This progress in education was instrumental in establishing universities in India.

The Charles Wood dispatch of 1854 popularly known as the 'Magna Carta of English Education' in India also paved the way for the establishment of the universities in the presidency towns. Sir John Colville introduced the Bill to establish universities in India and it was passed by the Governor General of India Lord Dalhousie on 24th January 1857, paved the way for the foundation of three universities based on the London Universities Model in the Presidency towns of Calcutta, Madras and Bombay.

Indian Education Commission, popularly known as Hunter Commission was appointed by the British Indian Government in 1882 to study the progress of education under the new policy adopted in 1854 by the East India Company and transferred to the Crown and accepted by the Secretary of State in 1859. Sir William W. Hunter in his report had clearly stated that the conditions of the libraries was in a very poor state and declared them "hardly creditable." The Commission paid special attention to the colleges and their libraries and other facilities.

The direct result of the Commission was the establishment of Panjab University, Lahore and Allahabad University in 1882 and 1887 respectively but still the condition of the education and libraries remained in a poor state.

The Raleigh Commission 1902 appointed by Lord Curzon to investigate the conditions and prospects of the Indian universities and to recommend measures to improve their constitution and working and standards of teaching also paid special attention to the academic libraries and found that, "the library is little used by graduates and hardly at all by other students." Further, the Commission commented, "In a college where library is inadequate or ill arranged, the students have no opportunity of forming the habit of independent and intelligent reading."

Thus, the Commission specifically recommended that reference services must be made an integral part of all libraries in colleges and universities, and that one of the prerequisite conditions for the grant of university affiliation to a college be the accessibility of students to the library of the institution.

The recommendations of the Raleigh Commission were included in the Universities Act of 1904 and provided the power to all universities to require that all colleges applying for affiliation maintain proper libraries, equipment, library building, and lend books to all students but the situation and the status of libraries could not be improved much simply because the recommendations made by the Commission and the provisions made in the act could not be implemented properly. The Calcutta University Commission popularly known as Sadler Commission was appointed by the government in 1917 to study the situation and the status of education in the country and to make recommendations to solve the existing problems.

The Commission noticed that "one of the greatest weak-nesses of the existing system is the extraordinarily unimportant part which is played by the library" and found that "in some colleges the library is regarded not as an essential part of teaching equipment but merely as a more or less useless conventional accessory." The Commission made the recommendations regarding the libraries that college libraries be strengthened and that training should be given to the students and occasionally to the teachers about use of the library.

One of the immediate result of the Calcutta University Commission was the establishment of a few new teaching-cum-residential universities at Patna in 1917, Osmania in Hyderabad in 1918, Dacca, Aligarh, and Lucknow in 1921, Delhi in 1922 and Nagpur in 1923 and all of them were established along with the establishment of libraries as an integral part of the university system.

As stated earlier, the impact of the Commission could very well be seen in the establishment of several universities along with their libraries. This was the period when in the libraries scenario, a person appeared who at a later stage turned the entire scene and become the father of library science in India.

The man was none other than Dr. S.R. Ranganathan. The University of Madras appointed Dr. S.R. Ranganathan as its Librarian in 1924. He was trained at the University of London Library School before joining his duties at Madras. Things did change rapidly after his joining. For example, he introduced the lending and reference services at the Madras University Library and extended the library hours for the benefit of the readers.

Whereas the hours had previously been 7 a.m. to 4 p.m., they were changed to 7 a.m. to 6 p.m. He delivered a series of lectures to about two thousand teachers at the conference of the South Indian Teachers' Union in 1929 regarding the use and importance of the library services.

The Madras Library Association started a summer course in librarianship and the lectures for this course were mainly delivered by Dr. Ranganathan. The main objective of the course in its beginning was to spread the ideas of the value of good library services and modern library methods among potential users of the library. The budget of the university library of Madras had been very poor from the beginning and it was really a difficult task to manage, run and administer the library effectively within it.

Ranganathan brought this poor financial position to the notice of the then Chief Minister, Dr. P. Subbaroyan, when he delivered a speech during an educational conference held at Madras in 1926. In his speech, Ranganathan "gave a graphic account of the library network in Europe and the United States of America and compared it with the poor, appalling facilities existing in India.... added that paucity of funds prevented him developing his library."

The Chief Minister was highly impressed by Ranganathan's speech and promised to give more State help to the University Library. Its immediate result was a grant of rupees 6,000 which was added to the annual grant from the State, and, in addition, rupees 100,000 in lump sum were sanctioned by the Madras State Government in the same year to buy books and periodicals in pure sciences, humanities, and social sciences.

Provision was also made for additional grants to the library, as and when new departments of study and research were established. In the words of Ranganathan, "This was the first time when such a forward financial step in the history of the university libraries in India was taken in the second quarter of the 20th century."

The University of Madras library made a good start under Ranganathan's effective leadership and administration. In 1930, the library had five well-trained reference librarians to help the readers, and they "carried the work to a high pitch of efficiency."

This was the first time in the history of Indian libraries that a special reference service was introduced in a university library. The library collection increased to 93,000 volumes in 1935 and on September 3, 1936, the library was shifted to its first new and permanent functional building. By 1944, when Ranganathan resigned from the position of the Librarian, to become the University Librarian at the *Banaras Hindu University* (BHU), the collection of the Madras University Library had augmented to 1,20,000 volumes.

The contribution of Dr. Ranganathan to the growth and development of libraries in general and the Madras University Library in particular is undoubtedly tremendous and unforgettable. It will not be wrong to say that the Library School of Madras and the Madras University Library were the laboratories of Ranganathan to propound his ideas in library science and to test them practically.

Some of the important and major ideas of Ranganathan were the Five Laws of Library Science which were enunciated by him in 1924, and their formulation and publication in 1929 and 1931 respectively. These laws are still considered a unifying theory for all library practices and services, and set of guidelines for the dynamic development and study of library science as a whole.

The University of Bombay Library received a special grant of rupees 50,000 from the Central Government in 1939 to strengthen its collection for graduate studies. During the period from 1931 to 1939, a few more special grants were given to the library for its collection development. A very special grant of rupees 10,000 was given by Kikabhai and Maniklal, sons of the late Premchand Roychand, in 1931 to replace the electric clock of the library tower. The collection, which stood at 4,504 volumes in 1900, rose to 70,000 in 1939 and 73,582 in 1947. Though higher education and academic libraries made some progress during the first quarter of the present century, yet their growth and development was not very well organized.

Academic institutions and their growth after 1916 created a few problems also and the general feeling was that the "quality of Education was being sacrificed for quantity." While such a situation prevailed, the Indian Statutory Commission, popularly known as the Simon Commission, was appointed by the Government in 1927 to study the conditions prevailing in India.

The Simon Commission appointed an Auxiliary Committee to look into the growth of education in India. Sir Philip Hartog, a former member of the Calcutta University Commission, and a former Vice-Chancellor of the University of Dacca, was appointed its Chairman.

In its report, submitted in 1929, the Committee stated that "the dispersal of resources for university teaching among a number of colleges had made it difficult to build up university libraries of the type required for advanced work both at the Honours and the research stage majority of the university libraries were inadequate and all needed great additions."

In addition to want of books, libraries also lacked good current periodicals in their collections. The Committee also made a special note of the low academic standards in many colleges and universities and the "unhealthy competition for candidates between neighbouring universities". This report, however, did not offer any comprehensive, detailed, and realistic solutions to the problems. In 1935, Ministry of Education was formed in each province, as per the provisions of the dyarchy in the Montague-Chelmsford Reforms of 1919, supplemented by those of the new Government of India Act of 1935.

The Ministry of Education in India requested the Central Advisory Board of Education in 1944 to survey the educational conditions in the country. The Board's report, known as the Sargeant Report, after its Chairman, Sir Sargeant, the Educational Advisor to the Government of India, came up with a master-plan for the development of education in the post-World War II India. Its terms of reference covered education at all levels-primary, secondary, and higher. The Indian universities, as they existed then, despite many admirable features, did not fully satisfy the requirements of a national system of education. During the British rule, several committees and commissions set up periodically, paved way for the foundation of several colleges and the establishment of many universities and in many cases the libraries were also established along with them.

It is also true that as compared to the first two decades the development of university libraries after 1924 did make better progress but the college libraries were still neglected and were struggling to get their recognition.

There were only 12 universities in India in 1924 and their number swelled to 18 by the time India got freedom in 1947. In fact, the academic libraries during the British rule had no significance in the academic life of the institutions of higher education and the pivotal role that can be played by the academic libraries in the life of the institutions could very well be seen in the policy statement of higher education of the free India and the fact was also proven when at the time of national reconstruction, the importance of libraries in teaching and research was recognized, and libraries received the early attention of the Government of India.

ACADEMIC LIBRARIES IN INDIA AFTER INDEPENDENCE

The actual process for the development of university libraries in India can be said to have been set in motion with the appointment of the University Education Commission presided over by Dr. S. Radhakrishnan and its recommendations, such as, annual grants, open access system, working hours, organization of the library, staff, steps to make students book conscious and the need to give grants to teachers to buy books.

The section on libraries of the report opens with a powerful statement on the importance of libraries in university education and states, "teaching is a cooperative enterprise. Teachers must have the necessary tools for teaching purposes in the shape of libraries and laboratories as also the right type of students."

The Commission in the course of its study of the academic libraries, found that "libraries were hopelessly inadequate to serve the curricular needs of a modern university. They were ill-housed, illstocked, and ill-staffed and were totally lacking in standard literary and scientific journals. Service was in the hands of personnel that had hardly any notion of the objectives of university education. The annual appropriation for book purchase seldom exceeded the ten thousand mark."

In addition, the annual grant for these libraries were not sufficient. Therefore, the Commission recommended that at least six per cent of the total budget of each academic institution should be set aside for the library. It added that if institutions were not willing to allocate six per cent of their budget to libraries, they should spend ₹ 40 per student enrolled. The Commission also suggested that greater attention should be paid to improve the reference services in the university libraries. Documentation and biblio-graphical services must be developed in order to promote research among the faculty and students, make libraries proper centres for research activities, and to raise the standards of services.

As far as the library staff is concerned, the Commission was of the view that it is very important to have well-qualified staff, including the Director, in order to provide excellent service in any library. The Director's qualifications must include Ph.D. in Library Science and he must have the rank and salary of a professor, capabilities of organization and management, and should have full powers of an administrator to run the library effectively.

University Education Commission. There is no doubt that the recommendations of the Commission "were based on the needs of the modern library services in universities for the promotion of research and creative learning." It was for the first time that such detailed attention was paid to the library matters by a commission on university education in India.

Ranganathan Committee (1957)

The most comprehensive and significant document on the university and college libraries is the Report of the UGC library committee, chaired by Ranganathan. The Report was published by the University Grants Commission in 1959 entitled 'University and College Libraries.' It was perhaps the first attempt by any Library Committee in India to systematically survey the academic libraries on a national basis, and it was also the first time that the government of India had decided to seek advice from a professional librarian regarding academic libraries. The committee was to advice the UGC on the standards of libraries, building, pay scales, and library training.

After the survey the library committee invited all academic librarians to a seminar on "Work flow in university and college libraries," at Delhi from March 4 to 7, 1959 to keep them informed about the progress the committee had made surveying the academic libraries. It wanted to discuss its recommendations with them. Some of the recommendations of the Committee included the provision that the UGC and the State Government should help the college and the university libraries in the collection development of both books and periodicals.

The formula suggested by the committee was that funds be given "at the rate of ₹ 15 per enrolled student and ₹ 200 per teacher and research fellow. There should also be special initial library grants in the case of a new university and of a new department in an existing university, a similar scale should be followed for the college libraries. In order to promote co-operation among libraries, a Union Catalogue of books and a Union List of periodicals to be prepared. The Committee strongly recommended that an open access system be introduced in every academic library. Committee also stressed "that reference service is the essential human process of establishing contact between the right reader and the right book by personal service. Reference service is vital in promotion of reading habit in student each library should provide an adequate number of reference librarians to function as library hosts and human converters."

Other recommendations included building up a microfilm collection, copying facilities for microfilms and book material, appointment of a committee to look into the standards of teaching, examination and research in the library schools, and appointment of full-time teaching faculty members rather than asking librarians to teach part time in the library schools.

The Committee added that "the status and the salary of the library staff should be the same as that of the teaching and research staff', *i.e.*, Professor, Reader, and Lecturer etc." The recommendations of the committee had a farreaching effect on the development of the university libraries later.

They had not only provided a framework to the UGC to implement its grants-in-aid programmes but also given to the university authorities important guidelines. Particular mention, in this connection, may be made of the recommendations concerning the library finances which had helped libraries to secure enough finances by way of annual grants from the universities themselves and of development grants from the UGC.

The recommendations on the library personnel and staff strength have given to the library staff status and salaries equivalent to the academic staff and ensure provision for adequate staff for various library operations. The Committee submitted its report to the UGC with the hope that it will provide a blueprint for the systematic development of university libraries in the country.

Hence, inspite of many hurdles like education being a state subject in the Indian Constitution, considerable development in the university libraries has taken place and as such the condition of these libraries in 1953 was much better than in the 1940's and even the early 1950's.

Kothari Commission

The Education Commission under the chairmanship of Dr. D. S. Kothari marked another important stage in the history of university libraries in India.

The Commission devoted considerable attention to the development of the university libraries and made suitable recommendations on the following points:

- Norms for financial support;
- Long range planning for library development;

- The need for the establishment of a well equipped library before the starting of a university, college, or department;
- Suitable phasing over of the library grants;
- Encouraging the students in the use of books;
- Interdisciplinary communication; and
- Documentation service in libraries etc.

The Education Commission had also addressed itself to the role of libraries in adult education and recommended establish-ment of a network of public libraries. It wanted the school libraries to be integrated with public libraries for purposes of the adult education programmes. The Report, submitted by Dr. D. S. Kothari, on June 29, 1966, emphatically pointed out that "nothing can be more damaging than to ignore its library and to give it a low priority. No new college, university or department should be opened unless adequate number of books in the library are provided."

The Commission was shocked to note that the recommen-dations of the Radhakrishnan Commission had not been fully implemented, for only four universities in India has spent five per cent or more of their budget on books and periodicals acquisitions, though the 1948's Commission has suggested that six per cent of the total budget be spent on libraries. Other universities had spent less than five per cent of their budget on libraries, "Surprisingly enough there are five universities which spent even less than one per cent of the total budget on the libraries."

It was clear proof that the university libraries in India were not functioning properly to fulfil the needs of higher education. The Kothari Commission recommended that a long range plan for library development should be drawn up for each academic institution taking into consideration anticipated increase in enrollment, introduction of new subjects and research needs etc., and documentation service be encouraged in libraries, and documentation experts be appointed to help researchers and do indexing and abstracting. It was further recommended that "the book selection should be oriented towards supporting instruction and research." The library should "provide resources necessary for research in fields of special interest to the university; provide library facilities and services necessary for the success of all formal programmes of instruction."

Monetary guidelines were also suggested by the Commission. "As a norm, a university should spend each year about ₹ 25 per student registered and ₹ 300 per teacher depending on the stage of development of each university library." It was also suggested that "the foreign exchange needed for university and college libraries should be allowed separately to the UGC."

The Wheat Loan Programme

During the 1950's and early 1960's the Indian academic libraries received huge grants from the UGC amounting up to ₹ 100,000 for books, buildings, equipment and even for additional staff. At the same time many libraries got additional grants from a special US fund called the 'Wheat Loan Programme.' The American Congress passed a special Act, in 1951 known as the 'Public Law 480' to loan India $ 19,000,000 to buy much needed wheat from the US. Under the agreement of the loan, India had to buy American books, periodicals and scientific equipment worth $ 50,000 to be used for research purposes in the Indian libraries.

This, money India had to pay as interest on the loan. Part of the money was to be spent on the exchange of scholars, including librarians, between the two countries. The United States authorities bought some educational material and equipment from India for research purposes and higher education in the American Universities.

During 1951-1961 Indian libraries spent US $ 1,400,000 of the purchase of American books, US dollar 160,000 on libraries, US $ 40,000 on the travel and study grants for thirty three Indian librarians to visit the United States and US $ 75,000 on the travel and study grants of the five Americans.

College Libraries

The College libraries in India have a significant role to play in higher education. Majority of the undergraduate students, *i.e.*, 88.5 per cent and graduate students, *i.e.*, 53 per cent, attend these colleges. When India attained Independence many among the 533 affiliated colleges did not have their own libraries, but at present, every college in the country has a library.

Majority of the college libraries do not have proper facilities to meet the needs of their users. Their collections are not up-to-date, budgets are their very inadequate and limited, and a large number of them are single libraries. In many colleges, there is neither a library hall nor a sufficient big room, not to think of a separate building for the library.

Any unused room, quite often somewhere out of sight, would be considered adequate to house a few shelves of books. And in most college libraries there is complete darkness even during the day time, as the windows are closed out of a fear that the books may be stolen.. Different studies, conducted by scholars and Srivastva have explicitly established that the condition of the college libraries in India are far from satisfactory.

The college libraries are open only six to eight hours a day. Many do not have any qualified librarian on their staff and have closed stacks only. The several commissions and committees, like the Radhakrishnan Commission of 1948, did not stress the importance of the college libraries in their reports. However, the University Grants Commission gives more importance to the college libraries.

As the quality of higher education and research, especially at the graduate level, depends upon, among other things, the standard of the college libraries and their services. Therefore, the UGC has played a significant role in the growth and development of college libraries since 1953 by giving grants for books, equipment, staff and library buildings and has done a remarkable job in salary improvement of the college librarians. The UGC's contribution to the college libraries is at the rate of ₹ 15 per student with a maximum of ₹ 10,000 with some additional and special grants for text books, when a new subject is introduced in the Curriculum.

On the other hand, the colleges and the state governments have failed to provide their equal share. The total Expenditure on the college libraries according to the recommendation of the Education Commission should be 6.25 per cent of the total budgets of the colleges, but in most cases it has remained between 1.5 per cent and 2.3 per cent.

Sardana Collection development of the college libraries are done without taking into consideration the actual needs of the faculty and the students of the colleges as sixty per cent of them consist of text books and 20 per cent cover fiction.

Even this small inadequate collection, in depth and content, is not used effectively due to the closed stacks system and lack of staff and facilities for instruction concerning their use. The net result is that the utility factor of the college libraries comes practically to nothing.

In most college libraries, books are neither properly classified nor catalogued. In several libraries no systematic classification is followed for collection arrangements. The only service the college library renders to its clientele is book-lending. There are colleges where students are not even allowed inside the library.

The UGC is aware of the slow progress of the college libraries. In addition to providing financial help for development, it has also from time to time organized seminars to keep the college librarians aware of the new developments in the field. But these seminars have made only a limited effect on the progress of the college libraries. The condition of the college libraries in the country should be a cause for alarm among the academic community.

In the interests of the development of higher education in the country along proper lines, it is important to make a detailed study of the style of functioning of the college libraries and of the utilization of the library resources and facilities by the students and teachers. This will help in the preparation of more realistic and operational policies and programmes for ensuring the proper functioning, utilization and development of the college libraries. The college library has to be made the intellectual hub of the institution, serving equally, both the students and teachers.

This is all the more necessary because about 90 per cent of the students in higher education in India pursue their studies in colleges and they have only very small and substandard college library resources to fall back upon. Although, owing to various efforts of the UGC as well as other forces, the traditional concept that the college library is a custodian of books has changed, yet there is evidence enough to show that the condition of the college libraries is generally poor, their development is rather slow and that the position of the college libraries and their librarians in India, with a few exceptions, is pitiable.

UNIVERSITY LIBRARIES

University libraries all over the world have their own place of importance in the scheme of higher learning. Libraries are not only repositories of knowledge but also dispensers of such knowledge. There is no doubt that where libraries of universities and institutions of higher learning are ignored or not given due recognition, the country as a whole suffers because the standards of study, teaching and research very heavily depend upon the qualitative and quantitative service rendered by the university libraries.

The Radhakrishnan Commission expressed that "the library is the heart of all the university's work, directly so, as regards its research work and indirectly as regards its educational work, which derives its life from research. Scientific research needs the library as well as its laboratories while for humanistic research the library is both library and the laboratory in one. Both for humanistic and scientific studies, a first class library is essential in a university."

The growth of university libraries since Independence can be seen in respect of the initiatives taken by the Central Government considering the vital importance of higher education and role of libraries in the educational development, commitment to fulfill the demand of higher education, and the foundation of the UGC in 1953 by an Act of Parliament. The Radhakrishnan Commission recognized the value and importance of a well equipped and organized library system and its role in higher education.

It had found many drawbacks and pitfalls in the university libraries and had made many recommendations for the improvement of library facilities. The Ranganathan Committee, appointed by the UGC in 1957, made some outstanding recommendations, which included standards for library building, collection development, staff and services and furniture etc. These recommendations were accepted by the UGC and forwarded for implementation.

The Kothari Commission also made valuable recommen-dations for this purpose, but the role of the University Grants Commission deserves special mention, because it has played a vital role by "regularly providing appropriate grants and funds to all universities for development of libraries, to purchase books and journals...., construction of new library buildings and for library equipment and furniture."

Dr. D. S. Kothari, the Chairman of University Grants Commission, said, "Libraries play a vital role in the development of institutions of higher learning.

The University Grants Commission attaches great importance to the strengthening of library facilities in the universities and colleges and their efficient administration. The commission has also been giving grants to institutions for books and journals construction of library building and appointment of library staff."

One of the most remarkable and identifiable development in the history of higher education and libraries was the foundation of the INFLIBNET in 1991. Information and Library Network Centre is an autonomous Inter-University Centre of the UGC of India. It is a major National Programme initiated by the UGC in 1991 with its Head Quarters at Gujarat University Campus, Ahmedabad. Initially started as a project under the IUCAA, it became an independent Inter-University Centre in 1966.

Its objectives are:

- To promote and establish communication facilities to improve capability in information transfer and access, that provides support to scholarship, learning, research and academic pursuit through cooperation and involvement of agencies concerned.
- *To establish Inflibnet*: Information and Library Network a computer communication network for linking libraries and information centres in universities, deemed to be universities, colleges, UGC information centres, institutions of national importance and R&D institutions, etc. avoiding duplication of efforts.

Inflibnet performs following major activities:

- Provides grants to universities to automate the libraries, establishing the network facilities and create an information technology environment.
- Developed and distributed Software for University Libraries (Soul) which is an integrated userfriendly library management software. The latest version of the software is 2.0 which is competent to operate with the latest technologies and international standards such as MARC21, Unicode based and NCIP 2.0 based protocols for electronic surveillance and control.
- Indian Catalogue of University Libraries in India (IndCat) is Online Library Catalogue of books, theses and journals available in major university libraries in India which provides bibliographic description, location of the material in all subjects available in more than 112 university libraries. Thus, IndCat has over 10 million bibliographical records of books from more than 113 universities. In addition, the database of theses, expert databases, project databases and Sewakoffline database access facilities are also extended to the libraries of higher learning institutions.
- To enhance the skills of university library staff for implementation of

Inflibnet programme, it conducts training programme for library staff, onsite training for member library staff, training on SOUL software, holding Calibre convention every year and workshops for senior level staff of the university libraries are conducted.

- It has brought out a document entitled 'Inflibnet Standards and Guideline for Data Capturing' prepared by a task force of experts based on Common Communication Format (CCF).

Another very important and significant landmark in the history of higher education and development of libraries in India is the establishment of "Ugcinfonet Digial Library Consortium" by the UGC on the concluding day of its Golden jubilee celebrations by his Excellency the then President of India, Dr. A.P.J Abdul Kalam at Vigyan Bhawan on 28th December 2003. UGC-Infonet is an innovative project launched by UGC to facilitate scholarly e-resources to Indian academies through joint partnership of UGC, Inflibnet and Ernet.

This includes interlinking of universities and colleges in the country electronically with a view to achieve maximum efficiency through Internet enabled teaching, learning and governance. The UGC-Infonet is overlaid on Ernet infrastructure in a manner so as to provide assured quality of service and optimum utilization of bandwidth resources. The network will be run and managed by Ernet India.

The project is funded by UGC with 100 per cent capital investment and up to 90 per cent of recurring costs. UGC and Ernet India have signed the necessary MoU for this purpose. A joint technical and tariff committee, has been setup to guide and monitor the design, implementation and operations of Ugcinfonet. Information for Library Network (Inflibnet) an autonomous Inter-University Centre of UGC, is the nodal agency for coordination and facilitation of the linkage between Ernet and the Universities.

Under this programme, information and communication technologies (ICT) and internet will be used to transform learning environment from a monodimensional one to a multidimensional one. This was created to help and benefit more than 310 universities and about 14,000 colleges affiliated with these universities and approximately 10 million students with the e-journals, thus, is a boon to higher education system in many ways.

The UGC-Infonet digital Library consortium has the following objectives: Bhatt,

- To subscribe electronic resources for the members of the consortium at highly discounted rates of subscription and with the best terms and conditions.
- Promote the rational use of funds.
- Guarantee local storage of the information acquired for continuous use by present and future users.
- To impart training to the users, librarians, research scholars and

faculty members of the institutions on the electronic resources with an aim to optimize the usage of the electronic resources.
- To have more interaction amongst the member libraries.
- To increase the research productivity of the institutions in terms of quality and quantity of publications
- Strategic alliance with institutions that have common interests resulting reduced information cost and improved resource sharing.

National Knowledge Commission

The National Knowledge Commission was set up by the Government of India on 13th June 2005 with a time-frame of three years, from 2nd October 2005 to 2nd October 2008. As a high-level advisory body to the Prime Minister of India, the National Knowledge Commission was given a mandate to guide policy and direct reforms, focusing on certain key areas such as education, science and technology, agriculture, industry, e-governance etc. Easy access to knowledge, creation and preservation of knowledge systems, dissemination of knowledge and better knowledge services are core concerns of the Commission.

The Commission envisaged the future road map for the growth and development of academic libraries by imbibing core issues such as, set up a national commission on libraries, prepare a national census of all libraries, revamp LIS education, training and research facilities, re-assess staffing of libraries, set up a central library fund, modernize library management, encourage greater community participation in library management, promote information communication technology applications in all libraries, facilitate donation and maintenance of private collections, and encourage public private partnerships in LIS development, etc.

3

Digital Library Science

INFORMATION SCIENCE

What is information science? The question, while seemingly simple, begs another, more complex one: *How is information science, or for that matter any field, to be defined?* This is a complex problem dealt with at length in philosophy and in other fields. Lexical definitions are necessary for providing a broad description and boundaries of the subjects covered by a field, but they cannot provide for a deeper understanding. Webster does not a field define. This is not to reject clear lexical definitions—not at all—just to establish their limitations.

In approaching the discussion of information science, I am taking the problem point of view as elaborated by Popper who argued that:

- [S]ubject matter or kind of things do not, I hold, constitute a basis for distinguishing disciplines....*We are not students of some subject matter, but students of problems*. Any problem may cut right across the border of any subject matter or discipline.

Our emphasis is on problems addressed by information science. Although we provide definitions of information science and other fields in interdisciplinary relations with information science later in the chapter, we are doing this solely to advance the understanding of problems addressed by different fields and their relation to information science problems.

Debates over the "proper" definition of information science, as of any field, are fruitless, and in expectations naive. Information science, as a science and as a profession, is defined by the problems it has addressed and the methods it has used for their solutions over time.

Any advances in information science depend on whether the field is indeed progressing in relation to problems addressed and methods used. Any "fixing," if in order, will have to be approached by redefining or refocusing either the problems addressed, or the methods for their solutions, or both.

Information science has three general characteristics that are the leitmotif of its evolution and existence. These are shared with many modern fields.

They can also be viewed as problem areas with which infor-mation science has to deal on a general level:

- First, information science is interdisciplinary in nature; however, the relations with various disciplines are changing. The interdisciplinary evolution is far from over.
- Second, information science is inexorably connected to information technology. A technological imperative is compelling and constraining the evolution of information science, as is the evolution of a number of other fields, and moreover, of the information society as a whole.
- Third, information science is, with many other fields, an active participant in the evolution of the infor-mation society. Information science has a strong social and human dimension, above and beyond technology.

A number of works that I freely consulted dealt with various historical aspects of information science.

Among those works are:

- Shera and Cleveland,
- Bourne,
- Herner,
- Salton,
- Cleverdon,
- Swanson,
- Lilley and Trice,
- Farkas-Conn,
- Buckland and Liu, and
- Rayward.

Still, a comprehensive history of information science is a project for a future historian of science. As yet only historical pieces and different perspectives of pieces exist. A history of any field is a history of a few powerful ideas.

I suggest that information science has three such powerful ideas, so far. These ideas deal with processing of information in a radically different way than was done previously or elsewhere. The first and the original idea, emerging in 1950s, is *information retrieval*, providing for processing of information based on formal logic. The second, emerging shortly thereafter, is *relevance*, directly orienting and associating the process with human information needs and assessments.

The third, derived from elsewhere some two decades later, is *interaction*, enabling direct exchanges and feedback between systems and people engaged in IR processes. So far, no powerful ideas have emerged about *information*, as the underlying phenomenon, or *"literature"*, as the object of processing.

However, one can argue that the idea of mapping of "literature," that started with exploitation of citation indexes in 1960s, may also qualify as a powerful idea. In a non-historical sense this stage deals with these powerful ideas and with leitmotifs. They form a framework for understanding the past, present, and future of information science.

DEFINITION OF DIGITAL LIBRARIES AND PERSONALISED SERVICES

While reviewing the definitions of digital libraries, Borgman noted that "in general, researchers (who primarily come from computer science and/or engineering backgrounds) focus on digital libraries as content collected on behalf of user communities, while librarians focus on digital libraries as institutions or services"'. She further stressed that the current state of digital library research and development, especially in the USA, is influenced by the research definition of digital libraries.

The emphasis on the "enabling technologies" for access to digital resources rather than on the services traditionally provided by libraries becomes quite evident when one looks at the two special issues of the *Journal of the American Society for Information Science*, The two issues contain excellent articles reflecting the state of digital library research but none focus on digital library services *per se*. Even the editor of the two special issues did not discuss reference and information services.

He mentioned that "digital libraries have the ability to provide a previously unattainable level of service". He emphasised access to information and suggested the various methods, tools and techniques that facilitate improved access to information in digital libraries. However, this is in sharp contrast to the views of the two editors of the special issue of *Information Processing and Management* on digital libraries. Marchionini and Fox in their editorial stated that "digital library work occurs in the context of a complex design space shaped by four dimensions: community, technology, services and content".

The fact that digital libraries should not be regarded only as point of access to digital information was emphasised by a definition of digital libraries given by Borgman as early as in 1992 whereby she contended that a digital library are:

- A service;
- An architecture;
- A set of information resources, databases of text, numbers, graphics, sound, video, etc. and
- A set of tools and capabilities to locate, retrieve and utilise the information resources available.

The definition of a digital library that came up in the March 1994 Digital Library Workshop emphasised that a full service digital library must accomplish all the essential services of traditional libraries and also exploit the well-known advantages of digital storage, searching and communication.

There are many other definitions of digital libraries that mention the services aspect, either explicitly or implicitly. Pointing out the lack of emphasis on reference and information services, Sloan lamented that "human interaction in the digital library is discussed far less frequently. One would almost get the impression that the service tradition of the physical library will be unnecessary and redundant in the digital library environment".

He emphasised the point that "technology and information resources, on their own, cannot make up an effective digital library". Emphasising the need for personalised services in digital libraries, Lombardi mentioned that, "helping clients find resources in a digitally chaotic world is the first priority". In a Delphi study of digital libraries it was revealed that "the primary roles librarians play in digital libraries include organisation, selection and acquisition and acting as gateways to the provision of services involving information". This study also revealed that "the best reasons for developing a digital library include: increasing access to information, serving end users' needs and bringing organisation to the unstructured universe of electronically available information".

Thus, this study shows the importance of "serving end users' needs", and the need for the librarians to act as "gateways to the provision of services involving information" in a digital library. Another study conducted by Downs and Friedman indicated that "in the absence of human intermediaries, there is a need for end-user instruction on the use of digital libraries". Covi pointed out that "digital libraries will be used only when workers can readily integrate into social legimitated and legitimatable ways of working". She further suggested that subject specialists, as digital library service providers, help users formulate disciplinary search strategies and provide assistance in developing new resources.

Arms, while trying to answer the question "whether or not we need reference librarians in a digital library", pointed out that automatic tools are steadily reducing the need for reference librarians in fields like medicine that required a significant amount of intermediation in information searching. The essence of Arms' paper is that while computers can do a lot in performing most of the traditional jobs of reference librarians, their skills may be required in case of complex information searches.

Arms, however, believes that there have been significant improvements in the end-user search facilities, provided by electronic database search services and Web search engines, and hence, the need for human intermediaries in information searching has reduced significantly. Perhaps the most comprehensive view of the need for and the nature of personalised services in a digital library has been delineated by researchers.

They maintained that:

- Services reflect the functionality afforded by systems serving the community of users. Access services that facilitate search and browsing have been central to digital library research thus far, but there is great need for attention to reference and question-answering, on-demand help, and fostering of citisenship and literacy and mechanisms to simplify participatory involvement of user communities.

REFERENCE AND INFORMATION SERVICES ON THE WEB

A number of reference and information services are now available on the Web. Interestingly, many of these services are provided by non-library and commercial organisations. While some are free, others need payment.

Detailed discussions on such services are available in a number of publications, McKiernan maintains a site that provides categorised listing of libraries that offer real-time reference services using chat software, live interactive communication tools, call centre management software, bulletin board services and other Internet technologies.

Most of these services are designed for registered users of the libraries concerned.

Researchers categorised online reference and information services into three broad groups:

- Reference and information services from publishers, database search services, and specialised institutions;
- Reference services provided by libraries and/or experts through the Internet; and
- Reference and information services where users need to conduct a search and find information through theWeb.

Researchers discussed several online information services that belong to the first category.

They have listed various current awareness and SDI services such as: the contents page service from commercial publishers, such as Elsevier's

- Contents Direct Service, IDEAL Alert from Academic Press, and so on;
- Information on new books available free from publishers and vendors, such as the *Wiley Book Notification Service* and Amazon.com;
- SDI services fromonline search service providers, such as Dialog;
- *Current Contents* and *ISI Alerting Services* from ISI, and so on.

Some of these services, particularly the contents page services from publishers of journals, are free, while for others, such as *Dialog Alerts* or *Current Contents* from ISI, users need to register and pay.

Table provides a quick overview of some online reference and information services currently available. This is not an exhaustive list, but the table shows the different types of services and some of their characteristics.

It provides the following facts about the Web-based reference services listed there:

- The listed Web-based reference services are offered by dotcom companies;
- These services use the Web only for communication between the user and the system/answer provider, while the information service is provided by a human expert;
- While most services are free, some charge as high as $250 per question;
- in many cases services are provided by (self-proclaimed?) volunteer experts;
- There are some services offered in specific subject fields.

In addition to those in table, there are also some Web-based reference services where users need to conduct a search for a reference query. Such services provide free access to various online reference sources, and allow users either to select a specific source or conduct a search on a range, or all, of the reference sources.

Examples of such services include the following:

- Internet Public Library.
- Infoplease
- Britannica
- Bartleby Reference.
- Internet Library for Librarians.
- Electric Library.
- Mediaeater Reference Desk.
- ReferenceDesk.
- Xrefer.

While most of these Web-based reference services are available free, some charge a small fee. For example, the Electric Library charges $79.95 for an entire year of unlimited access. Janes *et al.* reported a study of 20 Web-based "expert services". By asking 240 questions to 20 selected expert services, they noted that the sites gave verifiable answers to 69 per cent of factual questions. An interesting observation of this study was that the kind of reference interview that takes place in traditional reference service environments is non-existent in Web-based reference services.

In fact, the sites did not come back for any discussion or clarification after receiving the initial queries. As a justification, the authors suggested that Web-based information services have been built mainly to answer factual questions, and therefore the experts concerned do not need to go through the reference interview process.

Nevertheless, the high rate of success of factual questions shows that more and more end-users will move towards these expert services rather than to libraries for answers to simple types of questions.

SEARCH ENGINE SERVICES

Although Ask Jeeves is basically a search engine, many researchers also see it as aWeb-based information service because of two reasons:

- Unlike in other search and metasearch engines, users can ask a question in Ask Jeeves, and in many cases can get an answer right away; and
- Users can ask a question on a given topic, and Ask Jeeves comes up with a list of questions on the same or similar topics; the user can select any of the those predefined questions, and then Ask Jeeves provides answers to that.

This is an interesting service and may be considered as a useful model for digital library reference and information services.

The Ask Jeeves site maintains that:

- Ask Jeeves is a unique question-answering system that allows users to ask questions in plain English, and then delivers the answer. As one of the most sophisticated navigation systems on the Internet, Ask Jeeves combines a unique natural language engine with a proprietary knowledgebase.Taken together, this mechanism processes the meaning and grammar of real questions in plain English; provides intelligent responses for user confirmation; links directly to relevant, high-quality answers; and, perhaps most exciting of all, becomesmore intelligent as its knowledgebase expands with each question asked and each answer delivered.

The site further says that Ask Jeeves processes each query syntactically and semantically, and then Ask Jeeves' answer-processing engine provides the question template response. When the user clicks on a response, the answer-processing engine retrieves the answer template that contains links to the answer locations. Thus, Ask Jeeves helps users select a query from a pre-defined set of queries on a given topic.

However, there is a debate on whether the kind of service provided by Ask Jeeves matches reference services provided by libraries. Kresh reported an interesting finding: "One consortial system in northern California conducted an informal test of Ask Jeeves by sending it 12 questions its libraries had answered. There were no trick questions, none were arcane, just questions typically received by those libraries. Jeeves was unable to answer any of the questions".

Nevertheless, the techniques and the technology used by Ask Jeeves may be very useful for introducing reference services in digital libraries. Webhelp.com is another service that claims to offer "real-time search assistance with a real live expert I any time, day or night". About.com is a service that shows a number of pre-defined categories related to a search topic given by the user. For example, a simple search on "e-commerce" not only produces a list of sites, but also provides a set of topics related to "e-commerce", such as e-commerce definition, e-commerce security, advantages of e-commerce, e-commerce disadvantages, e-commerce statistics, etc.

DIGITAL REFERENCE SERVICES AND LIBRARIES

A number of libraries have now begun to offer Web-based reference services and a number of recent studies report the current practice of reference services provided by libraries. Although this is not an exhaustive review of all the Web-based reference services provided by libraries, the following section provides a quick overview of some that are currently available.

DIGITAL REFERENCE SERVICES FOR THE GENERAL PUBLIC

Ask A Librarian is a Web-based reference service, primarily designed for UK residents, provided by a network of public libraries in the UK. The site says: "Mail us your factual question and we'll send you an answer within two working days, if not before".

A user has to put the query through an enquiry page, which is automatically routed to one of the participating libraries, which receives it as an e-mail message. Within two days the library sends an e-mail message to the user with its response to the enquiry. The British Library provides special reference services for business, patent, scientific, technical, medical and environmental information. These services range from answering simple questions to finding answers to complex questions involving online database searching, etc. While some of these services are free, for others users need to pay. For example, users can ask simple business questions using a form, and can expect an answer within ten working days. Similarly, users can send e-mails with simple environmental queries.

A typical answer in such a case may include:

- A list of bibliographies from a British Library catalogue literature search; and/or;
- A list of organisations to contact for more detailed information, and/or
- Information retrieved from Internet sources.

Users are not charged for this kind of service. However, for complex queries users need to pay.

For example, the British Library provides a Science Technology Medicine (STM) search service for which users need to pay at the following rate:

- J 82.00 per hour of staff time divided into 15-minute periods;
- Plus costs of online searching;
- Plus Value Added Tax (VAT).

As stated in the Web site most searches take at least 30 minutes and therefore cost J 41.00 for staff time + costs for online searching + VAT. The site also mentions that the average list of references costs J 80.00 for medical subjects, and between J 100.00 and J 150.00 for other subjects. Users are also charged a fee if the results are to be faxed. In order to obtain an STM search service, the user has to fill in a form that has three parts. In the first part users need to fill in their personal details, etc., in the second part, users need to enter the query, and in the third part they need to specify the modes of delivery, payment, etc. In the second part of the form, users can enter the detail specification of the query using Boolean operators and specifying date, language, etc., as limiting factors.

TYPES OF DIGITAL LIBRARIES

The term digital library is diffuse enough to be applied to a wide range of collections and organizations, but, to be considered a digital library, an online collection of information must be managed by and made accessible to a community of users. Thus, some web sites can be considered digital libraries, but far from all. Many of the best known digital libraries are older than the web including Project Perseus, Project Gutenberg, and ibiblio. Nevertheless, as a result of the development of the internet and its search potential, digital libraries such as the European Library and the Library of Congress are now developing in a Web-based environment. Public, school and college libraries are also able to develop digital download web sites, featuring eBooks, audiobooks, music and video.

A distinction is often made between content that was created in a digital format, known as born-digital, and information that has been converted from a physical medium, *e.g.*, paper, by digitizing. The term hybrid library is sometimes used for libraries that have both physical collections and digital collections. For example, American Memory is a digital library within the Library of Congress. Some important digital libraries also serve as long term archives, for example, the ePrint arXiv, and the Internet Archive.

ACADEMIC REPOSITORIES

Many academic libraries are actively involved in building institutional repositories of the institution's books, papers, theses, and other works which can be digitized or were 'born digital'. Many of these repositories are made available to the general public with few restrictions, in accordance with the goals of open access, in contrast to the publication of research in commercial journals, where the publishers often limit access rights. Institutional, truly free, and corporate repositories are sometimes referred to as digital libraries.

DIGITAL ARCHIVES

Physical archives differ from physical libraries in several ways.

Traditionally, archives were defined as:

- Containing primary sources of information (typically letters and papers directly produced by an individual or organization) rather than the secondary sources found in a library (books, periodicals, etc);

- Having their contents organized in groups rather than individual items;
- Having unique contents.

The technology used to create digital libraries has been even more revolutionary for archives since it breaks down the second and third of these general rules.

In other words, "digital archives" or "online archives" will still generally contain primary sources, but they are likely to be described individually rather than (or in addition to) in groups or collections, and because they are digital their contents are easily reproducible and may indeed have been reproduced from elsewhere. The Oxford Text Archive is generally considered to be the oldest digital archive of academic physical primary source materials.

LEADERS IN THE FIELD

Project Gutenberg, Google Book Search, Windows Live Search Books(shutdown), Internet Archive, Cornell University, The Library of Congress World Digital Library, The Digital Library at the University of Michigan, and Carnegie Mellon University's Million Book Project are considered leaders in the field of digital library creation and management.

THE FUTURE

Large scale digitization projects are underway at Google, the Million Book Project, and Internet Archive. With continued improvements in book handling and presentation technologies such as optical character recognition and ebooks, and development of alternative depositories and business models, digital libraries are rapidly growing in popularity as demonstrated by Google, Yahoo!, and MSN's efforts. Just as libraries have ventured into audio and video collections, so have digital libraries such as the Internet Archive.

SEARCHING

Most digital libraries provide a search interface which allows resources to be found. These resources are typically deep web (or invisible web) resources since they frequently cannot be located by search engine crawlers. Some digital libraries create special pages or sitemaps to allow search engines to find all their resources. Digital libraries frequently use the Open Archives Initiative Protocol for Metadata Harvesting (OAI-PMH) to expose their metadata to other digital libraries, and search engines like Google Scholar, Yahoo! and Scirus can also use OAI-PMH to find these deep web resources.

There are two general strategies for searching a federation of digital libraries:

- Distributed searching, and
- Searching previously harvested metadata.

Distributed searching typically involves a client sending multiple search requests in parallel to a number of servers in the federation. The results are gathered, duplicates are eliminated or clustered, and the remaining items are sorted and presented back to the client. Protocols like Z39.50 are frequently used in distributed searching. A benefit to this approach is that the resource-intensive tasks of indexing and storage are left to the respective servers in the federation. A drawback to this approach is that the search mechanism is limited by the different indexing and ranking capabilities of each database, making it difficult to assemble a combined result consisting of the most relevant found items. Searching over previously harvested metadata involves searching a locally stored index of information that has previously been collected from the libraries in the federation. When a search is performed, the search mechanism does not need to make connections with the digital libraries it is searching - it already has a local representation of the information.

This approach requires the creation of an indexing and harvesting mechanism which operates regularly, connecting to all the digital libraries and querying the whole collection in order to discover new and updated resources. OAI-PMH is frequently used by digital libraries for allowing metadata to be harvested. A benefit to this approach is that the search mechanism has full control over indexing and ranking algorithms, possibly allowing more consistent results. A drawback is that harvesting and indexing systems are more resource-intensive and therefore expensive.

MEASUREMENT OF USE AND PERFORMANCE INDICATORS IN THE DIGITAL LIBRARY

INTERNATIONAL STANDARDS FOR PERFORMANCE MEASUREMENT

The ability to monitor use and interpret the results is essential if any information resource or service is to be deemed a success or otherwise. Internationally standardised performance indicators have been developed for traditional library services. However, recent studies of usage measurement and performance indicators for digital libraries have found no evidence of standardisation and continue to recommend that international standards be developed and applied. An initiative in this direction has been taken by the ICOLC who have published guidelines for statistical measures of usage of electronic resources. An eLib supporting study published in 1997 investigated Management Information Systems and Performance Measurement for the Electronic Library. The authors described a three-fold approach to library management with regard to performance measurement:

- The day-to-day needs of library managers;
- The need for information that can be used by planners for forecasting;
- The need for indicators of value for strategic review.

Although they found that some indicators used in traditional libraries can be adapted, it was necessary to devise other 57 new indicators. For example, the number of documents accessed was considered not to be important in an electronic environment; the range and depth of resources available was deemed far more important.

Furthermore, Brophy and Wynne identified a number of issues which must be addressed if progress is to be made in this area. While acknowledging the significant contribution of the eLib programme in this regard, they called for a clearer definition and understanding of what is meant by the term 'electronic library'.

Non-standard Usage Measurement

A requirement for international standards is clear but development of such standards is a lengthy process. While this process is ongoing, each individual digital library initiative requires feedback to inform development and, thus, must unilaterally adopt an approach to performance measurement.

Electronic library projects in the UK, Europe and the USA have used a variety of different definitions and methods of usage measurement and analysis. Thus, neither analyses nor data from different projects can be compared.

Most Internet usage analysis tools are applicable to digital library activities and WWW server log file analysis programmes still predominate. In 1997 the eLib supporting study referred to above found that most work in the electronic library field relied on transaction logging for management information.

If users are authenticated (*i.e.* have usernames and passwords), it is possible using these tools, to monitor individual use by logging the username alongside the URL. Hits can also be time stamped. In this way, an individual's progress can be tracked from page to page. It is possible also, using cookies, for a service supplier to track an individual's movements on the Internet beyond that supplier's site. However, this is likely to be considered a breach of privacy and librarians 58 make it an issue in negotiation with content suppliers.

To comply with the library ethos, performance indicators should not rely on information about individuals' reading habits. Many academic subscription services authenticate whole sites by registering and restricting access a list of IP addresses.

Not only does this overcome privacy issues related to individual users as names and time stamps cannot be recorded on accesses, but it also removes the need for costly password management. An alternative means of reducing the cost of authentication in the UK is use of the ATHENS service which provides an individual with a username and password which may be used to access a variety of services.

Unfortunately, use of ATHENS greatly reduces the management information that can be gathered by individual service suppliers. This is deliberate to protect the privacy of individual users. For example, it is not possible for a supplier to monitor use of her service within a specific discipline if neither individuals nor even whole classes are identifiable by user ID.

Limitations of Current usage Measurement Tools

It is important when designing performance measurement activities that they be justified in terms of the benefits derived. Because it is automatic, transaction logging is a cheap way of gathering data in an electronic environment.

Unfortunately, the type of data that can be collected is often restricted by the delivery format. In 1996, when Michigan University intended to test economic models during the TULIP Project, it was unable to do so because 'the Web does not support the kind of data collection required to test economic models'.

Project MUSE is still unable to distinguish between downloading/printing and browsing as the Web is a stateless environment. SuperJournal know that although users claim to prefer HTML documents for onscreen viewing, given a choice of formats, a large majority 59 chooses PDF over HTML. As most users print documents if they intend to read more than a few lines, it can be assumed that they select PDF as a superior format for printing.

Unfortunately, SuperJournal cannot verify this assumption by monitoring use as it is not possible to differentiate downloading from printing. Thus, although data gathering is cheap, as yet, it is also limited. Furthermore, analysis of such data tends to be time consuming and thus expensive and interpretation is not always straightforward.

For example, it may be assumed that more hits indicate a better service, as a high number suggests that users return and that they recommend a site to others but, of course, this may not always be the case. A subject-based gateway which generates search results that closely match a users needs will record very few hits before that user leaves the site satisfied with the result.

If the search results supplied are poor and include a number of extraneous links or if the user is required to conduct several searches before she retrieves useful links, the gateway will record many more hits before the user leaves.

However, if a subject-based gateway offers not only access to a database of catalogue records but also holds a local archive, it should record a larger number of hits as users are likely both to search the database and to retrieve local resources. Furthermore, attempts to make more efficient use of internet bandwidth by caching and mirroring can subvert attempts to monitor use. Access to resources from site A from a cache or mirror held at site B will not be included in usage measurement unless site B informs site A about the cache and agrees to supply site A with use data. This type of shortfall makes WWW statistics unreliable or, worse, misleading.

Inferring user Behaviour from Transaction Logs

Use of transaction logs for performance measurement requires digital library practitioners to infer meaning from specific types of user act in a digital environment. For example, A. Dawson of the BUBL service (http://www.bubl.ac.uk) suggests that to view a list of journal issues with dates and contents is the equivalent of browsing a library shelf. He also asserts that searching is a deliberate activity which is not easily mistaken and that to access full-text is a likely indication that the user is reading the article.

The latter assertion is qualified by the acknowledgement that the reader may access text to scan for relevance rather than, necessarily, to read the article. However, Dawson argues that this ambiguity need not influence the accuracy of any performance measure as it applies to all journals.

This type of inference helps digital library practitioners to make sense of quantitative data. However, knowledge of user behaviour in the digital environment is limited and it can be dangerous to base inference entirely on assumptions and prior experience.

For example, Dawson's assumption that the frequency with which a reader accessing full text is in fact scanning for relevance will apply equally to all journals is contradicted by the findings of the SuperJournal project.

SuperJournal found evidence that the way in which scientists and social scientists use journal elements differs. For example, scientists are more likely than social scientists to identify a relevant article from its title and to print it on that basis. Social scientists more often read the abstract to establish relevance because article titles in the social sciences can be more ambiguous. There may be similar differences in the way that scientists and social scientists approach full text.

It is clearly difficult to derive qualitative research findings from quantitative information. Qualitative methods such as interviews and 61 observation should be used to inform assumptions about the meaning of quantitative information and for triangulation.

Training and Awareness

Some of the eLib projects in the Training and Awareness programme area have now migrated to a service model and offer training courses in the use of new technologies for teaching and learning. HEIs are likely to continue to pay for this type of training from staff development budgets.

Training of users in the use of IT is unlikely to fall within the remit of libraries although libraries will probably continue to offer training in information skills and the use of specific resources.

It is beyond the scope of this project to explore the economics of this activity and compare the costs and benefits of training academics and students in the use of electronic and print resources. Clearly, the transition from a traditional to a digital or hybrid library involves dramatic changes in the infrastructure that supports the production and use of information resources. At present people prefer not to read on screen so they print articles from electronic journals.

As resources for teaching, learning and research are increasingly delivered in electronic form there is likely to be a mass shift from photocopying to printing; the latter is more expensive than the former but the total opportunity cost of an individual operating a photocopier is not incurred so costs are probably very similar.

As people become more familiar with technology, users may no longer need print copies.

This could lead to a net reduction in the cost of using information. The report of a recent study on the impact of electronic journals on networked printing suggested that one of the reasons for printing material from the Internet is to ensure future access; networked access is not always reliable.

In effect users create a personal print cache of networked resources. The report predicted that improved access to networked resources would 62 reduce the need to print but suggested that it may also increase use of the network, which in turn would increase the print load. The net effect of a combination of such changes is virtually impossible to predict.

Another factor impacting on the economics of digital information is the pace of technological change; new technologies become obsolete at an alarming rate, making it expensive for organisations to meet the changing needs of users. However, technological advances are reducing some costs, for example the cost of storing digital resources.

It is not possible within the scope of this project to estimate the infrastructure costs associated with delivering electronic resources in such an unstable and unpredictable climate. Investment in infrastructure that effectively enables all stakeholders to conduct much of their business electronically will be required. The models described here will be based on the assumption that the HE sector will invest in sufficient infrastructure to support digital/hybrid library activities.

At present there is no coherent model of the digital library, nor is there yet any developed model of the hybrid library. Furthermore, economic issues tend to be tested after solutions have been found to the more pressing technical, cultural and legal issues. Many specific digital library activities are insufficiently mature to have generated economic models. Where a model exists it has been evaluated and where alternatives exist these have been compared.

It is clear that a great deal of progress has been made over the last decade towards a greater understanding of how digital library activities may be integrated in HE. Nevertheless, a considerable amount of work remains, specifically in the areas of preservation and archiving and in standardisation of usage measurement and performance indicators. Conclusions regarding specific issues relating to digital library activities are outlined in the remainder of this report.

SEMANTIC RESEARCH FOR DIGITAL LIBRARIES

During the DLI, which ran from 1994 to 1998, significant research was conducted at all six projects in the area of semantic retrieval and analysis for digital libraries. Among the semantic indexing and analysis techniques that are considered scalable and domain independent, the following classes of algorithms and methods have been examined and subjected to experimentation in various digital library, multimedia database, and information science applications:

Object Recognition, Segmentation, and Indexing

The most fundamental techniques in Information Retrieval involve identifying key features in objects. For example, automatic indexing and natural language processing (*e.g.*, noun phrase extraction or object type tagging) are frequently used to extract meaningful keywords or phrases from texts automatically. Texture, colour, or shape-based indexing and segmentation techniques are often used to identify images. For audio and video applications, voice recognition, speech recognition, and scene segmentation, techniques can be used to identify meaningful descriptors in audio or video streams.

Semantic Analysis

Several classes of techniques have been used for semantic analysis of texts or multimedia objects. Symbolic machine learning (*e.g.*, ID3 decision tree algorithm, version space), graph-based clustering and classification (*e.g.*, Ward's hierarchical clustering), statistics-based multivariate analyses (*e.g.*, latent semantic indexing, multi-dimensional scaling, regressions), artificial neural network-based computing (*e.g.*, backpropagation networks, Kohonen self-organizing maps), and evolution-based programming (*e.g.*, genetic algorithms) are among the popular techniques.

In this information age, we believe such techniques will serve as good alternatives for processing, analyzing, and summarizing large amounts of diverse and rapidly changing multimedia information.

Knowledge Representations

The results from a semantic analysis process could be represented in the form of semantic networks, decision rules, or predicate logic. Many researchers have attempted to integrate such results with existing human-created knowledge structures such as ontologies, subject headings, or thesauri. Spreading activation based inferencing methods often are used to traverse various large-scale knowledge structures.

Human-computer Interactions (HCI) and Information Visualization:

One of the major trends in almost all emerging information systems applications is the focus on user-friendly, graphical, and seamless Human Computer Interactions. The Web-based browsers for texts, images, and videos have raised user expectations of rendering and manipulation of information.

Recent advances in development languages and platforms such as Java, OpenGL, and VRML and the availability of advanced graphical workstations at affordable prices have also made information visualization a promising area for research.

Several digital library research teams including Arizona/Illinois, Xerox PARC, Berkeley, and Stanford, are pushing the boundary of visualization techniques for dynamic displays of large-scale information collections.

The Illinois DLI Project: Federating Repositories of Scientific Literature

The Artificial Intelligence Lab at the University of Arizona was a major partner in the University of Illinois DLI Project, one of six projects funded by the NSF/DARPA/NASA DLI (Phase 1). The project consisted of two major components:

- A production testbed based in a real library
- Fundamental technology research for semantic interoperability (semantic indexes across subjects and media developed at the University of Arizona).

The Testbed

The Illinois DLI production testbed was developed in the Grainger Engineering Library at the University of Illinois at Urbana-Champaign (UIUC). It supports full federated searching on the structure of journal articles, as specified by SGML markup, using an experimental Web-based interface.

The initial rollout was available at the UIUC campus in October 1997 and has been integrated with the library information services. The testbed consists of materials from 5 publishers, 55 engineering journals, and 40,000 full-text articles.

The primary partners of the project include: American Institute of Physics, American Physical Society, American Astronomical Society, American Society of Civil Engineers, American Society of Mechanical Engineers, American Society of Agricultural Engineers, American Institute of Aeronautics and Astronautics, Institute of Electrical and Electronic Engineers, Institute of Electrical Engineers, and IEEE Computer Society.

The testbed was implemented using Soft Quad (SGML rendering) and Open Text (full-text search), both commercial software.

The Illinois DLI project developers and evaluators have worked together very closely on needs assessment and usability studies. The production testbed has been evaluated since October 1997. Six hundred UIUC user subjects enrolled in introductory computer science classes have used the system; and their feedback has been collected and analyzed. We expect to have collected usage data for about 1500 subjects at the end of the study. Usage data consists of session observations and transaction logs.

After four years of research effort, the testbed successes include:

- Willingness to build custom encoding procedures for SGML. This enabled the testbed to succeed in federating journals from different publishers with differing use of SGML, where Elsevier and OCLC failed.
- Canonical encoding for structure tags. The testbed can federate across publishers and journals.
- Willingness to build custom software for searching. The Illinois DLI system is able to show multiple views on the Web and has advanced structure search capabilities.
- Production repositories for real publishers. The project became the R&D arm of several scientific publishers and generated valuable contributions to the scientific publishing industry.
- Changing the nature of libraries with research. The project enables a research prototype to become a standard service capability for engineering libraries.

However, in the nature of research, we also have experienced many testbed difficulties:

For the user interface, the project originally planned to modify the Mosaic Web browser (which was developed at UIUC). When the Web became commercial, Mosaic was quickly taken out of the control of the developers. Custom software is hard to deploy widely: the Web browser interface has widespread support, but the functionality was too primitive for professional full-text search and display.

Several practical difficulties were found in using SGML for this project. Plans to use standard BRS as full-text backend had to be abandoned. It proved essential to use an SGML-specific search engine.

Good-quality SGML simply was not available. We had to work with every publisher, since nothing was ready for SGML publishing.

SGML interactive display proved not to be of journal quality. Physics requires good-quality display of mathematics, which is very difficult to achieve.

As the project comes to its end, several future directions are being explored:

- Technology transfer to publisher partners: Several partners have expressed interest in receiving the testbed technologies. A contract has been developed with the American Institute of Physics to clone the testbed software and processing. A similar contract is under development with American Society of Civil Engineers.

- Testbed continuance by university library: An industrial partnership programme has been established between the UIUC Library and publishers. A UIUC spin-off company has been formed to provide software and future services.

Semantic Research in Illinois DLI Project

The University of Illinois DLI project, through the partnership with the Artificial Intelligence Lab at the University of Arizona, has conducted research in semantic retrieval and analysis.

In particular, natural language processing, statistical analysis, neural network clustering, and information visualization techniques have been developed for different subject domains and media types.

Scalable Semantics become Feasible

Statistical and neural network clustering proves useful and feasible interactively and for large-scale collections.

Specifically, the AI lab has developed a noun phrasing technique for concept extraction, a concept space technique for building automatic thesauri, and a self-organizing map (SOM) algorithm for building category maps. More details are provided below.

Semantic indexes for large collections

Two large-scale semantic indexing simulations were performed in 1996 and 1997, respectively. We analyzed 400,000 Inspec abstracts and 4,000,000 Compendex abstracts to generate about 1,000 engineering-specific concept spaces (automatic thesauri) using the NCSA supercomputers (Convex Exemplar and SGI Origin 2000).

Results of such computations could be used for semantic retrieval and vocabulary switching across domains.

An Example

In this section we present an example of selected semantic retrieval and analysis techniques developed by the University of Arizona Artificial Intelligence Lab (AI Lab) for the Illinois DLI project. A textual semantic analysis pyramid was developed by AI Lab to assist in semantic indexing, analysis, and visualization of textual documents.

The pyramid, as depicted in Figure, consists of 4 layers of techniques, from bottom to top: noun phrasing indexing, concept association, automatic categorization, and advanced visualization.

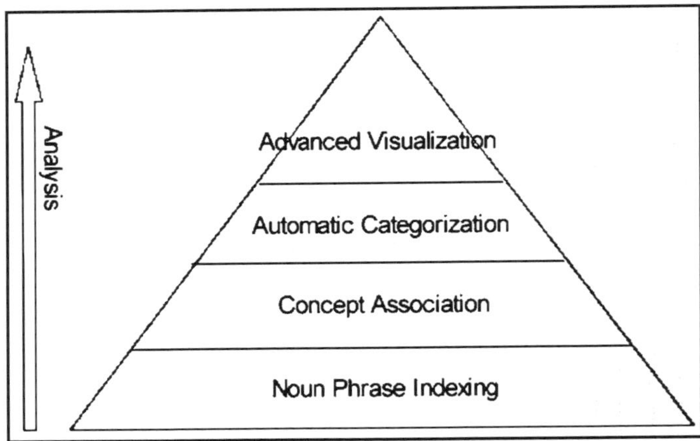

Fig. A Textual Semantic Analysis Pyramid

Noun Phrase Indexing

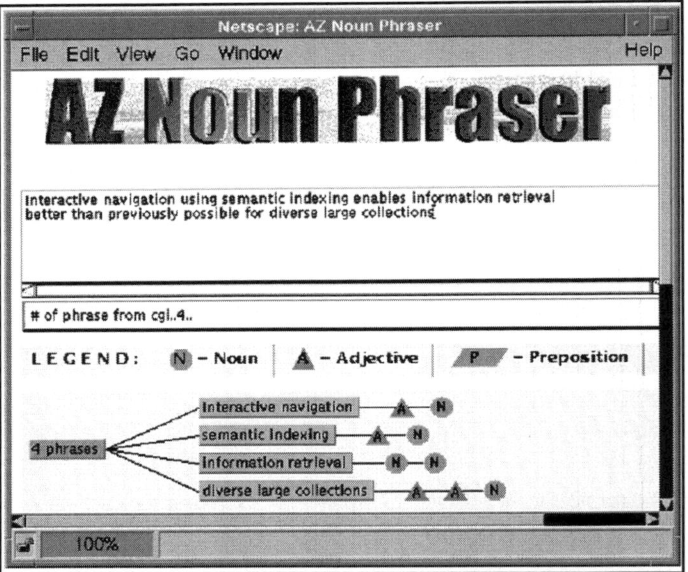

Fig. Tagged noun phrases.

Noun phrase indexing aims to identify concepts (grammatically correct noun phrases) from a collection for term indexing. Known as AZ Noun Phraser, the programme begins with a text tokenization process to separate punctuations and symbols and is followed by part-of-speech-tagging (POST) using variations of the Brill tagger and 30-plus grammatic noun phrasing rules. Figure shows an example of tagged noun phrases for a simple sentence. For example, "interactive navigation" is a noun phrase that consists of an adjective (A) and a noun (N).

Concept Association

Concept association attempts to generate weighted, contextual concept (term) association in a collection to assist in concept-based associative retrieval. It adopts several heuristic term weighting rules and a weighted co-occurrence analysis algorithm. Figure shows the associated terms for "information retrieval" in a sample collection of project reports of the DARPA/ITO Programme - TP (Term Phrase) such as "IR system," "information retrieval engine," "speech collection," etc.

Automatic Categorization

A category map is the result of performing a neural network based clustering (self-organizing) of similar documents followed by automatic category labeling. Documents that are similar to each other (in noun phrase terms) are grouped together in a neighbourhood on a two-dimensional display. As shown in the colored jigsaw-puzzle display in Figure, each colored region represents a unique topic that contains similar documents. Topics that are more important often occupy larger regions.

By clicking on each region, a searcher can browse documents grouped in that region. An alphabetical list that is a summary of the 2D result is also displayed on the left-hand-side of Figure, *e.g.*, Adaptive Computing System (13 documents), Architectural Design (9 documents), etc.

Advanced Visualization

In addition to the 2D display, the same clustering result can also be displayed in a 3D helicopter fly-through landscape as shown in Figure, where cylinder height represents the number of documents in each region. Similar documents are grouped in a same-colored region. Using a VRML plug-in (COSMO player), a searcher is then able to "fly" through the information landscape and explore interesting topics and documents. Clicking on a cylinder will display the underlying clustered documents.

Discussions and Future Directions

The techniques discussed above were developed in the context of the Illinois DLI project, especially for the engineering domain. The techniques appear scalable and promising. We are currently in the process of fine-tuning these techniques for collections of different sizes and domains. Significant semantic research effort for multimedia content has been funded continuously by a multi-year DARPA project (1997-2000).

In the new Digital Libraries Initiative Phase 2 project entitled: "High-Performance Digital Library Classification Systems: From Information Retrieval to Knowledge Management," we will continue to experiment with various scalable textual analysis, clustering, and visualization techniques to automatically categorize large document collections, *e.g.*, NLM's Medline collection (9 million abstracts) and the indexable web pages (50 million web pages). Such system-generated classification systems will be integrated with human-created ontologies (NLM's Unified Medical Language Systems and the Yahoo directory).

Selected semantic analysis techniques discussed above have recently been integrated with several Internet spider applications. In CI (Competitive Intelligence) Spider, users supply keywords and starting URLs for fetching web pages. The graphical CI Spider automatically summarizes and categorizes the content in fetched pages using noun phrases and graphical concept maps. In Meta Spider, users supply keywords to extract web pages from several major search engines (*e.g.*, Alta Vista, Lycos, Goto, Snap). The Meta Spider then summarizes content in all web pages, similar to CI Spider.

DIGITAL LIBRARIES AND THE EVOLVING WEB

In addition to the technical incompatibilities between the digital library and web architectures that were described in the previous part, there is a widening gap between their underlying information models. The web that Tim Berners-Lee invented in 1989 has undergone an explosive growth in scale, measured in terms of number of URLs, servers, and traffic.

At the same time, it has experienced a radical change in form and impact, referred to as Web 2.0. In contrast to the relatively passive and transactional search/access paradigm characteristic of the library and Web 1.0 in which the delineation between authors and consumers was relatively distinct, information interactions in Web 2.0 are highly inter-active and participatory.

Rather than just browsing and reading web pages, web users, acting as both authors and readers are writing reviews on Amazon, annotating and tagging pictures on Flickr, writing and updating articles on Wikipedia, publishing observations and research results in blogs, and mashing up online content into new content. This part examines the evolving web and the coexistence of digital libraries within that context.

The metaphor of versions – Web 1.0, Web 2.0, and the recently coined Web 3.0–is obviously artificial and overly simplistic. However, it is a useful rhetorical device. The predominant "features" of these versions are as follows. *Web 1.0*–called the document web, the "web of cognition", or the "read-only" web.

The time span of this version roughly extends from the invention of the web until 2000. It primarily consisted of hyperlinked, semi-static, atomic documents (HTML, PDF, GIF or JPEG images). Interaction and collaboration were minimal except for document authoring and querying. Content creation required specialized tools and, as a result, was restricted to a small subset of web users. *Web 2.0*-called the "web of communication" or the "read/write" web.

This "version" includes participation-oriented tools such as wikis, blogs, social applications like Flickr, and instant communication tools like Twitter. Another prominent feature is the notion of a "mash-up" whereby new information objects are created via the dynamic combination of existing information resources.

These features enable a phenomenon that Engestrom calls "object-centered sociality", in which information objects, people, and social exchanges are linked together in web space. This has effected a phase transition in the web's impact on economics, scholarship, learning, and most recently politics.

The effect of this impact on national politics is exemplified by the recent observation that "... Barack Obama's victories in the Democratic primary and in the presidential election would not have been possible without Internet-empowered fund-raising and social networking". *Web 3.0*–called the "web of meaning" or the "contextual web", this currently emerging web function-ality incorporates concepts of the semantic web, the under-pinnings of which Tim Berners-Lee and the W3C have been developing since the late 1990's.

The key features of the semantic web include machine readability and interpretation of web data and the ability to reason over that data. The technological foundation of the semantic web is the Resource Description Framework (RDF) a data model for expressing statements about entities (web resources) and their properties (ontologically defined relationships).

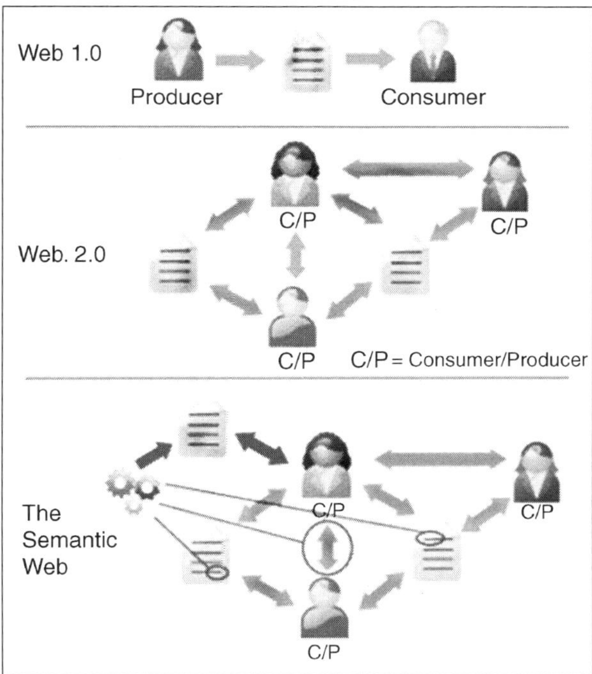

Fig. Expansion of Web Functionality

Raffl *et al.* adopt the language of Evolutionary Systems Theory to illustrate how the features of these versions are cumulative: "[E]ach new layer is built upon a preceding one and ...the new stage comprises not only the new layer, but parts of the old one". Figure illustrates the changing nature of the web through these versions.

As shown, Web 1.0 was primarily a one-way channel from producers to consumers. In Web 2.0, the bifurcation of web participants blurs into consumer/ producers who collaboratively author, manage, and annotate content. This is enhanced in the Semantic Web (Web 3.0) in which machines (agents) process and interpret this collaboratively produced content and contribute new content back on the web.

The participatory nature Web 2.0 should not be dismissed as just a popular phenomenon, manifested in increased use of mainly social sites like FaceBook. Many experts in the field, we are witnessing a fundamental change in the prevailing information paradigm that is transforming all aspects of our culture. Notably, this impact extends to the nature of scholarly research and communication, one of the backbones of the research library.

As pointed out by Paul Ginsparg, who create arXiv and is considered one of the icons of Internet-based scholarship:

- ...There are...objective reasons to believe that we are witnessing an essential change in the way information is accessed, the way it is communicated to and from the general public, and among research professionals-fundamental methodological changes that will lead to a terrain 10-20 years from now more different than it was 10-20 years ago than in any comparable time period.

Timo Hannay of Nature, one of the most prestigious scientific journals, makes the following observation of the impact of the current and future of the web on science scholarship:

- For all but a very small number of widely read titles, the day of the print journal seems to be almost over. Yet to see this development as the major impact of the web on science would be extremely narrow-minded–equivalent to viewing the web primarily as an efficient PDF distribution network... Though it will take longer to have its full effect, the web's major impact will be on the way that science itself is practiced.

In addition, there is mounting evidence that, for a number of important informationoriented activities such as education, the participatory information paradigm in Web 2.0 has advantages over the traditional consumption-based model. Fuchs and Raffl argue that Web 2.0 paradigms of collaboration, construction, and participation are more closely aligned with recognized models of human cognition and knowledge development than the more restrictive and controlled library model.

Downes and Ullrich describe the utility of the Web 2.0 model for education because of the manner in which it facilitates activities such as group collaboration, exploration, and manipulation that are key to learning according to cognitively-oriented constructivist theories.

Gee argues that the "affinity spaces" facilitated by the Web 2.0 environment are powerful tools for learning. Black identifies the notion of "beta-reading" in online fan communities where contributors grow as readers and writers based on mutual feedback. Finally, others see the general benefits of the "wisdom of crowds" that is enabled by the collaborative nature of Web 2.0.

INFLUENCE OF THE LIBRARY ON DIGITAL LIBRARY TECHNOLOGY

The previous part described the set of assumptions about libraries and networked information that led to the choice of the term "digital libraries." This part describes the manner in which that term and the presumptions underlying it have affected the nature of the technical artifacts produced by digital library research. This effect is reflected in both the overall architectural framework and on the individual architectural components of that framework.

Table. Comparison of Digital Library and Web Architectures

	Digital Libraries	Web Architecture
Core Architecture	Repository-centric	Resource-centric
User Model	Portal Searching	Browsing
Content Model	Digital Objects	Resources
Indexing Model	Surrogates	Full-text and links
Identification	Persistent IDs	URIs
Federation Model	Federated Search, Metadata Harvesting	Centralized Indexing

CORE ARCHITECTURE: REPOSITORY-CENTRIC VERSUS RESOURCE-CENTRIC

Digital library systems are by and large based on the notion of the institutionallymanaged *repository* as the central architec-tural entity. The repository acts as the container for storage of and access to "digital objects", the content "within" the library. In this manner, the repository is a virtual boundary defining the locus of institutional management, curation, and preservation of the contained digital objects.

This virtual boundary is the functional equivalent of the physical boundary in the "bricks and mortar" library in which the physical structure defines the limits of library curation and stewardship of the information resources within it. In contrast, the *resource* is the central entity in the web architecture.

Uniquely identified resources are the nodes in a virtual directed graph, in which the edges are the hyperlinks that connect resources. Notably absent from this graph model is the notion of containment or location. There is no first-class entity that corresponds to the repository in digital architecture. Although repositories are sometimes compared to web sites, the comparison is incorrect due to the nature of the latter. A web site is an ambiguously defined, second-class technical artifact – it may be all the web pages served within the same DNS domain, or those accessible through a single server. Technically, it has no identity (URI) and therefore it cannot be the target of any protocol requests. Conceptually, it does not imply control or management in the same manner as a repository. The remainder of this part describes the major components of digital library systems that support this repository-centric architectural core.

PORTALS

The portal, or the "front door of the digital library", serves the same purpose as the physical entry to the traditional library. It provides the user with the clear notion of being "inside" the digital library. Services and content within the portal are thereby blessed with the imprimatur of the library, endowing them with a level of trust and integrity. This is commonly known as "branding". Correspondingly, most digital library applications clearly indicate to the user when they are "leaving the library", for example by traversing a hyperlink to a page outside the boundary of the library. The focus of a portal is usually a search interface, that in most cases is field-based, providing more functionality than the single text box search paradigm employed by most web search engines.

This allows users to search on specific bibliographic fields such as title, author, or subject. This search paradigm reflects the influence of the library cataloguing tradition, which eschews simple keyword searching that is predominant in mainstream crawler-based search engines (*e.g.*, Google) in favour of more targeted search capabilities.

Metadata, which is the basis of this field-based searching. In contrast to this "front-door" paradigm, the web user metaphorically "surfs" among linked information resources without regard for their location on the network. The informal notion of a "homepage" for a web site does exist, but there is no presumption or enforcement of this as the uniform entry point to the collection of pages of that site. The notion of uniform, location-independent sources has proven to be quite powerful. In its simplest form it makes it possible to aggregate information from multiple sources in a single webpage, in the manner that a page may include an image that is stored in some other location on the net. As I will describe later, location independence is leveraged in Web 2.0 in a much more powerful manner in the form of "mash-ups."

METADATA–CATALOGUING IN THE DIGITAL CONTEXT

The shaping effect of the library tradition on digital libraries is perhaps most evident in the focus on descriptive metadata. This focus has its roots in cataloguing, one of the core functions of the modern library. The traditional catalogue developed for a number of reasons. At the simplest level, in a library of physical resources it gave users an easy and compact tool for finding information resources without having to traverse the shelves.

However, describing the catalogue as merely a compact shelf list trivializes its complexity and intellectual content. Underlying cataloguing is the concept of information entities having uniform attributes, such as author, title, or subject classification, and the utility of those attributes for logical organization of those entities. This organization presents multiple *access points* based on those uniform attributes, and allows users to search and browse within those access points.

For example, a user may search for information by author name and then traverse the resources associated with that author, or alternatively they may search for information by subject classification and traverse the resources associated within that class. As a result, the organization of the catalogue and the manner in which it is made available to the user (*e.g.*, cards in drawers or screens in an electronic catalogue) is independent of the manner in which the physical, or digital, resources are organized on shelves, or in repositories.

Furthermore, an individual information resource (*e.g.*, a book) may have multiple catalogue instances, each accessible through specific access points (*e.g.*, title, author, subject, etc.). Efforts to extend the practice of cataloguing into the context of online information reflects an ongoing belief that in a world where even the books that are part of library collections have been digitized and are available for full-text search, structured search over surrogates is more functional and ultimately preferred by users.

This is despite empirical evidence that users seem to prefer the "one text box" search paradigm of Google to the fielded-search paradigm employed in most digital library portals and online catalogs, and decades-old evidence of the frequent superiority in recall and precision of automated full-text search to human-assisted indexing and cataloguing.

Traditional library cataloguing is both complex and expensive, especially when applied to the rapidly expanding and diverse set of digital resources. The notion of metadata emerged as a simpler and less expensive alternative to traditional cataloguing records, perhaps making it possible for non-profess-ionals to create structured bibliographic information.

The predominant digital library metadata effort is the Dublin Core Metadata Initiative. Ironically, the origins of Dublin Core lie in improving search and retrieval on the general web. However, this effort to develop easy-to-use bibliographic standards for networked information objects has been deemed irrelevant, ill-conceived, or even counterproductive by the mainstream web community and most notably the search engines that dominate it.

As I describe later, the attempts to translate the benefits of cataloguing to the online domain via metadata have been compromised by problems with ensuring the quality of the metadata records that are produced by non-professionals and preventing so-called "metadata spamming" by unscrupulous agents trying to falsely lead information consumers to their sites.

DIGITAL OBJECTS — CONTAINERS FOR COMPLEX DATA AND METADATA

The content model of most digital library architectures is based on the notion of a *digital object*. an identified (first-class) information resource that is an aggregation of multiple information units consisting of multiple formats, multiple subsidiary units, versions, or document components (*e.g.*, the text, data, images, etc. of a scholarly paper).

These are generally known as *compound objects*. These object models reflect an ongoing effort by the library community to account for the complexity of information in both its abstract form and the physical or digital manifestations of it.

These efforts have focused on mechanisms to represent the various relationships among information resources. and to describe those resources at multiple levels of granularity, for various purposes, and in various descriptive formats. Access to compound objects and their components is frequently mediated by protocols unique to the particular repository architecture.

These protocols are usually embedded in the URLs that carry user requests from the digital library portal to the repository. These protocols allow operations such as access a digital object in a specific form, access a portion of a digital object such as its descriptive metadata, and the like.

The proliferation of these architecture-specific access protocols has spawned a virtual cottage industry of repository interoperability initiatives in the digital library community. In contrast, the web architecture includes a quite simple information model based on the atomic resource.

"Interoperability" is defined in the simple terms of the web architecture–resources, URIs, and HTTP. There is no architectural notion of a compound object, or aggregation of resources. Ad hoc and de facto aggregations exist, for example a logical document split into a set of interlinked web pages.

However, these aggregations are not first-class objects. they do not have a unique identity and are essentially ephemeral. There is, in fact, an increased awareness in the web community that more complex information models are appropriate in a number of instances. for example, scholarly publishing.

FEDERATION

The issue of federation arises because digital library systems are conceived as discrete institutionally-managed entities with distinct boundaries accessible to the user through branded portals. Sometimes, a user might want to search across multiple digital libraries when a selected resource is not available in their "local" library. In the physical library domain, this problem is solved by union catalogs such as WorldCat and by interlibrary loan.

Digital library applications employ two mechanisms to allow users to search for and access information outside the confines of a single digital library. The first is federated searching or meta-searching, in which a single search query is multicast to several digital library search engines.

The query is then individually processed at those search engines. the individual result sets are then returned and integrated at the site from which the original query was multicast. Federated searching was the subject of substantial work in the early years of digital library research describes our own work in this area.

Although instances of federated search still exist, the technique has fallen into some disfavour because of problems with dependence on the reliability of multiple search sites and the problems with the ranking of search results from several sources. The second is metadata harvesting, in which bibliographic records from several distributed institutional sources are combined at a single indexing site, which provides a search interface across the resulting "union catalogue". The most widely deployed mechanism for metadata harvesting is the Open Archives Protocol for Metadata Harvesting (OAI-PMH). That same chapter describes complica-tions with metadata harvesting. Neither of these techniques has achieved widespread deployment in the general web information space.

Boundaries and the repositories that implement them are not a part of the web architecture. Web search engines such as Google crawl the web via graph traversal, ignoring the notion of the location of a webpage, except as a tool for optimizing graph traversal strategies. In addition, ranking algorithms such as PageRank are designed to operate over a centralized index, and are difficult if not impossible in the context of distributed methods such as federated search,

PERSISTENT IDENTITY FOR NETWORK INFORMATION

A final example of the difference between digital library and web architecture is the notion of "persistent identity" for information stored in digital repositories. The attention to this issue in the digital library contexts reflects concerns about both preservation and control of intellectual property. The Handle System is the best known of this class of technologies.

Like many persistent naming systems, the Handle System depends on a hierarchy of identity resolvers, and therefore the notion of a central *root* name server. These efforts have gained little traction in the mainstream web community, which has historically resisted centralization and has comfortably adapted to the fragility of URLs, deeming identity persistence as a policy problem rather than a technical problem.

EMERGENCE OF DIGITAL LIBRARY SERVICES IN INDIA

The digital library is an electronic or virtual library where information is selected, acquired, processed, organised, stored and retrieved in digital form. The developed countries have already digitized their libraries. The developing countries are in the process of digitization of their libraries. The users of digital libraries are the universal users who should have facility to access to all created and acquired digital sources of information in the form of electronic text, image, map, sound, video and multimedia. Thus the digital libraries are attributed to electronic databases and capable of handling large data and servicing users effectively in resource sharing environment.

DIGITAL LIBRARY INFRASTRUCTURE

A digital library has certain technological requirements such as:

- Locally developed database
- Local library system with adequate personal computers having LAN and CD-ROM Drives.
- Electronic mail service
- Network connection to have access to other data bases
- Various functions to coordinate, manage the entry and retrieve data.
- Multimedia Kit
- Well trained manpower
- Computer Hardware with Audio-Visuals, Video Conferencing Kit, Pentium Web Server, Laser Printer, Scanner, Barcode Scanner, Barcode Printer, Digital graphic printer and UPS.
- Software and its accessories.

The super structure of digital library rests on some important factors like:

- The human need for information especially that is timely and relevant and
- Accumulation of information, and all the supporting infrastructure that includes research community, professional associations, libraries and publishers, advances in methods and technology leading to developments in net working, information science, information storage and retireval, hyper-media, human-computer interaction, artificial intelligence and other areas of computer science that make digital libraries a possible proposition.

Digital Library Services

Always library services are followed by library works. But now the advancement in information technology has brought changes in the concept of traditional library work as well as service. The recent trend and change in the information related field especially in collection, storing, processing and dissemination of information have resulted in to the evolution of digital libraries. Now most of the reference books like encyclopaedias, dictionaries, directories, hand books, etc. are published in electronic form.

Similarly about 50 per cent of the existing secondary resources like abstracting and indexing services are available in electronic form for example, Chemical Abstracts Service, Index Medicus, Engineering Index. At present most of the digital libraries have been highlighted mainly on providing access to diverse digital information resources. The provision of personalized reference and information services is considered as one of the important characteristics of the library and information profession.

However reference services include:

- Either finding the required information on behalf of users, or assisting users in finding information themselves;
- Instruction in the use of library resources and services, and
- User guidance in which users are guided in selecting the most appropriate information sources and services.

In this changing scenario, reference works of modern libraries are influenced by a set of related technical and economic factors, especially the increasing use of technology and techniques. To cite some examples, the recent developments in the INTERNET and in Web Technologies have brought significant changes in the concept of traditional reference services and a number of web-based "expert services", that are now offered by many non-library organisation.

Information services are provided to the users on demand as well as anticipating the user needs including various forms of current awareness and selective dissemination of informa-tion services. Such services are provided to the users to keep them abreast of the latest developments in their field of interest through on-line search services in digital information environment, even by the non-library organisations like Dialog.

PERSONALIZED SERVICES

Most of the researches on digital library development have focused on access to and retrieval of digital information but they have overlooked the personalized service aspects, as primary goal of library information services. However the technology and information resources, on their own, can not make up an effective digital library. On priority basis the personalized services in a digital library environment would help the users to find information resources available in a digitally chaotic world.

In a Delphy study it was revealed that:

- The primary roles library professionals play in digital libraries include organization of macro and micro-documents, selection and acquisition and acting as gateways to the provision of information services, and

- The best reasons of developing a digital library include: increasing access to information serving and users needs and bringing organization to the unstructured universe of electronically available information.

However there is a demand for end-user instruction on the use of digital libraries and the digital library professionals who are subject specialists should help users to formulate disciplinary search strategies and provide assistance in developing new digital information resources.

Web-based Reference and Information Services

Several reference and information services are now available on the web and many of these services are provided by non-library organization. Also a web site that provides a categorized listing of libraries that offer real-time reference services using specific software, live interactive communication tools, call centre management software, bulletin board services and other INTERNET technologies.

Of course, most of these services are designed for registered users of some specific libraries in-digital information environment. HodgKin has made an aggregation approach to reference and information services. According to which more than one reference sources is made accessible digitally and also it is more practicable in terms of visibility and profitability than a single reference source.

Further:

- It's reference service becomes much better known to professional users and thus easier to find, by providing access to several reference works,
- By tackling a number of reference works at a time, the publishers can achieve economics of scale in production and development
- The user's search session is likely to be much more powerful and fruitful.

Online reference and information services can be broadly categorized into three groups:

- Those from publishers, database search services and specialized institutions
- Those provided by libraries and/or experts through the INTERNET and
- Where the users need to conduct a search and find information through the web.

Also they have listed several online information services that belong to the first category comprising various current awareness, and SDI services, for example:

- Contents pages services from commercial publishers, such as Elsevier's Contents Direct Service and IDEAL Alert from Academic Press.

- Information on new books available for free from publishers and vendors, such as Wiley Book, Notification Service from Wiley, and Amazon.com.
- SDI services from online search services providers, such as Dialog (Dialog Alerts)
- Current contents and ISI Alerting Services from ISI and so on.

However some of these services, particularly the contents page services from publishers of journals, are free, while for others, such as Dialog Alerts, or Current Contents from ISI, users need to register and pay for the services. There are also some web-based reference services where users need to conduct a search in order to answer their reference query.

For example:

- The Internet Public Library,
- Britannica,
- The Electric Library and
- The Internet Library for librarians.

Most of these web-based reference services are available free of charge but some charge a small amount as fee. For example, the Electric Library charges an annual subscription fee.

SEARCH ENGINE SERVICES

Sherman made a comparision among three web-based reference services like:

- Ask Jeeves basically a search engine, is useful for complex questions and is a good choice for searchers who lack Boolean or other searching skills, because of its strong natural language parser and question-and-answer template structure. The users can ask a question on a given topic and it comes up with a list of questions on the same or similar topics; the users can select any of those predefined questions and then it provides further answers. It processes each query syntactically and semantically and then its answer processing engine provides the question template response. When the users click on a response, the answer-processing engine retrieves the answer template that contains links to the answer locations. Thus Ask Jeeves can help users to select a query from a pre-defined set of queries on a given topic. So it is considered as a useful model for reference and infor-mation services in digital libraries.
- The Electric Library is an excellent choice for a serious researcher in need of timely content from a wide array of otherwise unavailable sources. It provides access to various on line reference sources and allows users to either select a specific source or conduct a search on a range, or all, of the sources.

- Information please is a suitable tool for students and other researchers, as an authoritative source of facts and pointers for further investigation.

Moreover Chowdhury and Chowdhury have suggested some other useful search engine services like:

- Web help.com that claims to offer real time search assistance with a real live expertany time, day or night,
- About.com is a service that shows a number of pre-defined categories related to a search topic given by the user.

For example, a simple search on 'e-commerce' not only produces a list of sites, but also provides a set of topics related to e-commerce, such as e-commercedefinition, e-commerce security, the advantages and disadvantages of e-commerce, e-commerce statistics and so on.

DIGITAL REFERENCE SERVICES FOR GENERAL PUBLIC

Today web-based digital reference services are being provided by a network of public libraries. The users make their query on an enquiry page and it is automatically routed to one of the participating libraries which records it as an e-mail message to the user containing necessary and available information. For example, the British Library, London provides special reference services for business, scientific, technical, medical, patent and environmental information which range from answering simple queries up to complex questions involving on line data base searches. Of course some of these services are free if users put simple queries, but for complex queries users need to pay at the prescribed rate which covers the costs of staff time, on-line searching and value added tax (VAT). The British Library provides STM (Science, Technology and Medicine) Search Service for which users need to pay. Similarly New York Public Library (Digital Library), American Library of Congress, Alexandria Digital Library, Berkeley Digital Library, Bibliotheque Nationale de France, Victoria State Library, Vatican Library, etc. are some other libraries which provide digital reference services for users.

DIGITAL REFERENCE SERVICES OF ACADEMIC LIBRARIES

Web based reference services are also now being provided by academic libraries, Recently a study report on web-based reference services reflects the current practices of digital library services in seventy academic libraries of USA. The study shows that university libraries allow their patrons to put reference questions in a variety ways: 99 per cent offer e-mail reference, 96 per cent offer reference services by appointment while 29 per cent of the libraries offer real-time virtual reference. These libraries use *customer relationship management* (CRM) software packages for providing web-based reference services in the virtual reference environment.

CO-OPERATIVE DIGITAL LIBRARY SERVICES

The rising cost of digital reference sources and its proper processing by the trained manpower and also the initial infrastructural investment for introducing new services in libraries have influenced different organisations to choose a co-operative model of digital reference services. As a result some co-operative projects have been launched for providing web-based reference services to the users who can ask for such services from a remote location at any time. The Library of Congress, USA has launched the collaborative digital reference service with a mission to provide the users, anywhere anytime through an international digital network of libraries.

This network has three main components consisting of:

- Member Profiles
- Request Manager-Software for entering, routing and answering reference queries; and
- Knowledge Base-a searchable database of questions and answer sets.

In this network a participating library sends a question to the system on behalf of a user and the system looks in to the knowledge base for a match. Then a reply is sent to the relevant library through e-mail. Incase the question and its corresponding answer is not found in the knowledge base, then it is passed on to the Request Manager where using the profiles of participating libraries and their information resources collection, expertise etc, relevant query is passed on to an appropriate library.

This library receives the query, finds an answer and sends back reply to the results store and answer to the knowledge base. Thus the Knowledge Base and Request Manager become able to provide reference service in digital environment. However, the Library of Congress and OCLC have developed a co-operative "Question Point" the advanced generation of *collaborative Digital Reference Service* (CDTS) in June 2002 which integrates local as well as global electronic reference networks.

PRESENT SCENARIO IN INDIA

All the six IITs (Indian Institute of Technology) created as centres of excellence for higher training, research and development in science, engineering and technology, have automated their libraries and now they have access to more than one thousand electronic journals. The Central Library IIT, Delhi has switched over to the Silver Platter's Electronics Reference Library (ERL) technology for providing access to bibliographic databases subscribed on CD-ROM.

The technology facilitates simultaneous and integrated access to ERL complaint reference databases to multiple users across the LAN/WAN Via TCP/IP. This library offers network-based CD-ROM search services from the CD-ROM databases subscribed in the central library. Most of its databases have now been transferred to ERL technology and its CD-NET system has been installed for searching of CD-ROM databases on the campus intranet. This Library has started subscribing to the web-based full-text electronic journals with availability of high speed INTERNET connection and about 1330 electronic journals are accessible full text.

In most of the higher learning and research institutes in India such as:

- The Regional Engineering Colleges (RECs),
- Tata Institute of Fundamental Research (TFIR),
- Indian Institute of Science (IIS),
- Indian Statistical Institute (ISI),
- Indian Agricultural Research Institute (IARI),
- Institute of Veterinary Research of India (IVRI),
- All India Institute of Medical Science (AIMS),
- Indian Institute of Management (IIMs),
- Institute of Physics, Institute of Life Science,
- Shaha Institute Nuclear Physics,
- The Medical College Libraries etc., have automated their library systems.

Some of them are in the process of digitization of rare and valuable documents. Digital library services in India are in developing stage. At present most of the university libraries have taken steps to provide web-based reference and information services in digital environment in addition to their traditional library services.

These services include:

- Access to library catalogues and union catalogues.
- Access to bibliographic databases
- Access to subject gate ways in specific disciplines
- Providing links to web sites
- Accessing and procuring e-reference sources
- Subscribing to e-journals
- Reference services provided by librarians and experts on the web
- Document delivery services
- On-line current awareness services
- Digitization of library resources, considering their intellectual value.

The University Grants Commission (UGC) of India has launched the major initiative for setting up nation wide communication network for Indian universities called UGC-Infonet. Each university was to establish a LAN in its campus linking all the teaching departments including library. ERNET of India and INFLIBNET Centre, Ahmedabad are conducting a series of training programmes for technical staff of each participating university library for managing and maintaining the network at their premises. The INFLIBNET Centre will administer and monitor the E-Journal programme and will have independent electronic access to all the publications to help with the process. The INFLIBNET Centre has carried out training programmes in various places to spread awareness and to develop expertise in the University community in the use of E-Resoures under the networked environment. The INFLIBNET Centre has developed and also recently released library automation software package new version for university libraries (SOUL) for building up digital library services. Soul is Windows based user friendly software, based on client server architecture with multi-user and multi language facilities which supports internationally known standards such as CCF, AACR-II andMARC-21, etc.

Thus INFLIBNET centre is patronizing for digitization of college and university libraries and encouraging e-subscription and e-learning in Indian Universities and colleges. The DELNET (Delhi Library Network) created as a metropolitan network in 1988, has changed its name to Developing Library New Work (DELNET) in 2000. The main objectives of DELNET are to promote resource sharing among its member libraries, develop a network of member libraries, collect store and disseminate information, offer computerized information services in digital environment

The DELNET presently avails the high speed satellite communication facilities of NIC spread across the country and its 620 member libraries can access about 35 lakh bibliographic records in machine readable form. Also it maintains an online union catalogue of books available in its member libraries in CCF format. Its union catalogue is continuously updated. DELNET has been networking the libraries of about 400 affiliated institutes of AICTE, New Delhi. DELNET presents two management software packages *i.e.* DELMARC and DELPLUS.

4

Library Classification Systems

MEANING OF CLASSIFICATION

Systematic grouping of entities (both abstract and concrete) to meet one's requirement is known as classification. Classification lies at the root of all human activities. Our daily life is very much dependent on the process of classification, however, elementary this process may appear. You can surely recall a number of activities around you where classification plays its part. Take, for example, the arrangement of contents in a railway time table, the display of goods in a grocery shop, the arrangement of modules in a departmental store to facilitate the selection of goods by customers, the seating arrangement in a theatre or stadium, the assignment of registration numbers to various motor vehicles by a state transport authority, or the sorting of letters by postmen first by the city, then by the street and lastly by the house numbers for quick delivery of post. These are simple examples of how we use classification in our activities.

The word 'classification' was derived from the Latin word classes which meant order or rank of mobility in Roman society based upon birth and wealth. Classification is a mental process by which we group or separate things on the basis of common characteristics.

For example, things grouped together on the basis of a common characteristic like writing material. In other words, classification is an attempt to identify a class for like things. We succeed in our attempt by applying a characteristic and isolating all like things on that basis from unlike things. Classification in essence means dividing into groups, grouping, sorting, arranging, ordering, ranking and relating one entity to the others.

Dr. S.R. Ranganathan, in his *Prolegomena to Library Classification (1967)*, elaborately discusses the meaning of classification. In the case of physical objects, division and assortment are the two results of classification, According to Ranganathan, while division implies sorting objects into two or more groups, assortment additionally denotes arrangement of these groups in a predetermined sequence. Further, in library classification, the sequence of objects, *i.e.*, documents, is so mechanised by the use of notation that it is reflected in the notation when a document is withdrawn or added.

Thus, one can see that the term 'classification' is a homonym.

Ranganathan, therefore, tried to resolve the homonym by examining the various ways in which the term has been used:

- Classification in Sense 1 is DIVISION.
- Classification in Sense 2 is ASSORTMENT.
- Classification in Sense 3 is CLASSIFICATION IN SENSE 2 plus representing each entity by an ordinal number taken out of a system of ordinal numbers, designed to mechanise the maintenance of the sequence,
- Classification in Sense 4 is CLASSIFICATION IN SENSE 3 when complete assortment is made of an amplified universe - that is when the entities and the pseudo-entities arising in the process of successive assortment stand arranged in one filiatory sequence.
- Classification in Sense 5 is CLASSIFICATION IN SENSE 4 with all the entities removed but only the pseudo-entities or classes retained.

It is classification in Sense 5 that is used:

- Either when the universe classified is infinite,
- When some of the entities are unknown and unknowable at any moment, even though the universe classified is finite.

It is classification in Sense 5 that is practised by the library profession. The primary,concern of libraries is to establish the most helpful arrangement of documents. Library classification, therefore, presupposes the use of notation, *i.e.*, a brief symbol for the names of subjects. It is in this sense that the word classification is used in this and other units.

Definition of Library Classification

Having understood the meaning of classification in library science, let us now go through a few well-known definitions of library classification.

Library classification has been defined by both the classificationists and the critics, all necessarily underlying its utilitarian aspect. According to Margaret Mann, classification is "the arranging of things according to likeness and unlikeness. It is the sorting and grouping of things, but in addition, classification of books is a knowledge classification with adjustments made necessary by the physical form of books".

W.C. Berwick Sayers defines it as the arrangement of books on shelves or description of them in the manner which is most helpful to those who read". Arthur Maltby revises Sayers definition as "the systematic arrangement of books and other material on shelves or of catalogue and index entries in the manner which is most useful to those who read or who seek a definite piece of information". Ranganathan is more elaborate in his definition.

According to Ranganathan:

- "it is the translation of the name of the subject of a book into the preferred artificial language of ordinal numbers, and the individualisation of several books dealing with the same specific subject by means of a further set of ordinal numbers which represent some features of the book other than their thought content".

In this definition, we find three important phrases, *viz.*,

- Artificial language,
- Ordinal numbers, and
- Specific subject.

These three phrases need some explanation.

Artificial Language

In library classification we use symbols to denote subjects. The names of subjects are in ordinary language understandable to an ordinary person. Therefore, we call it the natural language which comes naturally to the human being living in a society. On the other hand, the symbols that we may use to denote a subject, say B, or 510, or QA for mathematics, are artificial in the sense that the common man will not ordinarily understand the meaning of these symbols. Hence these are artificial and intelligible to a specifically trained class of professionals. Their value is only ordinal, which means that these symbols have no quantitative or qualitative value; they only determine the sequence/order of documents on the shelves. These symbols also maintain/preserve the chosen sequence as the books will be replaced at their proper place after taking them out for reading or lending. These symbols do not indicate anything except the order/sequence of these documents on the shelves.

Ordinal Numbers

These are used not for the purpose of counting but ordering and mechanising the arrangement of things. For example, participants in a conference can be listed in a desired sequence on the basis of some suitable principle and then this sequence can be mechanised with the help of ordinal numbers.

Melvil Dewey (1851-1931), the father of modern library classification, was the first classificationist to use simple Indo-Arabic numerals (0-9) as ordinal numbers for the systematic listing of subjects both broader and narrower, in his Decimal Classification first published in 1876. Since then the system of ordinal numbers-notation as it is called in library classification-has been the principal element in the design and use of library classification schemes.

Specific Subject

The contents of a document may deal with some field of knowledge. It is a prerequisite for a classifier to know what subject matter the document exactly contains. After ascertaining the exact subject, or specific subject, the classifier translates that specific subject into the artificial language or ordinal numbers of the classification scheme used. In order to know the specific subject of the document the classifier has to examine its title, contents page, preface and introduction, and to scan through some chapters, and, if necessary to go through the entire book. There may be certain occasions where a classifier has to consult an expert to ascertain the specific subject of a document.

Ranganathan defines the specific subject of a document as "that division of knowledge whose extension and intension are equal to those of its thought content". Extension means the scope (if the subject treatment and intension means the depth of the subject treatment in a given document. Palmer and Wells define it as "that division of knowledge which exactly comprehends all the major factors that go in its making". Let us take an example and perform an analysis to ascertain the specific subject.

It is possible to interpret the contents of this book as '*Mstory*' or '*History of India*' or 'History of India during the Mughal Period'. All these possible subjects are not specific enough and are too broad to convey the actual thought content of the book. It is, therefore, necessary to add one more phrase to the analysis to make it complete, and that phrase is 'Reign of Akbar'. All these aspects should now be brought into the class number. If you omit any of these aspects, the extension and intension will not be equal to the thought content of the book.

The specific subject of the book can be arrived at as follows History:

- Indian History
- Mughal Period
- Akbar
- Reign

When you analyse the thought content of the document on the lines, the extension (scope) decreases and the intension (depth) increases with every successive division. This sort of subject ordering is called "general to specific". Ranganathan's definition of classification refers to two objectives: Translation of the subject into an ordinal number and individualisation of a given document in the total order of documents in a library. The subject of the document is translated into a class number with the help of a notation. But, several documents are likely to bear the same class number and the problem of individualisation arises. The class number is, therefore, not enough. It has to be supplemented by one, or if necessary, by two, additional elements.

These additional elements are:

- Book number and
- Collection number.

Class number, book number and collection number constitute the call number of a document. It is only the call number that individualises a given document in a library.

Call Number

The call numbers' for a document consists of three elements, *viz.*, class number, book number and collection number. The following example will show the presence of these three elements in a call number.

Jawaharlal Nehru: An Autobiography with Musings on Recent Events in India, Bombay, Allied. 1962.

The call number for this book by Dewey Decimal classification is:

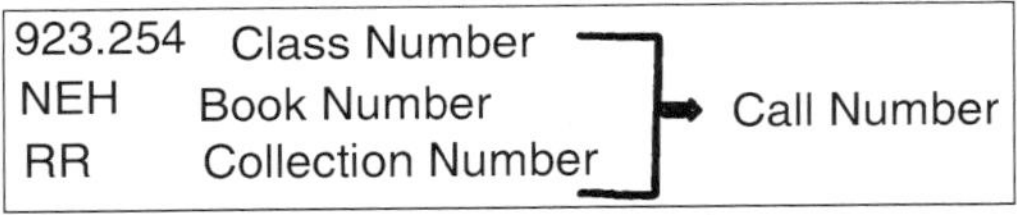

The explanation of the above call number is:

- *923254*: Biography of an Indian statesman (that is the subject of the book, *i.e.*, Class number
- *NEH*: Nerhu (the first three letters from surname of the author, Book number)
- *RR*: Reading Room Collection (the nature of the collection in the library *i.e.*, collection number

Thus, with the help of book number and collection number a document is fully individualised. It means that the call number of a document is unique. Different methods are in use to devise book number and collection number. It is left to individual 'libraries to follow one of these methods, or, if possible, devise their own method or practice.

Purpose and Function

We have so far studied the meaning of classification. We also have studied the importance of a call number. We would now do well to see what exactly is achieved by classifying documents and arranging them in a systematic way in a library.

In the era of the information revolution, the role of libraries in acquiring and organising various types of documents hardly needs any emphasis - Libraries as service institutions acquire documents for use. These acquisitions should systematically be arranged so as to meet the ever growing needs of readers precisely, exhaustively and expeditiously.

If documents are arranged in library on the basis of factors other than subject matter, the arrangement will not be helpful in meeting the requirements of the majority of readers who usually approach a library for subject material. In other words, documents should be classified and arranged on the basis of their subject content.

We are witness to the information revolution. Documents are published in various languages in various disciplines in diverse forms. Libraries have always been acquiring books and adding them to their collections. Therefore, the collection of an active library continues to grow year after year. Ranganathan compares active and effective libraries with growing organisms, In an unclassified library, when the collection grows steadily into thousands and lakhs of volumes, it t would be difficult for the library staff to lay hands on a particular document required by a reader.

To meet the subject approach of readers the collection must necessarily be classified by subject. In libraries where the collection is arranged by accession number, or author or title, and not by subject, books on the same subject will be scattered throughout the collection. Even if the books are arranged alphabetically by subject, the resultant sequence will not be helpful, as unrelated material will come together.

For example:

- Adult education
- Agriculture
- Algebra
- Alloys
- American history
- Anthropology
- Applied mechanics
- Arithmetic
- Astronomy
- Atomic energy
- Australian history.

This type of sequence of subjects surely is far less useful and will fail to meet the requirements of readers. Alphabetical sequence leads to alphabetical scattering of logically related subjects; as shown in the example. It is through systematic arrangement that a filiatory sequence or collection of closely related subjects can be achieved.

For this we require a scheme of library classification. Here is an example of arranging documents on the basis of Dewey Decimal Classification which brings documents dealing with different aspects of economics systematically one after another at one place in a collection.

•	330	Economics explained	by R.L. Heibroner
•	331	The economics of work and pay	by Albert Reas
•	332	Essentials of finance	by R.G. Jones
•	333	The economics of natural resources	by R. Leconber
•	334	Cooperative housing	by M. Digby
•	335	Socialism without the state	by E.Lurd
•	336	The fiscal system of HongKong	by H.C.Y. Ho
•	337	Building Europe: Britain's parterns in EEC	by K.J. Twitchett
•	338	Production economics	by M. Fuss
•	339	Macroeconomics	by J.B. Beare

Within each class the arrangement is carried out finally and minutely, *e.g.*,

•	300	Social sciences
•	330	Economics
•	332	Financial economics
•	332.1	Banks and banking
•	332.11	Central banks
•	331.110 954	Reserve Bank of India

Libraries stock various types of documents for different purposes. Classification helps achieve a 'systematic arrangement of different types of documents'.

In big libraries, the collection is segregated in different parts or departments. This is done for the efficient and effective use of library collections and for the convenience of different types of readers. In each department, the collection requires a classified arrangement. An Classification unclassified collection, even though equipped with necessary guides, would be of no use as the readers feel lost in the ocean of books wasting their valuable time to find documents.

It has rightly been said that to locate a book in an unclassified library is as difficult as to locate a needle in a hystack. On the other hand, a systematic arrangement helps readers to get documents without loss of time. Thus the time saved by the library staff can be utilised for rendering personalized reference service for the benefit of readers. A systematic arrangement of documents creates order out of chaos. It provides a panoramic view of documents available in a library on a given subject along with those on closely related subjects. This filiatory sequence of subjects facilitates readers not only in getting his/her documents, but also helps them know the strength and weakness of the collection.

The second, third and fourth Laws of Library Science, *viz.*, Every reader his/her document, Every document its reader and Save the time of the reader, as expounded by Ranganathan, can be practised by libraries through the systematic arrangement of documents.

The First and Fifth Laws, *i.e.*, Books are for use and A library is a growing organism also advocate a systematic classification of books in libraries. The arrangement of documents on the shelves is in a progressive order of complexity, *i.e.*, from the general to the specific. Colon Classification is able to arrange documents in an APUPA pattern. Such an arrangement is in pedagogical order, *i.e.*, it is self-educative and reflects the progress of that subject in an evolutionary order.

In the light of the discussion in this subsection, the functions of library classification can be summarised as follows:

- Library classification helps to arrange documents in a systematic order, which is most convenient to the reader and the library staff. It brings related subjects in close proximity, called collocation by Henry Bliss.

- It helps the identification and location of a document on a given subject wanted by a reader whatever may be the size of the library collection. Documents can be quickly retrieved from and replaced to their original positions. The location, lending and replacement of documents are completed mechanically in libraries.
- It helps to arrange documents into organised groups, like pigeonholes; and when a new document is added to the collection, classification finds an appropriate place for the newly added documents among the other documents on the same subject.
- The universe of knowledge is dynamic, continuous, infinite and ever growing. New areas or subjects are being continuously added to the sum total of human knowledge, When the first document on a new subject is added to the library collection, it finds itself at the appropriate place among the already existing related subjects, *i.e.*, among its kith and kin and according to the level of its relationship to them. The functions stated in (ii), (iii), and (iv) are also known as mechanisation of the arrangement.
- It helps to organise book displays and exhibitions. It facilitates withdrawal of certain documents from the main collection for special purposes and occasions such as book talks, seminars, symposia, conferences and special exhibitions, on a given topic.
- It helps in recording the daily issue and return of documents on various subjects at the circulation counter of a library. This facilitates the compilation of statistics on issues, which reflect the pattern of use and demand of documents on different subjects. The feedback helps in the allocation of funds to various subjects and guides the book selection policy of the library. The statistics so collected can be included in the annual report of the library.
- Stock verification is a very important aspect of library administration. Library classification, through the medium of shelflists, facilitates an efficient and thorough stock verification of the library's holdings.
- It helps in the compilation of reading lists. This facilitates facet analysis of the reference queries on various aspects and 'indirectly helps in an efficient reference service.
- It helps in the compilation of subject union catalogues and bibliographies of books and other reading material. The union catalogues are very important tools for resource 'sharing and cooperation among libraries.
- Classified catalogues are only possible with a classification scheme. In a research library classified catalogues are preferred over dictionary catalogues.
- It assists in systematically deriving subject entries. It also aids

the cataloguer to use the alphabetical list of subject headings for deriving specific subject headings through class numbers, *i.e.*, by the chain procedure.

- Classificatory principles are used in subject headings and thesaurus construction.
- It helps the library staff, especially the classifiers, to be aware of and comprehend the complexities in the development of the universe of knowledge, which is the basis for a systematic arrangement of documents in libraries.
- Nowadays classification finds immense uses in OPACs (*i.e.*, online public access catalogues). In a computerised catalogue, the class number field can be used in combination with other fields such as language, date or even subject heading and can be used with logical operators such as AND/OR/NOT or the Boolean logical operators. Class numbers can be used to broaden or narrow the searches. Class number searches in combination with other fields increase the efficiency (recall and precision ratios) of the information retrieval system, of which classification is a tool.
- It is the basis for the organisation of knowledge emb6died in documents for maximum use. It is the basis for efficient bibliographic control and retrieval of documents. It is a great time saving device for the reader and the library staff. As Hulme puts it, "it is a mechanical time saving device for the discovery of knowledge in books".

NEED AND PURPOSE OF LIBRARY CLASSIFICATION

As a participant in this course you are either a library worker or wish to be one. You are aware that libraries keep various types of documents. At the outset, it is necessary to know that libraries hold several types of collections like printed books, journals, manuscripts, maps, charts, micro-documents, CD-ROMs, video and audio cassettes. etc. All these collections should necessarily be arranged systematically. There are three possible ways in which a reader may demand library material. He may ask by the name of the author whose works he wishes to read, or by the title of the book. The third situation is that he may need book(s) on a particular subject. This last one is known as subject approach. In short, subject approach is the means of securing unknown items from the collection, and classification is the means of facilitating it. Library classification yields subject-wise arrangement of library materials in which documents are arranged by subject and each subject is followed by another subject related to it, *e.g.*, physics following mathematics. This is known as systematic arrangement.

The other important activities in a library such as book selection, circulation and reference services are somewhat indirectly dependent upon library classification. It is thus no wonder that classification is widely regarded as the foundation of librarianship. Classification can ensure full exploitation of library material and strengthen other services in a library. The need for classification is all the greater in modern libraries, as they store different types of documents requiring diverse storage media. In other words, documents on the same subject(s) get scattered throughout the collection because of their diverse physical forms. Classification, however, is the means of bringing books on the shelves and their entries in a catalogue or index at one place. Let us, therefore, acquaint ourselves with these different types of documents that modern libraries acquire and store.

DOCUMENTS

We find in libraries various types of documents, *viz.*, manuscripts, printed books, periodicals, pamphlets, reports, photo reproductions, sound records, films, musical scores, microfilms, maps, atlases, charts, illustrations and electronic media items, such as CD-ROMs, through which human thought is communicated and preserved. Proper collection, storage and maximum use of these documents is the prime concern of present day libraries.

Nature of Documents

The problem of collection, storage and retrieval of documents has been complicated by the following factors:

- The steady growth in the output of various types of documents popularly known as the "knowledge explosion" or "information explosion" or "information flood" or "information boom or bloom".
- The publication of documents in various languages of the world. The production of documents in diverse physical forms. '
- The nature and complexity of the thought content of the subject matter presented in various forms of documents.
- The complexity of readers' approach to documents and libraries.

Each document, like an individual, is not only unique but also exhibits relations of considerable complexity with other documents. Extrinsic features like size, colour, volume, binding, year of publication and intrinsic features like thought content and their arrangement inside the document, or the nature of information, *i.e.*, textual, numeric, bibliographic or graphic, also add to the complexity of the problem of libraries for achieving the objective of maximum utilisation of their collections. The complexity of thought content and the nature of relationships between various types of documents must be known and clearly established for their maximum use.

The maximum use of documents can be ensured by:

- Personal assistance to readers,
- Systematic arrangement, and
- Proper display of materials in the library.

If the collection of a library is arranged in a systematic way documents can be located and retrieved easily. A classification scheme is the map or device for the arrangement of books in the library.

Collection and Storage of Documents

From the dawn of civilization man has recognised the need for collecting and preserving the records of human thought. Books and other graphic material are the records of human thoughts, action and achievement and can serve as the basis for future achievement. Their value to society, thus, cannot be exaggerated. These records are collected and preserved in libraries for the benefit of present and future generations. These records, diverse in form and content, are referred to by the generic term documents.

Factors Determining Arrangement of Documents

Documents can be arranged in various ways in a library, *e.g.*, by author, or by title, or by, subject or by basis such as size, language, colour of binding or any other such criterion. The needs of the readers may be the criterion one can consider for arrangement of documents in a library. Mills, in his book Modern Outline of Library Classification, lists the following possible characteristics determining the arrangements of documents:

- *Age of reader*: Children's books are distinguished from adult's books.
- *Conditions attached to the use of the material*: Books for lending are distinguished from those to be consulted within the library. Generally "Reference Books" come under this category.
- *Documents of unusual size*: Documents of an abnormal size, oversize or undersize, are shelved separately. This is done to conserve space in the stack area.
- *Documents of unusual gross body*: Micro cards, gramophone records, tapes, slides and other audio-visual material and electronic documents are shelved separately.
- *Thought content of the document (subject matter)*: Factual literature is arranged by subject, imaginative literature by language or author.
- *Language of the document*: Documents in foreign languages are separately arranged in their original languages.
- *Value of the document*: Manuscripts and rare and costly documents are shelved separately.
- *Peculiarities of form of presentation*: Files of bound periodicals are separately shelved.
- *Date of printing*: Incunabula - early printed books - are shelved separately.
- *Local history collection*: Documents dealing with various aspects of a place, locality or region are shelved separately.

- *Gift collection*: A large number of hooks may be gifted with the condition to shelve them separately.

The factors influence the arrangement of documents in libraries. But thought content or subject arrangement (fifth in Mill's list) is still the dominant and important facto- for deciding the sequence of documents. All other factors in the list are functional. Though a collection can be divided into several parts on the basis of any of the functional factors, it would still be helpful to arrange documents in each part on the basis of subject matter. This leads to parallel sequences in the various collections in libraries.

In any library, the total collection gets divided into some separate collections of general books and reference books, textbooks, journals, etc. There are, thus, many sequences of books on one and the same subject in the library. These sequences are known as "parallel sequences".

Arrangement of Documents in Libraries

Until the end of the 19th century library collections were small in size. Not as many subject fields had developed as one notice now, and publishing was not as wide spread. The readership was not as large as we notice in the present times. Libraries of yesteryear attempted to arrange their collections on the basis of fixed locations. This method was employed to allocate each and every document a particular and permanent place on a particular shelf of the library. Each new document, irrespective of its thought content, was assigned to the place immediately next to the one previously added to the collection.

The fixed location failed to bring together documents embodying the same subject. Fixed location implied chronological order of accession under broad subject categories.

In some of the older libraries, attempts where made to arrange the collection on the basis of extrinsic characteristics such as colour, size, year of publication and type of binding of documents. All these arrangements or sequences are not as helpful as the subject arrangement.

Approach of Readers for Documents

As stated earlier, documents can be arranged in libraries on the basis of the colour of the binding, the size, the language, the year of publication, the accession number and so on. But these methods are outdated and unhelpful, as they cannot bring to the notice of the reader the author, the title or the subject matter of a document. There is little or no chance of your finding today a library, which arranges its collection on the basis of colour, size, year of publication or even the name of the publisher. It was possible to use these characteris-tics for arranging books when the collections were very small in size.

There are a few libraries where the collections are arranged on the basis of accession number or serial number. The other methods by which documents are usually arranged are by title, author or subject. This is because in present-day libraries, the reader's approach for a specific document is by title or author or subject. It is common practice that fiction is arranged by author, periodicals by title and scientific factual literature by subject. In some libraries, you can find that even imaginative literature (belles letters) is arranged first by language, and within each language by form followed by author and, if necessary, by work number.

It has already been explained, that a reader may demand a document by a particular author or of a particular title or on a particular subject. There are, thus, mainly three approaches to a collection, *viz.*, author, title and subject.

Author Approach

Generally readers go to a library to find:

- A particular document whose author is known or
- What documents by a particular author are in the library.

But the arrangement of documents on the basis of the author is not always helpful. If you want a particular document, or documents on a particular subject, the author arrangement fails to bring documents having the same specific subject and related subjects at one place. Here is an example:

•	Marsten, R.B.	:	Communication Technology
•	Marston, A.N.	:	Encyclopaedia of Angling
•	Marston, E.H.	:	Dynamic Environment
•	Marston, Elizabeth	:	Rain Forest
•	Marston, John	:	Dutch Courtesan
•	Marston, J.E.	:	Nature of Public Relations
•	Marston, Phillip	:	Breeder of Democracy
•	Marston, P.B.	:	Collected Poems
•	Marst, R.M.	:	Electronic Projects
•	Martell, P.	:	World Military Leaders

Title Approach

Sometimes you may go to a library to get a document whose title you know. If the books in the library are arranged by title, it will meet your requirement. But the method of arranging documents on the basis of title is also not very helpful. There is always a chance of a title being misquoted. Titles sometimes change from one edition to another. The title of the same document would differ when translated from one language to another. Sometimes the same document is published in different countries under different titles, though the language may remain the same. Title arrangement, like author arrangement, fails to bring together documents having the same specific subject at one place. Because of these limitations; the arrangement of documents on the basis of title is not very helpful.

Here is an example:

- Instant Astrology by Jack London

- Instant Beauty Tricks by P. Brooks
- Instant Book Keeping by D.C. Conaway
- Instant Chicago by J. Graham
- Instant College by R.W. Graham Classification
- Instant Divorce by S. Rosen
- Instant English Handbook by M. Semmelmeyer
- Instant Medical Advisor by J. Smith
- Instant Paintings by N. Koni
- Instant Quotation Dictionary by B.O. Bolander

Subject Approach

In academic, special, technical and research libraries, and to a large extent even in public libraries, you will find that the majority of readers approach documents on the basis of the subject. This subject approach by readers has increased due to the growth in science and technology and also to a large extent in social sciences where the author and the title of a document are important but not adequate. Due to the enormous output of documents in these fields, it is often difficult to recall a specific title or author correctly except in the case of classics.

Therefore, one finds that in well organised libraries documents are arranged on the basis of subject matter. This arrangement helps to bring documents embodying the same specific subject together and those on related subjects in their close proximity on the shelves. This would result, as Ranganathan puts it, into an APUPA arrangement that will give reader the greatest satisfaction at the moment in full conformity to all the Five Laws of Library Science. In this arrangement, the focal point of one's main interest is the UMBRAL REGION.

This is followed on, either side by the PENUMBRAL REGION represented by subjects on either side of the UMBRAL region having successfully a decreasing bearing on the umbral region. The penumbral region will ultimately thin into ALIEN REGIONS. This is helpful and convenient especially on open access libraries. Readers can directly go to the shelves and browse through the library collection. Generally, the objective of libraries is to have an APUPA ARRANGEMENT EVERYWHERE.

Subject arrangement, hence, helps bring together on the shelves documents on one and the same subject followed by those of related subjects. Suppose you are looking for a specific document on say, physics, you can find, where subject arrangement exists, documents not only on physics, but also those related to it in close proximity, *i.e.*, chemistry. It may so happen that if a specific title wanted by you is not available, you can find another title on the subject that may very well meet your requirement. Some scholars may need everything available on their topic. You will notice that near the books on chemistry, you will also find books on related subjects like mathematics and astronomy on one side and chemistry and biology on the other.

Subject arrangement of documents enables you to know:

- What documents the library has on a specific subject; and
- What is the quality of collection on that subject, and what are the gaps in the collection?

This kind of arrangement is known as 'filiatory sequence'.

In large and special libraries, having several parts such as:

- Text books
- Reference books
- Theses and dissertations
- Pamphlets
- Bound volumes of periodicals

You will find that all these different collections are arranged by subject using a scheme of library classification:

It has been the considered opinion of experts that the arrangement of documents on a basis other than subject may not meet the requirements of the majority of readers in modem libraries. Nowadays the subject approach to books is predominant. Eminent classificationists like Melvil Dewey, J.D. Brown, C.A. Cutter, W.C.B. Sayers, S.R. Ranganathan, H. E. Bliss and others advocate the subject arrangement of documents. Subject arrangement, however, does not mean that there is no scope for the author and title approaches. These approaches are taken care of through the author and title catalogues. Subject arrangement, then, is paramount and the basis for it is the subject content of documents. Library classification is the technique used in libraries for mechanising of this subject content documents: It is a technique for making libraries more helpful.

UNIVERSAL DECIMAL CLASSIFICATION

The *Universal Decimal Classification* (UDC) is a bibliographic and library classification developed by the Belgian bibliogra-phers Paul Otlet and Henri La Fontaine at the end of the 19th century. The UDC provides a systematic arrangement of all branches of human knowledge organized as a coherent system in which knowledge fields are related and inter-linked. Originally based on the Dewey Decimal Classification, the UDC was developed as a new analytico-synthetic classification system with a significantly larger vocabulary and syntax that enables very detailed content indexing and information retrieval in large collections.

In its first edition in 1905, the UDC already included many features that were revolutionary in the context of knowledge classifications.

- Tables of generally applicable concepts - called common auxiliary tables;

- A series of special auxiliary tables with specific but re-usable attributes in a particular field of knowledge;
- An expressive notational system with connecting symbols and syntax rules to enable coordination of subjects and the creation of a documentation language proper.

Although originally designed as an indexing and retrieval system, due to its logical structure and scalability, they UDC has become one of the most widely used knowledge organization systems in libraries, where it is used for either shelf arrangement, content indexing or both. UDC codes can describe any type of document or object to any desired level of detail. These can include textual documents and other media such as films, video and sound recordings, illustrations, maps as well as realia such as museum objects. Since the first edition in French "Manuel du Répertoire bibliographique universel", the UDC has been translated and published in various editions in 40 languages. UDC Summary, an abridged Web version of the scheme is available in over 45 languages. The classification has been modified and extended over the years to cope with increasing output in all areas of human knowledge, and is still under continuous review to take account of new developments.

The Application of UDC

UDC is used in around 150,000 libraries in 130 countries and in many bibliographical services which require detailed content indexing. In a number of countries it is the main classification system for information exchange and is used in all type of libraries: public, school, academic and special libraries. UDC is also used in national bibliographies of around 30 countries. Examples of large databases indexed by UDC include: NEBIS - 2.6 million records, COBIB.SI - 3.5 million records; Hungarian National Union Catalogue - 2.9 million records; VINITI RAS database with 28 million records; *Meteorological and Geoastrophysical Abstracts* (MGA) with 600 journal titles; PORBASE with 1.5 million records, etc. UDC has traditionally been used for the indexing of scientific articles which was an important source of information of scientific output in the period predating electronic publishing. Collections of research articles in many countries covering decades of scientific output contain UDC codes.

Examples of journal articles indexed by UDC:

- UDC code 663.12:57.06 in the article "Yeast Systematics: from Phenotype to Genotype" in the journal Food Technology and Biotechnology
- UDC code 37.037:796.56, provided in the article "The game method as means of interface of technical-tactical and psychological preparation in sports orienteering" in the Russian journal "Pedagogico-psychological and medico-biological problems of the physical culture and sport".

- UDC code 621.715:621.924:539.3 in the article Residual Stress in Shot-Peened Sheets of AlMg4.5Mn Alloy - in the journal Materials and technology.

The design of UDC lends itself to machine readability, and the system has been used both with early automatic mechanical sorting devices, and modern library OPACs. From 1993, a standard version of UDC is maintained and is distributed in a database format: UDC Master Reference File (UDC MRF) which is updated and released annually. The 2010 version of the MRF contains over 69,000 classes. In the past full printed editions used to have around 220,000 subdivisions.

UDC structure and Content

Notation

A notation is a code commonly used in classification schemes to represent a class, *i.e.* a subject and its position in the hierarchy, to enable mechanical sorting and filing of subjects. UDC uses Arabic numerals arranged decimally. Every number is thought of as a decimal fraction with the initial decimal point omitted, which determines the filing order. An advantage of decimal notational systems is that they are infinitely extensible, and when new subdivisions are introduced, they need not disturb the existing allocation of numbers. For ease of reading, a UDC notation is usually punctuated after every third digit:

Notation	Caption (Class description)
539.120	Theoretical problems of elementary particles physics. Theories and models of fundamental interactions
539.120.2	Symmetries of quantum physics
539.120.22	Conservation laws
539.120.222	Translations. Rotations
539.120.224	Reflection in time and space
539.120.226	Space-time symmetries
539.120.23	Internal symmetries
539.120.3	Currents
539.120.4	Unified field theories
539.120.5	Strings

In UDC the notation has two features that make the scheme easier to browse and work with:

- *Hierarchically expressive*: The longer the notation, the more specific the class: removing the final digit automatically produces a broader class code.
- *Syntactically expressive*: When UDC codes are combined, the sequence of digits is interrupted by a precise type of punctuation sign which indicates that the expression is a combination of classes rather than a simple class *e.g.* the colon in 34:32 indicates that there are two distinct notational elements: 34 Law. Jurisprudence and 32 Politics; the closing

and opening parentheses and double quotes in the following code 91(574.22)"19"(084.3) indicate four separate notational elements: 913 Regional geography, (574.22) North Kazakhstan; "19" 20th century and (084.3) Maps (document form)

Basic Features and Syntax

The UDC is an anlytico-synthetic and/or faceted classification. It allows an unlimited combination of attributes of a subject and relationships between subjects to be expressed. UDC codes from different tables can be combined to present various aspects of document content and form, *e.g.* 94(410)"19"(075) History *(main subject)* of United Kingdom *(place)* in 20th century *(time)*, a textbook *(document form)*. Or: 37:2 Relationship between Education and Religion. Complex UDC expressions can be accurately parsed into constituent elements. UDC is also a disciplinary classification covering the entire universe of knowledge. This type of classification can also be described as *aspect* or *perspective*, which means that concepts are subsumed and placed under the field in which they are studied.

Thus, the same concept can appear in different fields of knowledge. This particular feature is usually implemented in UDC by re-using the same concept in various combinations with the main subject, *e.g.* a code for language in common auxiliaries of language is used to derive numbers for ethnic grouping, individual languages in linguistics and individual literatures. Or, a code from the auxiliaries of place, *e.g. (410) United Kingdom*, uniquely representing the concept of United Kingdom can be used to express *911(410) Regional geography of United Kingdom* and *94(410) History of United Kingdom*.

Organization of Classes

Concepts are organized in two kinds of tables in UDC. Common auxiliary tables (including certain auxiliary signs). These tables contain facets of concepts representing, general recurrent characteristics, applicable over a range of subjects throughout the main tables, including notions such as place, language of the text and physical form of the document, which may occur in almost any subject. UDC numbers from these tables, called common auxiliaries are simply added at the end of the number for the subject taken from the main tables. There are over 15,000 of common auxiliaries in UDC.

The main tables or main schedules containing the various disciplines and branches of knowledge, arranged in 9 main classes, numbered from 0 to 9. At the beginning of each class there are also series of special auxiliaries, which express aspects that are recurrent within this specific class. Main tables in UDC contain more than 60,000 subdivisions.

Main Classes

- 0 Science and Knowledge. Organization. Computer Science. Information. Documentation. Librarianship. Institu-tions. Publications

- 1 Philosophy. Psychology
- 2 Religion. Theology
- 3 Social Sciences
- 4 vacant
- 5 Mathematics. Natural Sciences
- 6 Applied Sciences. Medicine, Technology
- 7 The Arts. Recreation. Entertainment. Sport
- 8 Language, Linguistics, Literature
- 9 Geography, Biography, History

The vacant class 4 is the result of a planned schedule expansion. This class was freed by moving linguistics into class 8 in 1960s to make space for future developments in the rapidly expanding fields of knowledge; primarily natural sciences and technology.

Common Auxiliary Tables

Common auxiliaries are aspect-free concepts that can be used in combination with any other UDC code from the main classes or with other common auxiliaries. They have unique notational representations that makes them stand out in complex expressions. Common auxiliary numbers always begin with a certain symbol known as a facet indicator, *e.g.* = (equal sign) always introduces concepts representing the language of a document; (0...) numbers enclosed in parentheses starting with zero always represent a concept designating document form. Thus (075) Textbook and =111 English can be combined to express, *e.g.* (075)=111 Textbooks in English, and when combined with numbers from the main UDC tables they can be used as follows:

2(075)=111 Religion textbooks in English, 51(075)=111 Mathematics textbooks in English etc.

- =... Common auxiliaries of language.
- (0...) Common auxiliaries of form.
- (1/9) Common auxiliaries of place.
- (=...) Common auxiliaries of human ancestry, ethnic grouping and nationality.
- "..." Common auxiliaries of time.
- -0... Common auxiliaries of general characteristics: Properties, Materials, Relations/Processes and Persons.
- -02 Common auxiliaries of properties.
- -03 Common auxiliaries of materials.
- -04 Common auxiliaries of relations, processes and operations.
- -05 Common auxilaries of persons and personal characteristics.

Connecting Signs

In order to preserve the precise meaning and enable accurate parsing of complex UDC expressions, a number of connecting symbols are made available to relate and extend UDC numbers. These are:

Symbol	Symbol Name	Meaning	Example
+	plus	addition	e.g. 59+636 zoology and animal breeding
/	stroke	consecutive extension	e.g. 592/599 Systematic zoology (everything from 592 to 599 inclusive)
:	colon	relation	e.g. 17:7 Relation of ethics to art
[ ]	square brackets	subgrouping	e.g. 311:[622+669](485) statistics of mining and metallurgy in Sweden (the auxiliary qualifiers 622+669 considered as a unit)
*	asterisk	Introduces non UDC notation	e.g. 523.4*433 Planetology, minor planet Eros (IAU authorized number after the asterisk)
A/Z	alphabetic extension	Direct alphabetical specification	e.g. 821.133.1MOL French literature, works of Molière

UDC Outline

UDC classes in this outline are taken from the Multilingual Universal Decimal Classification Summary released on the by the UDC Consortium under the Creative Commons Attribution Share Alike 3.0 licence.

DEWEY DECIMAL CLASSIFICATION

Of modern library classification schemes, the *Dewey Decimal Classification* (*DDC*) is both the oldest and the most widely used in the United States. It also has a substantial following abroad. Such widespread use is a tribute to Melville Louis Kossuth Dewey, whose original plan was adaptable enough to incorporate new subjects as they emerged and flexible enough to withstand the changes imposed by the passage of time. Dewey was born on December 10, 1851, and graduated from Amherst College in 1874, where he became assistant college librarian. He actually began developing the first draft of his system for arranging books while working as a student assistant in the college library in 1873. He soon became a leader in American librarianship, helping to found both the *American Library Association* (ALA) and the first American library school at Columbia University. Being a man of many interests, he was also an advocate of spelling reform.

He shortened his forename to "Melvil", dropped his two middle names, and even attempted to change the spelling of his surname to "Dui". Throughout his career he promoted librarianship by his teaching, writing, and speaking. In recognizing and acting upon the need to systematize library collections for effective use, he knew of various previous attempts, but found them inadequate. Dewey never claimed to have originated decimals for classification notation, but earlier systems used them merely as shelf location devices with no significant relation to the subject matter.

What Dewey did claim as original, and with some justification, was his "relativ index", compiled as a key to the "diverse material" included in his tables. His most significant contribution was perhaps the use of decimals for hierarchical divisions. Combined with the digits 0 to 9, decimals provide a pure notation that can be subdivided indefinitely. The first edition of Dewey's scheme, prepared for the Amherst College Library, was issued anonymously in 1876 under the title *A Classification and Subject Index for Cataloguing and Arranging the Books and Pamphlets of a Library*.

It included schedules to 1000 divisions numbered 000–999, together with a relative index and prefatory matter—a total of 44 pages. The second, "revised and greatly enlarged" edition was published under Dewey's name in 1885. Since that time 20 more full editions and 14 abridgments have appeared. The fourteenth edition, published in 1942, remained the standard edition for many years because an experimental index to the fifteenth edition, published in 1951, was unsuccessful. In 1958 the sixteenth edition appeared with many changes and additions, "Inorganic and Organic Chemistry."

Since that time each successive edition has carried, besides other, less sweeping changes, totally new developments of one or more targeted portions of the system. The present twenty-second edition was published in 2003; the associated fourteenth abridged edition was published in 2004. *DDC* notations are assigned the tag 082 in *MARC 21* when they have been created for a particular item by the *Library of Congress* (LC) or other national cataloging agency.

A *DDC* notation created by a local library participating in a network is placed in MARC field 092. *DDC* complete call numbers are also placed in field 092, regardless of who assigned the *DDC* notation to the item involved. Closely related to *DDC* is the *Universal Decimal Classification* (*UDC*), which was based originally on *DDC*. It is discussed briefly at the end of this chapter.

DEWEY DECIMAL CLASSIFICATION SYSTEM

In 1876 Melvil Dewey divided all fields of knowledge into ten major categories. Fiction and biography aren't included in these categories and are shelved separately. Fiction books are on the shelves in alphabetical order according to the author's last name. Biographies are in alphabetical order according to the last name of the person who is the subject of the book. Many public libraries in the United States still use the Dewey Decimal System because this is the system they have historically used, and because it is an easy system to use and master.

It arranges the contents of a library based on the division of all knowledge into 10 groups, with each group assigned 100 numbers.

These 10 main groups are then subdivided again and again to provide more specific subject groups.

- 000 GENERALITIES
  - 010 Bibliography
  - 020 Library and Information Sciences
  - 030 General encyclopedic works
  - 040 General reference works
  - 050 General Serials and their indexes
  - 060 General organizations and museology
  - 070 News media, journalism, publishing

- 080 General collections
- 090 Manuscripts and rare books

• 100 PHILOSOPHY and RELATED DISCIPLINES
- 110 Metaphysics
- 120 Epistemology, causation, mankind
- 130 Paranormal phenomena and arts
- 140 Specific philosophical schools
- 150 Psychology
- 160 Logic
- 170 Ethics
- 180 Ancient, medieval, Oriental philosophy
- 190 Modern Western philosophy

• 200 RELIGION
- 210 Natural theology
- 220 Bible
- 230 Christian theology
- 240 Christian moral and devotional theology
- 250 Christian orders and local church
- 260 Christian social history
- 270 Christian church history
- 280 Christian denominations and sects
- 290 Other and comparative religions

• 300 SOCIAL SCIENCES
- 310 General statistics
- 320 Political Science
- 330 Economics
- 340 Law
- 350 Public Administration
- 360 Social problems and services
- 380 Commerce
- 390 Customs, etiquette, folklore

• 400 LANGUAGE
- 410 Linguistics
- 420 English and Old English
- 430 Germanic languages
- 440 Romance languages
- 450 Italian, Romanian, Rhaeto-Romanic
- 460 Spanish and Portuguese languages
- 470 Italic languages
- 480 Hellenic languages
- 490 Other Languages

• 500 PURE SCIENCES

- 510 Mathematics
- 520 Astronomy
- 530 Physics
- 540 Chemistry
- 550 Earth sciences
- 560 Paleontology
- 570 Life sciences
- 580 Botany
- 590 Zoology

• 600 TECHNOLOGY
  - 610 Medical sciences
  - 620 Engineering
  - 630 Agriculture
  - 640 Home Economics
  - 650 Management
  - 660 Chemical engineering
  - 670 Manufacturing
  - 680 Manufacture for specific uses
  - 690 Building

• 700 THE ARTS
  - 710 Civic and Landscape arts
  - 720 Architecture
  - 730 Pottery, Sculpture
  - 740 Drawing, decorative arts
  - 750 Painting
  - 760 Graphic arts
  - 770 Photography
  - 780 Music
  - 790 Performing and recreational arts

• 800 LITERATURE
  - 810 American literature
  - 820 English literature
  - 830 Germanic literatures
  - 840 Romance Language literatures
  - 850 Italian, Romanian, Rhaeto-Romanic literatures
  - 860 Spanish literatures
  - 870 Italic literatures
  - 880 Classical Greek Literature
  - 890 Literatures of other languages

• 900 GENERAL GEOGRAPHY and HISTORY
  - 910 Geography and Travel
  - 920 Biography and Genealogy

- 930 Ancient History
- 940 History - Europe
- 950 History - Asia
- 960 History - Africa
- 970 History - North America
- 980 History - South America
- 990 History - other areas

COLON CLASSIFICATION (CC)

You have now studied in detail the Dewey Decimal Classification and Universal Decimal Classification schemes. This chapter attempts to familiarise you with the underlying principles of Colon Classification. The CC differs in several respects from the other two schemes, which you have already studied in this Block. S.R. Ranganathan, the author of CC, was well aware that a scheme of classification should be able to meet the challenge of ever rowing universe of knowledge and it should 'be able to accommodate, at an appropriate' place, any new subject without disturbing the arrays already formed. The seventh edition of CC has succeeded to a large extent in fulfilling this objective;

Two basic strategies for number building in CC are:

- Subject analysis, and
- Synthesis.

The analysis of a given subject results in the facetisation of the subject, as treated in the document, on the basis of five fundamental categories and their manifestation in it. Synthesis consists of bringing together the facets manifest in a subject to represent, as completely as possible, the description of that subject. Synthesis also has another connotation. It consists of connecting to the core subject those other aspects, which it shares with other subjects. By dint of its capabilities of analysis and synthesis, CC is known as an analytico-synthetic scheme. It is also described as a Freely Faceted Scheme.

Under a rigidly faceted scheme, each main class was given a facet formula and the numbers were coined with the help of a connecting digit, colon. The drawback under a rigidly faceted scheme, with a single connecting symbol, resulted from the cluttering of the connecting symbol, *i.e.*, whether a facet was present or absent, it had to be represented by a colon. With the introduction of 'separate connecting digits for personality, matter and energy facets in the fourth edition of CC, it became possible to represent only those facets in the number that are manifested in the subject treated in the document. Because of this facility, CC has since been called Freely Faceted.

Genesis of Colon Classification

Ranganathan was a mathematics lecturer. It was a mere accident that he was appointed Librarian of the Madras University Library in the year 1924. He was soon deputed to Britain for an observational tour of British libraries. While in Britain he also attended classes in the School of Librarianship, University of London. Berwick Sayers, known as' the grammarian of library classification, was one of the teachers at the School. During his tour of Britain; Ranganathan visited several libraries and was quick to notice the lacunae in the classification schemes in use then. A chance visit to a departmental store in London gave Ranganathan a clue for evolving a scheme of classification. He saw the demonstration of a toy called meccano set.

The meccano set consists of several slotted strips, rods, wheels, screws, nuts and bolts with which several different models could be made. This gave him the idea that in a classification scheme there should be standard units that could be joined by connecting symbols. Ranganathan's standard units resembled the strips and his connecting symbols resembled the nuts and bolts of the meccano set. The standard units became the schedules. Thus, a class number could be constructed with the different elements enumerated in the schedules with a connecting symbol and he chose the colon as the connecting symbol. This was, dip, Ranganathan's conception of Colon Classification. The foundation of Colon Classification was laid in Britain in the year 1924. In 1925, his journey back to India gave Ranganathan ample time to work on the schedules. The library on the ship he was travelling in and the Madras University Library's book catalogue, which he was carrying with him served as the working equipment for him.

First Edition

On reaching Madras he took up the work of classifying the Madras University Library collection. The years between 1925 and 1932 were devoted mainly to the 'construction' of the schedules of CC. In 1929, he also established a library school at the University. Both teaching and library work at the University contributed immensely to the publication in 1933 of the first edition of Colon Classification. It had three distinct part: 127 pages of rules explaining the underlying principles, 135 pages of schedules and 106 pages of index. The notation was mixed, consisting of the 26 Roman capital letters denoting main classes, Indo-Arabic numerals and also Roman lower case letters. The colon (:) was used as the connecting symbol for joining facets. Each main class was provided with a facet formula.

Search for Theory

Ranganathan was aware of several inconsistencies in his scheme and did not fight shy of consulting subjects experts to know the gamut of each discipline. At the same time he tried to evolve a theory of library classification. The years from 1933 to 1939 were spent in working on the theory of classification. It was during these years that several Canons of Classification were formulated. The result was the publication of Prolegomena to Library Classification in 1937. Based on this theory, the second edition of Colon Classification was published in 1939. The changes from the first to the second edition were not substantial. In this edition, two new concepts of Octave principles and auto-bias device were introduced.

A new main class 8 Spiritual Experience and Mysticism carne into being. The first edition, as already said, had three parts. A fourth part was added in the second edition. This additional part contained about 3,000 examples, which were illustrative of the rules given in the first part.

Subsequent Editions

In 1945, Ranganathan shifted to Banaras. He spent two years at Banaras Hindu University from 1945 to 1947. He was, however, bogged down in administrative work and all research came to a standstill. It was Sir Maurice Gwyer, the then Vice-Chancellor of Delhi University, who invited, Ranganathan to Delhi and gave him all facilities to devote himself to serious research. The eight years from 1947 to 1955 that he stayed at Delhi University were productive. Team research became possible, and a quarterly journal, Abgila, became the instrument to publish the research findings.

After a lapse of eleven years the third edition of Colon Classification appeared in 1950 without any major modifications. There were, however, a few changes in terminology. The findings of research at Delhi culminated in a dynamic theory of library classification. A major finding was that in any subject there could be only five ingredients. This gave rise to the Postulate of Five Fundamental Categories, which were stated as *Personality, Matter, Energy, Space and Time* (PMEST).

The postulate further stated that these five fundamental categories; fall in the sequence of P M E S T. Each fundamental category was assigned an indicator digit as shown below:

Fundamental Category	Indicator Digit '
Personality	, (Comma)
Matter	; (Semi-colon)
Energy	: (Colon)
Space	. (Dot)
Time	. (Dot)

The indicator digit for time was later changed to a single inverted comma ('). The ordinal value of the connecting symbols was also determined. These findings were included in the fourth edition of Colon Classification and the second edition of Prolegomena to Library Classification, published in 1957. The fifth edition appeared in the year 1957. The fifth edition had made several changes both in the rules and also in the schedules. Many Greek letters were introduced in the fourth edition to expand the base of the main classes.

These were found to be irritants and were replaced in the sixth edition by empty and emptying digits. Some changes were also effected in a few main classes. In addition, the second level of space and time facets was introduced. Meanwhile, the sixth edition of Colon Classification, was published in 1960. At about this time, Ranganathan had shifted to Bangalore.

A new centre, *Documentation Research and Training Centre* (DRTC), was established by the Indian Statistical Institute with Ranganathan as its honourary professor. At DRTC, Ranganathan was assisted by a team of researchers. The DRTC brought out they several special schedules of classification based on the new research findings. In 1963, a reprint of the sixth edition was published with a few corrections and amendments. At that time an announcement was made that the seventh edition would be, brought out incorporating all the new findings. Unfortunately, Ranganathan passed away in 1972 and the work was delayed. The long awaited seventh edition of Colon Classification with substantial changes from the earlier editions appeared in 1987, without an Index.

Basic Principles in Colon Classification

The CC, like other schemes of classification, starts with a set of main classes which form the first order array, of classes. Each main class is divided into facets. All facets are regarded as manifestations of five fundamental categories.

The terms are:

- Main classes,
- Array,
- Facet, and
- Fundamental categories.

Main Classes

The main classes in CC are like disciplines in DDC and theoretical subjects in UDC. They are the traditional subjects, which you are well acquainted with, like mathematics, physics, history, political science and soon. The number of main classes in CC is greater than those in DDC and UDC.

Array

The dictionary meaning of array is 'a systematic arrangement of numbers or symbols in an orderly manner.' In CC also, it means the same as its dictionary meaning. The arrangement, however, is referred to as the preferred sequence. The numbers, in a classification refer to a division of a subject on the basis –of a, single characteristic. For example, in medicine, the organs of the human body form the array of organs.

Facet

A facet is a characteristic by which 'a class is divided/grouped, Each main class is divided into facets to signify the whole series of arrays based on, a set of related characteristics of division. In the main class Literature, all enumerated languages, after which the national literatures are known, constitute in DDC,, the language facet of that class.

In the same class, all literary forms constitute another facet. It may also be stated here that within a facet an individual member is called a focus. Hindi literature, for example, is a focus in the language facet of the class Literature.

Fundamental Categories

To understand the basic principles of CC you have to first understand some of the rules framed by Ranganathan. He calls them postulates. One postulate states that there are five fundamental categories (FC), *viz.*, personality [P], matter [M], energy [E], space [S], and time [T], PMEST for short. A postulate is a presumption or assumption, which is never put to test. It is a basis for argument and hence one is not supposed to question the veracity of the assumption. That is the meaning of a postulate. According to Ranganathan, in any given subject, there may be a maximum of five fundamental categories. There can be less, but in no case more than five. They also come in the order of PMEST according to their decreasing concreteness. If you are able to identify the fundamental categories irk a given subject, you can classify any subject. Hence, you must have a clear perception of each of the five fundamental categories. As suggested, take up the five fundamental categories one by one for discussion in the reverse order.

Time and Space

These two have the usual meaning known to you. A century, a decade, a year, a month, a day, an hour are all indicators of time. If the subject is stated as Economic conditions of India in the 19th century, you can identify the time element in it. In some subjects, it may not be stated explicitly, *e.g.*, Economic conditions during the reign of Akbar. In this example, the fundamental category time is concealed, but still identifiable.

In the same way, it is fairly simple to locate the space element in a subject. In the title *Economic conditions of India in the 19th century*, you can find the space facet, *i.e.* India. Space is indicated by terms like continent, country, city, village, etc. All these come under the facet space.

Energy

The next fundamental category is energy. Energy refers to some type of action. In the subject medicine, diagnosis or treatment falls under the facet energy. It shows action. In agriculture, ploughing is energy, in education teaching is energy, and in sociology relief work is energy,and so on.

Matter

There is a major change in the seventh edition of CC in the case of the fundamental category matter. Up to the sixth edition, Matter was present only in a few main classes. There is a complete reversal in the seventh edition. In certain cases, what was considered energy now forms part of the matter facet. Besides, the fundamental category matter has undergone some other changes. It is distinguished as Matter Property [MP], Matter Material [MMt] and Matter Method [MM].

It is only matter property, which has almost replaced the fundamental category energy. To explain matter with a concrete example, in the class medicine, anatomy, physiology and diseases are viewed as manifestations of matter property. Similarly, in the main class agriculture, soil, manure, propagation, etc. are treated as manifestations of matter property. In the main class fine arts, under the class drawing, pencil drawing, ink drawing, and cartoon drawing are considered as a manifestation of matter method. In technology, product, and in biology substance are manifestation of matter material. Hence, in a given subject, it is not difficult to recognise the fundamental categories of time, space, energy and matter.

Personality

The fundamental category personality has evaded definition. Ranganathan found a way out to recognise personality by the method of residue, *i.e.*, when it cannot be any other fundamental category it is assigned to personality. However, experience in the design of depth schedules suggests that it is possible to identify a core concept in compound subjects going with a basic subject, such as, 'Human Body' in Medicine. Such a care concept is deemed to be a manifestation of 'Personality'.

Postulates of Basic Facet

Once you determine the different fundamental categories, they are to be attached to. a basic class in the order of P M E S T. A basic facet in the traditional meaning stands for a 16; class, *e.g.*, philosophy, psychology, chemistry, literature, history, etc. In CC, originally there were nearly 30 such main classes. This number rose to 47 in the sixth edition. You can find that many of the main classes listed in the seventh edition are not exactly basic subjects as you know them. If you take, for example, B Mathematics, the different subjects listed under it appear more like its extensions. Similarly properties of matter, sound, heat, electricity, magnetism etc., under C Physics are only adjuncts to the main class C. But in classifying, it makes a difference. In C6 Electricity, 6 is not a fundamental category, but is part of the basic class, and hence a separate facet formula had to be given for it.

Planes of Work

According to Ranganathan, there are three planes of work through which a scheme of library classification passes. The three planes are Idea plane, Herbal plane and Notational plane. A scheme of library classification has to first enumerate the Universe of Subjects, state their inter-relations and fix their order. This is done in the idea plane. The findings of the idea plane are to be represented in terms. This is -the verbal plane of work. Lastly, these terms are transformed into a notation. This last plane of work is known as the notational plane. There are thus three planes of work: idea, verbal and notational.

Rounds and Levels

Having identified five fundamental categories, it was found that some of them manifest themselves more than once in a subject, for example personality, matter and energy. This phenomenon was handled by the introduction of the postulates of rounds and levels. Take, far instance, a subject like Treatment of brain tumour by radium therapy. In this, we have the fundamental, categories brain FET tumour [A], treatment [ER], and radium therapy [El. 11 (E), thus, repeats itself. Such repetition of any of to three (R M and E)' fundamental categories is called round of fundamental category. These rounds are indicated as [1PI], [2PI], [113], [2E],' [1Mi], [2M1] and so on.

Let us take another example: King Lear by Shakespeare. First you must find what fundamental categories are present in this subject. The basic class is, of course; literature. The isolates are, language, form of literature, author and his work. All these isolates, I under the fundamental category personality. They, therefore, belong to the personality facet. These occurrences are referred to as levels of personality and they all fall in the first round. They are therefore indicated as [1P1], [1P2], [1P3], [1P4]. They are read as first level; first round, second level; first round, third level; and first round, fourth level.

Postulates of Facet Sequence

We have been discussing so far five fundamental categories, their rounds and levels. The next question that arises is in what order are these to be arranged. This has been answered by Ranganathan by his postulates of facet sequence. He has given five postulates followed by some principles going with them.

Therefore, only the postulates are repeated here.

- *Postulate of first facet*: In any compound subject, the first facet should be the basic facet. It simply means that there should be a basic class or main class even if it is not stated explicitly in the title of the document. For example, if we take treatment of cancer as our subject, the badic facet is not stated. But, by implication, the basic facet in this case is medicine.
- *Postulate of concreteness*: The five fundamental categories appear in the sequence of PMEST only. This means they appear in the order of their decreasing concreteness. To explain this with an example, let us take a subject like Prevention of fungus diseases in oranges in Nagpur. Here, apart from supplying the basic facet we have to find

out other fundamental categories and arrange them in the sequence of PMEST. Obviously, agriculture is the basic facet and the other fundamental categories are oranges [P], prevention [E], fungus diseases [M], and Nagpur [S]. To put them in order, according to the postulate, it will be

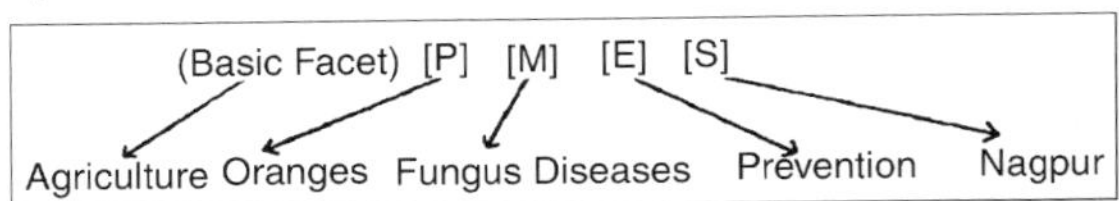

- *Postulate of facet sequence within a round*: In a compound subject, if any P, M and E occur in any round, they should be arranged in the order of P, M, E. For example, Preparation of soil for growing grapes has agriculture as the personality facet. As per the postulate, the sequence of the facet will be:
  - Agriculture (BF),
  - Grapes [P],
  - Soil [M], and
  - Preparation [E].
- *Postulate of facet sequence within the last round*: The fourth postulate states that in the last round of facets of a compound subject, in which each of the fundamental categories other than energy may occur, and occur only once, the sequence of facets should be P, M, S and T. Take, for instance, a little like: A study of the emotions of adults in 20th century USA. Here the basic facet is psychology and the other facets are emotions (matter), adults (personality), 20th century (time) and USA (space). In this, there is no manifestation of energy. Hence, as stated in the postulate, the sequence should be:
  - Psychology (BF),
  - Adults [P],
  - Emotions [M],
  - USA [S],
  - 20th century [T].
- *Postulate of level cluster*: The last postulate for the sequence of facets states that different levels of the same fundamental category within a round should be kept together. Let us take an example like Succession rights of minors in Hindu law. In this, the facets, succession, minor and Hindu law are all manifestations of personality. When arranged, they will be Law (B F), Hindu law [1P1], Minor [1P2], and succession [1P3].

This postulate is known as the postulate of level cluster.

Whatever we have studied so far in this chapter can be put in a nutshell as follows:

- Because of facetisation, CC differs tan other schemes to a very great extent.
- Each successive edition of CC displayed improve-ment in analysis over the previous edition.

- The basic principles worked out in CC axe
- Three planes of work.
- Five fundamental categories.
- Rounds and levels.
- Facet sequence.

Notation

Ranganathan, in his theory of library classification, introduced the concept of three planes of work, which you are already familiar with. Of these, the notational plane is beset with several difficulties. It is in this sphere that much research has taken place and several innovations have been made. You already know the meaning of notation, its function and its kinds. As suggested, now turn our attention to the notation in CC.

Mixed Notation—Indicator Digits

CC uses a mixed notation. It consists of

- Indo-Arabic numerals, 1-9
- Roman alphabet -both capitals and lower case, A to Z and a to z.
- Parentheses (}
- Indicator digits

Table. The Indicator Digits in the 7th Edition of CC

Digit/Symbol	Name of the Indicator Digit	Role of the Indicator Digit
•	Astenrisk	Indicates Agglomeration and Interpolation
←	Backward Arrow	Indicates backward range
"	Double Inverted Comma	Indicates Common Isolates
("The above three indicator digits have anteriorising value).		
&	Ampersand	Indicates phase relation
'	Single inverted Comma	Indicates phase relation
.	Dot	Indicates Space Facet
:	Colon	Indicates Energy Facet
;	Semi-colon	Indicates Matter Facet
,	Comma	Indicates Personlity Facet
-	Hyphen	Indicates Specator of kind 1
=	Equal Sign	Indicates Speciator of Kind 2
+	Plus Sign	and Addition
→	Forward Arrow	Indicates Forward range

Note: For the arrangement of the class numbers, all the notations and digits used in the scheme have given values, and, in the ascending sequence, they stand in the following order

) and '.;: - = ® a to z 01 to 9A to Z
(Asterisk),+ (Plus)," (Double Inverted Comma) and ←7- (backward arrow) have anteriorising value.

Empty Digit

To increase the capacity of an array, CC has introduced what is called an empty digit. An empty digit has no semantic value, but it retains the ordinal value. Let us see the meaning of empty digit with the help of an example. If you are using the Indo-Arabic numerals, you can use a maximum of nine numerals. If a subject and to be divided, we can divide it only up to nine places and the tenth and subsequent divisions cannot be accommodated. To overcome this difficulty, CC uses numerals 1 to 8 only and 9 is left as an empty digit. It has no value by itself, but regains its full value when it is used in combination as 91, 92, 93... 98 or 991, 992, 993... 998 and so on. This method has given tremendous potential to increase arrays in any given facet. The same principle has been used while using a to z, or A to Z. In lower case letters, z is made an empty digit, and in capital letters, T, V and X are postulated as empty-emptying digits and Z as empty digit. Also, CC uses a number of devices for increasing hospitality and facilitating synthesis.

Devices

We have seen that new subjects always crop up and a classification scheme should be able to find appropriate places for such new subjects within its framework. Ranganathan provided a number of devices for this purpose. The purpose of such a device is to form a new isolate or to sharpen an existing isolate in an array. This method has considerably reduced the size of the scheme.

The four major devices used in CC are:

- Chronological device
- Geographical device
- Subject device
- Alphabetical device

Chronological Device

The purpose of this device is to sharpen a facet number. It can sharpen. an isolate or form a new isolate. This is done by employing a chronological number from the schedule of time isolates. All numbers for authors in the class Literature are derived through this device. It is impracticable to enumerate all authors.

The chronological device has, however, taken care of such a contingency. To give an example, the number for Rabindranath Tagore is 0, 157,1M61. Here,-M61'stands for 1861, the year of birth of Rabindranath Tagore. This device has been used in several main classes like library science, mathematics, medicine, fine arts, psychology, education, economics, etc. This device can be used wherever warranted. The basic class of systems is derived through the chronological device.

Geographical Device

The purpose of all these devices, as stated earlier, 2 to form or to sharpen an isolate number in a schedule. Employing a geographical number from the schedule of space isolates is another mechanism of doing this. It has been used in library science, fine arts, religion, linguistics, history and in several other classes. The formation of an isolate using this device is as follows:

- 152 = d4437 means Rajasthani Hindi, where
  - 152 is Hindi
  - = is the connecting symbol
  - d is the symbol for dialect
  - 4437 is Rajasthan from the schedule of space isolates.
- Another example of the geographical device:
  - Early Egyptian religion for which the number is Q,8677.
  - Here, Q,8 is other religion, and
  - 677 is Egypt from the schedule of space isolates.

Subject Device

Subject device is used to form or sharpen a facet by adding to it another class number from elsewhere in the scheme. This device has been used in several train classes. The part of the number derived by the subject device should be enclosed in parenthesis. For example, Medical college library is 2, J3 (L). In the example, in library science, 2,J3 represents college libraries to which is added (L) from the main class L Medicine to derive medical college library by subject device. Let us take another example of subject device. Hindu Law is Z,(Q,2) where Z is law, and (Q,2) is Hindu religion from the main class Q Religion.

Alphabetical Device

Alphabetical device is also used to form or sharpen an isolate number. The device is used taking the first or the first two or three letters of the names of persons, or objects, or products widely accepted as such. The device can be used wherever warranted. The following are some examples where the device is used:

0, 157, 3M61,G	Gora, a novel by Rabindranath Tagore Here, G stands for Gora
0,157,3M61,H+W	Home and the world, a novel by Tagore. Here, the initial letters of the two words in the title are connected, using the plus sign (+). (H for Home and W for World)
D93CM	Maruti motor car. D93C is for motor cars and M stands for Maruti
J,381B	Basmati rice, where J,381 is rice' and B is for Basmati.

Phase Relations

Nowadays we come across several interdisciplinary subjects. This is the result of interaction between two or more subjects. For this purpose, CC has provided a device called Phase Relation.

A phase relation may occur between two or more main classes; it may also occur within one and the same facet of a main class, or within one and the same array isolates. These three types are called inter-subject, intra-facet and intra-array phase relations respectively. Besides, there are six kinds of phase relations indicated in CC. These six kinds are:

- General relation phase.
- Bias phase.
- Comparison phase.
- Difference phase.
- Tool phase:
- Influencing phase

The connecting symbol for a phase relation is composed of an ampersand and a relation indicator as shown in table:

Schedule of digits (CC 7 edition)

Kind of Phase Relation	Inter-subject	Infra-facet	Intra-array
General	a	j	t
Bias	b	k	u
Comparison	c	m	v
Difference	d	n	w
Tool	e	p	x
Influencing	G		

Following are a few examples to show the use of different kinds of phase relations in CC:

- A general study of special and university libraries - Type: intra-facet, Kind: general, No.2,14&jK
- Psychology for teachers - Type: Inter-subject, Kind: Nat, No.S&bT
- Comparison of Jainism and Buddhism - Type: intra-facet, Kind: comparison, No.61,3&m4
- Difference between undergraduate and postgraduate education Type: intra-array, Kidd: difference, No.T,181&w2
- Statistical analysis in library management - Type: inter-subject, Kind: tool, Nio.2:8&eBT
- Influence of music on literature - Type: inter-subject, Kind: influencing, No.O&gNR.

Systems and Specials

Up to the sixth edition of CC, systems and specials were enumerated along with the concerned main classes. In the seventh edition, they have been listed in the schedule of basic subjects. However, they have been separately defined.

Systems

The term system basic subjects denote a division of a main class expounded after a school of thought. A school of thought is a group, or succession of persons devoted to some cause or philosophy. The class number for a system is derived by the chronological device.

Some examples of system facets are:

- *B6-M8*: Hyperbolic geometry, where B6 is geometry and M8 means the 1880s. The number stands for a system of geometry expounded in the 1880s.
- *L-B*: Ayarveda. B is 999 to 1000 BC - a system of medicine that came into being prior to 1000 BC
- *S-N14*: Individualistic psychology. It means a school of psychology that came into being in 1914.
- *X-NI Communism*: The number stands for a system of economics that came into being in the 1910s.

Specials

The term special basic subjects denote a division of a main class in which the subject of study is restricted in some special manner. The class number of specials is derived by enumeration. Some of the examples of special basic subjects are:

Merits and Demerits of Colon Classification

Due to a sound theory and the provision of a hospitable notation, CC is capable of giving a unique number for almost every subject. The systematic order and the degree of detail due to analysis and synthesis are two great virtues of CC.

As a result, it has achieved two objectives:

1. Provision of a helpful order in each class, and
2. Facility in locating a given topic whether it is simple, compound or complex. It is claimed that CC can be effectively used in a computer-aided document finding system.

The major drawback of CC is that there exists no machinery to keep up the revision work as in the case of DDC and UDC. The guidance provided in the recently published seventh edition is not enough and lacks clarity at places. It calls for a manual with numerous examples to explain the application of various rules. It is far from simple, the virtue most cherished by the users.

THEORY LIBRARY CLASSIFICATION

In the beginning there was no theory; only practice was followed. Practice gave rise to descriptive theory. Thus, the descriptive theory was the first stage in the development of library classification. This theory was able.to meet the requirements of the universe of subjects, as it existed at that time. The descriptive theory was based on the practices in vogue based on different schemes of classification then available. The descriptive theory, distilled out of the contemporary schemes, held its sway until the early 1950s. The schemes designed before the 1950s were based on 'the flair or natural gift of the designers and not on any objectively worked out theory of library classification.

Their methods were empirical. The development of the descriptive theory is attributed to several stalwarts like Brown, Richardson, Hulme, Sayers, Bliss and Ranganathan. The period between 1898 and 1937 witnessed the genesis and development of this theory. These stalwarts, through their schemes and writings, enunciated certain principles of library classification which greatly contributed to the development of a General Theory of Library Classification.

J.D. BROWN (1862-1914)

J.D. Brown was an English librarian, whose contribution to the General Theory_ of Library Classification was small but significant. He brought out three different schemes of classification. The first of these three was developed in 1894 jointly with J.H. Quinn and was known as Guinn-Brown Scheme. This scheme did not make much impact. Three years later, in 1897, Brown independently brought out another scheme and called it Adjustable Classification. This scheme also proved inadequate even in those days. In the year 1906, Brown published the first edition of his Subject Classification, the scheme for which he is mostly known. Its second edition was brought out in 1914 and the third; edited by J.D. Stewart; in 1939.

Brown's Subject Classification was founded on the principle that every science and art spring from. Some.definite source. In the order of things, there were first two factors, *viz.*, matter and force. These, in turn, gave place to life. Life, in course of time, led to the mind, which in turn gave birth to records.

In addition to the shove principle, Brown also advocated -two other principles. The first of these two was his one place theory. According to this principle, each subject has only one place in the scheme inrespective of its' aspects and numerous manifestations. For example, the subject of rose may be viewed from the viewpoints of botany, horticulture, history, geography, decoration, -bibliography, etc. The subject of rose, according to Brown, is concrete, while the various viewpoints represent its aspects. He was of the opinion that the interest of the scholar in 'rose' is constant, unlike that of the bibliographer whose interest is only occasional. He, therefore, preferred to place rose under one concrete or specific heading. It means that his arrangement of books was not ht, discipline (as in the Dewey Decimal Classification (DDC) or Library of Congress, (LC); but by topic. It was an experiment, which failed.

The other principle advocated by Brown was the science and its applications theory. According to this principle, he places each subject as nearer as possible to the science from which it has sprung. Thus, rose is placed under botany, libraries under library economy, coal under mineralogy, and persons under biography. Theory and practice are collocated. As a result of this principle, Brown dispensed with "conven-tions, distinctions and groupings, which are arbitrary rather than scientific". for example, the distinction between Pure and Applied Sciences, between Fine Arts and Useful Arts, between Currency and Numismatics, between Architecture and Building and between Costume and Press was not made.

He faithfully followed these principles in his Subject Classification.

E.C RICHARDSON (1860-9939)

E.C. Richardson was the first librarian of Hartford Theological Seminary, USA, and later took over as librarian of the Princeton University Library. Richardson is regarded as the first classificationists to have ma4e a systematic attempt to set down a theory of library classification. In 1910, he published his book Classification, Theoretical and Practical. It was the first textbook on classification, which later influenced W.C.B. Sayers. In the introduction to this work, he enumerated basic laws and principles meant to guide the work of designing a scheme of classification.

These principles, called as Criteria of Classification, are as follows:

- Classification should follow the order of things; classes should be arranged in historical sequence.
- Division of classes should be minute.
- Arrange things according to likeness and unlikeness.
- Books are collected for use; they are administered for use, and hence, it is the use, which is the motive behind classification.
- A scheme of classification should be provided with a notation. The notation should be amenable to indefinite subdivisions preferably using a mixed symbol with decimal base and with mnemonic features.

Richardson asserted that "things: nature aye already classified and roan has to trace only the order -of the classification and record if."

E.W HULME (9659-1954)

Hulme was the librarian of the Patent Office Library, London. In 1911-1912, he published his book Principles of Book Classification in the library Association Record. Has principles influenced the later theories of book-classification. In the words of W.C.B. Sayers, the contribution of Hulme was " A valuable leadup to the more complete and satisfactory theories today".

According to Hulme, all classifications could be arranged into two groups (categories), *viz.*,

- Mechanical and-
- Philosophical

According to this categorisation, book classification is mechanical Hulme's principles of book classification are as follows:

- Book classification is the plotting of areas pre-existing in literature, and coincidence with a philosophical order is no guarantee of accuracy.
- Book classification-is mechanical assembly of material into classes.
- The division and coordination-of classes in literature is determined mainly upon formal and non-philosophical lines.
- Classification should be based literary warrant.

Hulme states that mechanical classifications are left uncoordinated. But in book classification, systematic coordination of classes is introduced. His theory of literary warrant immensely attracted the attention of later classificationists. E.A. Savage (1877-1966) revived the term. Hulme ragards books as "concrete aggregates of facts selected from the common stock of knowledge".

What Hulme meant by concrete aggregates is that if there are books on the subject of electricity and magnetism there is literary warrant for providing a number for such a class named "electricity and magnetism".

Literary warrant simply means that a subject cannot be listed in the scheme unless some literature has already appeared on it. Cr, the existing literature on a subject only justifies the inclusion of that subject in the scheme.

Hulme's principle of literary warrant greatly influenced the Library of Congress Classification (LC). Ranganathan also made use of this principle, but not exactly in the sense Hulme made, use of it. According to Ranganathan, when the literature on a particular subject grows in size, there may arise a need for providing a separate class for it in the scheme. Ranganathan's principle of literary warrant states that "the subjects in an array of subjects or the isolates in an array of isolates may be arranged in the sequence of decreasing quantity of the documents published or anticipated to be published on them, except when any other overwhelming consideration rules it out."

Hence, it requires that the various aspects of such a new subject should be so listed as to bring those aspects first on which more literature have appeared.

W.C.B. SAYERS (1881-1960)

William Charles Berwick Sayers, an English librarian and teacher of S.R. Ranganathan made a remarkable contribution to the development of the theory of classification. He is referred to as the first grammarian of library classification. He is responsible for interpreting and systematising the ideas of other theoreticians. He never designed any classification scheme, though, through his theory he has shown the way for others in the designing of classification schemes. His theory of book classification first appeared in 1915 under the title "Canons of Classification". He expanded the outline of the theory contained in this book in three other books, *viz.*, Grammar of

Classification, Introduction to Library Classification and Manual of Library Classification. It has now been revised by Rita Marcella and Robert Newton in 1994.

Sayers Canons of Classification

Sayers simplified his theory of classification by stating 29 principles. He called them canons, meaning rules, regulations, standard tests or criteria of classification. The 29-canons can be grouped under six categories as follows:

•	Canons of definition	... ...	6
•	Canons of divisions	... ...	7
•	Canons of terms	... ...	4
•	Canons of book classification	... ...	4
•	Canons of notation	... ...	4
•	Canons of book classification schemes	... ...	5

Definition

Classification is a mental process by which things or ideas are grouped according to their likeness. The likeness which exists in the universe of things and in ideas is called characteristic in classification. A characteristic is a basis of division or grouping of classes. In a scheme of classification, classes are to be arranged in a systematic order. The order is based on the theory of knowledge.

Division

Assembling things according to their degree of likeness and separating them according to their degree of unlikeness is the process of division. The chosen likeness or characteristic used to 'divide the given things may be natural or artificial.

A natural characteristic is the inherent quality of a thing and hence, is responsible for its very existence. An artificial characteristic may be possessed by a group of things. For example, colour of clothes is an artificial characteristic. The division should proceed from greater extension and smaller intension to smaller extension and greater intension. The process of division should be gradual moving from general to specific. The characteristic used must be consistent at each stage of division.

Terms

A scheme of classification is a statement of knowledge using verbal terms. A term is the name for a class. It may be a word or a phrase. The terms should be unambiguous and unique with the same meaning whenever they are used in a scheme of classification. In a scheme of classification the terms used should always be non-critical.

Book Classification

A book classification is a device for the arrangement of books by subject or form in a logical order. It must be capable of admitting any new subject without dislocating the class of subjects already drawn.

Book classification schemes must be equipped with

- A generalia class;
- Form classes like poetry, fiction, drama, etc.;
- Forms in which subjects are presented like theory, history, dictionary, etc.; -
- A notation; and
- An index.

Notation

A notation consists of signs representing the class names in a scheme of classification. A notation should be brief, simple and flexible and have a mnemonic value.

Book Classification Schemes:

A scheme of classification should provide columnar schedules in the order of precedence of subjects. It is necessary to explain how to use the scheme. There should be a machinery for the revision of the scheme to keep it up-to-date accommodating new developments in the knowledge.

H.E. BLISS (1370-1955)

He Evelyn Bliss devoted his entire active life to the intensive study of the art and science of classification. In addition; which he contributed in library journals, his theories and principles of classification were expanded in his first work, titled Organisation of Knowledge and the System of Science (1929). In this work, he formulated scientific, philosophical and logical grounds for the study of bibliographic classification.

This work is regarded as one of the basic texts on the theory of organisation of knowledge. He laid down the foundation for a relatively stable, scientifically acceptable and consistent scheme of classification. He also published another basic work on the theory of library classification titled Organisation of Knowledge in Libraries and the Subject Approach to Books. His work helped in establishing librarianship as a scholarly discipline. These two basic works convey to us the fundamental principles of classification which Bliss later tried to apply in his System of Bibliographic Classification (BC) whose outline was first published in 1935.

The basic concepts of classification as expounded by Bliss may broadly be categorised as:

- Consensus

- Subordination
- Collocation
- Alternative locations
- Notation.

Consensus

Bliss viewed book classification as basically knowledge classification. He felt that considerable agreement existed among the experts on the arrangement of various branches of human knowledge. He termed this as scientific and educational consensus. The growth, organisation and development of human knowledge are brought about through the process of science and education. The word consensus refers to a relative agreement on the major classes of knowledge, their scope, order of arrangement and the essential relation between them.

He believed that the natural order of main classes was close to this consensual order. Bliss felt that more closely a library classification reflected this consensus, the more stable, durable, flexible and efficient it would be. His order of main classes is based on this consensus.

Subordination

Bliss theorised that a classification scheme should observe two types of subordination, *viz.*,

- Subordination of the special to the general, and
- Gradation by speciality.

Subordination of the Special to the General

This is also referred to as the principle of decreasing extension. A scheme of classification should arrange subjects in the order of decreasing extension so that a general subject is followed by a special subject. The order of subjects in a scheme of classification should reflect the sequence from general to specific.

Gradation by Speciality

This concept is based on the philosophical notion of gradation by speciality. Gradation principle is employed for organising a series of topics of equal rank into a rational sequence. The principle is that some subject depend for their very existence on the works or findings of others, and those that so dependant should follow the disciplines upon which they rely. This is also known as the principle of dependency. For example, among the natural sciences, physics comes first because it deals with the fundamentals of natural phenomena. Chemical phenomena depend to some extent on the findings of the physicists and, therefore, chemistry follows physics. Bliss claims that "gradation by speciality is no mere arbitrary basis for classification but is a principle essential to the very process".

Thus, the order of classes will be:

- General treated generally.
- General treated specially.
- Special treated generally
- Special treated specially.

Collocation

It is a by product of the two principles. By collocation, Bliss means "bringing together in proximity subjects which are most closely related". Ranganathan termed this as filiatory sequence. The principles of subordination and gradation by speciality help to decide the sequence of broad subject fields or disciplines and, within each subject, the principle of decreasing extension and various orders in any array determine the sequence of the subject. It is also necessary for bringing together similar subjects, which are most closely related. Therefore, Bliss, in his Bibliographic Classification, collocated language with literature, because of their very close affinity with each other. Similarly, education is collocated with psychology, and chemical technology with chemistry. Collocation generally refers to coordinate classes. But, it may also refer to subordinate classes. Bliss subordinated sociology to anthropology and anthropology to biology.

Alternative Locations

A scheme of classification should meet the different needs and requirements of a special collection. Therefore, libraries may wish to- alter the order established by logical sequence. A scheme, if it is to be of maximum usefulness, should therefore provide for the adaptation of logical sequence to practical convenience in order to meet different views. Bliss did not believe in the rigid and unadaptable view of the order of knowledge. To meet this principle of practical convenience, provision has been made deliberately for alternative locations and treatments in his unique scheme, though it is somewhat contrary to the principle of consensus.

Provision has been made in notation for moving certain topics to other locations. For example, moving theology from the main class P religion to class AJ following philosophy; technologies like aeronautics or ship building from applied physics to useful arts and subordinating international law to political science or to law; and economic history to general history. This principle provides flexibility needed to solve certain problems in classification faced by all classifiers of all systems. But it also proves that there is no absolute consensus on the order of subjects.

Notation

Bliss recognised three important qualities of a good notation. These are:

- It should be correlative and subsidiary.

- It should be simple and brief, *i.e.*, a notation should remain reasonably simple. He even suggested an economic limit of three to four digits in a class number.
- It should use synthetic features. This is to achieve economy in the printing and display of schedules resulting in the simplicity of structure and convenience in use.

Bliss achieved this by the provision of general and special systematic schedules for construction of coextensive class numbers.

S.R. RANGANATHAN (1892-1972)

Right from 1924, S.R. Ranganathan had been developing his theory of library classification. In the first edition of *Prolegomena to Library Classification (1937)*, he provided an integrated theory, mainly descriptive and comparative, of the practices in classification then in vogue.

Ranganathan went ahead of those classificationists, mentioned in the preceding sub-sections, by extending the principles put forward by them. He also provided the largest list of normative principles named by -him as Fundamental Laws, Postulates, Principles and Canons and evolved a special terminology, which is evident from the first edition of Prolegomena. These rightly belong to stage-2 in the development of the General Theory of Library Classification. His theory is now synonymous with the General Theory of Library Classification.

S.R. Ranganathan was instrumental in revolutionising the *Theory of Classification*. He propounded certain fundamental ideas and concepts, which are the basis for the development of the *Theory of Classification*. The consistently advocated that library classification should conform to the *Laws of Library Science*. He worked vigourously towards the most helpful sequence of classes in a scheme of classification based on the concept of Facet Analysis and Fundamental Categories. He totally rejected the earlier schemes, based purely on enumeration. His laws, canons and principles of library classification have been presented in his *Prolegomena to Library Classification*. This is regarded as one of the seminal works on the *Theory of Library Classification*.

Mapping of Universe of Knowledge

Ranganathan visualised the problem of transforming the multi-dimensional universe of knowledge into a uni-dimensional one. This was the fundamental and perennial problem faced by the classificationists in the design of schemes of classification. To meet this problem squarely, Ranganathan formulated the General Theory of Classification, which was guided by Basic Laws, Laws of Library Science, Canons, Principles and Postulates. With the help of these laws, canons and principles, the mapping of the universe of knowledge in a scheme of classification could be successfully represented.

CLASSIFICATION RESEARCH GROUP (LONDON)

After the Royal Society Scientific Information Conference in 1948 and on the suggestion of the eminent scientist J.D. Bernel, the Classification Research Group (CRG) London was established in 1952. It is an unattached society of volunteers pursuing classification as an additional off the job work. They meet regularly in London. Upto 1996, they have held 308 meetings. Its founder members D.J. Foskett, Bernard Palmer (1910-1979), B.C. Vickery and A.J. Wells (1911-1994) were greatly influenced by Ranganathan's work.

They mostly came from special, industrial and academic libraries. Their deep and thorough study led them to believe that none of the published schemes provided a satisfactory system either in arrangement or depth of details. CRG accepted Ranganathan's method of facet analysis though it did not accept his views on the restriction of the number of categories to be five. They named their categories as Entities, Properties and Activities. Nevertheless, in Ranganathan's Dynamic Theory, they found a sound base to be built up.

They published their manifesto in the periodical Library Association Record (1955) which emphasises on the-need for a faceted classification as the basis of all methods of information retrieval. B.C. Vickery wrote a small volume on the methods of constructing a faceted classification. Members of CRG designed many faceted classification schemes for specialised subjects ranging from diamond technology to soil science; music to education. Experience gained in designing such schemes led them to believe that the right approach should be to seek new principles for library classification.

Though they never produced any new general classification system, their contributions to the development of classification techniques were many and innovating. A prominent member, Miss Barbara Kyle had a limited success in doing away with the necessity of main classes. Another member J.E.L. Farradane (1906-1989) incorporated the idea of relational analysis with operators into the construction of a faceted classification scheme. Later, a group member developed the Theory of Integrative Levels, which arranged entities in an evolving aggregation of complexities. Their work received publicity and wide discussion in their International Conference on Classification Research held at Dorking, England in 1957.

Another publication enshrining their work is Sayers Memorial Volume (1961) edited by D.J. Foskett and B.I. Palmer (London Library Association). At present, the CRG meetings are devoted to the discussion of the ensuing revised schedules of the Bibliographic Classification (BC2). Their major applied work remains in PRECIS formulated by Derek Austin, which had a classificatory approach. This Preserved Context Indexing System in 1971 replaced Ranganathan's Chain Procedure in the British National Bibliography - as required for the automated bibliography compilation work.

FACETED CLASSIFICATION

A faceted classification system allows the assignment of an object to multiple characteristics (attributes), enabling the classification to be ordered in multiple ways, rather than in a single, predetermined, taxonomic order. A facet comprises "clearly defined, mutually exclusive, and collectively exhaustive aspects, properties or characteristics of a class or specific subject". For example, a collection of books might be classified using an author facet, a subject facet, a date facet, etc.

Faceted classification is used in faceted search systems that enable a user to navigate information along multiple paths corresponding to different orderings of the facets. This contrasts with traditional taxonomies in which the hierarchy of categories is fixed and unchanging. The colon classification developed by S. R. Ranganathan is an example of faceted classification applied to the physical world, specifically for the purpose of organizing library materials. In the colon classification system, a book is assigned a set of values from independent facets.

It differs from traditional library classification schemas like the Dewey Decimal System and Library of Congress classification system, in which each document has a unique assignment in a single, hierarchically organized classification system. Faceted classification systems are also distinct from folksonomies or other tagging systems that do not break out the tags into independent facets.

FREINET CLASSIFICATION

The Freinet classification ("To organise everything") is used in the libraries of some elementary schools, and was invented by Célestin Freinet to facilitate the easy finding of documents, and the use of the "Bibliothèque de Travail". The principles are simple: Everything is split into 12 major divisions. 12 subdivisions along the principles of the Dewey decimal system are then divided into 10, and then 10 again.

Because of its logical classifications based on school work, this classification is seen by some educators to be more natural and more logical to students than official classifications based on organizational criteria. The last revision took place in 1984. It is still used, in addition to keywords, in IT and some data information organization systems.

THE 12 DIVISIONS

- 0. Reference:
  - 00 General
  - 01 English Dictionaries
  - 02 Dictionaries in foreign languages
  - 03 Bilingual, trilingual... dictionaries
  - 04 Other Dictionaries (proper names, places...)
  - 05 Encyclopaedias

   - 06 Repertory, bibliographies
   - 07 Reference works (textbooks)
- 1. Natural Environment:
   - 11 Land (geology)
   - 12 Relief
   - 13 Freshwater
   - 14 The oceans and seas
   - 15 The climates and vegetation
   - 16 Heaven (astronomy)
   - 17 Nature and Life (ecology)
- 2. Plants:
   - 21 Study of the plant
   - 22 The flowering plants
   - 23 The plants without flowers or seeds
   - 24 The microscopic beings
- 3. Animals:
   - 30 General study of the body (in humans and animals)
   - 31 The health of humans
   - 32 Mammals (except humans)
   - 33 Birds
   - 34 Reptiles and amphibians
   - 35 Fish
   - 36 Insects (articulated)
   - 37 Other articulated
   - 38 Shellfish
   - 39 Other animals
- 4. Other sciences:
   - 41 Mathematics
   - 42 Physical Sciences
   - 43 Chemistry
   - 44 Technology
- 5. Food and Agriculture:
   - 51 Working the earth
   - 52 Cultures
   - 53 Livestock
   - 54 Forestry
   - 55 Fishing
   - 56 Hunting
   - 57 Food industry
   - 58 Foods
   - 59 Drinks
- 6. Labour and Industry:

  - 60 General
  - 61 Sources of energy and engines
  - 62 Mining and quarrying
  - 63 Metals
  - 64 Chemical Industry
  - 65 Textile and clothing industry
  - 66 Building industry, housing and furniture
  - 67 Other Industries
- 7. The city and stock exchanges:
  - 71 The city, the municipality
  - 72 Trade
  - 73 Road Transport
  - 74 Rail transport
  - 75 Inland waterway transport
  - 76 Maritime Transport
  - 77 Air transportation and space
  - 78 Post, Telecommunications and IT
  - 79 Travel and Tourism
- 8. Society:
  - 81 People
  - 82 Contracts (environmental and social issues)
  - 83 Administrative organization of society
  - 84 Organisation of social policy
  - 85 Reports from nations
- 9. Culture and Recreation:
  - 91 Education and instructions
  - 92 Languages
  - 93 Literature and Philosophy
  - 94 Religions
  - 95 Arts and Entertainment
  - 96 Sports and Games
- G. Geography:
  - G0 The study of geography
  - G1 General Geography
  - G2 Geography locally and regionally
  - G3 Our country
  - G4 Europe
  - G5 Asia
  - G6 Africa
  - G7 America
  - G8 Oceania
  - G9 The Polar World

- H. History:
  - H1 Prehistory
  - H2 The East, Greece
  - H3 Rome and the early Middle Ages (from “700 to 987)
  - H4 Middle Ages (from 987 to 1492)
  - H5 Absolute monarchy (1492 to 1789)
  - H6 Struggles for Democracy (1789 to 1848)
  - H7 Organization of the Republic (1848 to 1914)
  - H8 Contemporary history (1914–present)

FRSAD

Functional Requirements for Subject Authority Data (FRSAD), previously known as Functional Requirements for Subject Authority Records, or FRSAR is a conceptual entity-relationship model currently being developed by a workgroup International Federation of Library Associations and Institutions (IFLA).

It is a continuation of the work done on the FRBR model, further explaining how the Group 3 entities, that consists of “entities that serve as subjects of intellectual or artistic endeavour” can be related and controlled within the bibliographic universe.

The model is meant to ease global sharing and use of subject authority data. The final draft of the report is to be presented in the spring of 2009 at the 75th IFLA General Conference and Council in Milan.

THE CONCEPTUAL MODEL

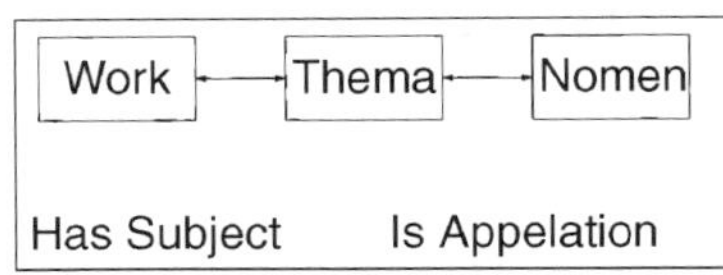

- *Work:* Work is a “distinct intellectual or artistic creation.
- *Thema:* Is anything that can be the subject of a work. This is the abstract idea of the aboutness of a given work. Thema is independent of language and disciplines.
- *Nomen:* Any alphanumeric, sound, visual, or any other symbol, sign or combination of symbols by which a thema is known, referred to or addressed. A nomen can be any expression of a thema. Ideally there will exist an authority file with every possible subject/thema. This means that it should be possible to exchange subject authority data between systems. If a user looks up a specific subject in a catalogue and wants to look in other places, he or she should not have to worry about translating the query, since the system would be able to recognize the underlying thema and automatically translate it into the relevant

nomen. One way to understand this is to think about how a subject can be described in different ways. For example, if one looks at a work about the city Stockholm, the capital of Sweden, there are many ways to describe Stockholm. First, one must distinguish between the city Stockholm and the many other meanings of the word. for example, Stockholm is also the name of other cities, a record label, and a syndrome. When the thema is established in an authority file, it is possible to translate across systems. The nomen for Stockholm could be anything from "Stockholm", "Stockholm (City)", "Tukholma"-the Finnish spelling of Stockholm-or a range of Zip-codes, or the longitude and latitude, or a picture of the city, or a sound. FRSAR, if implemented, enables users to perform specific and precise subject searching across multiple systems.

RELATIONSHIPS

Works and themas have a Many-to-many (data model) relationship, meaning that any work can have more than one subject, and any subject can be expressed in one or more works. The same is true for the relationship between thema and nomen. A thema can be expressed in many different ways and a nomen can express many different themas, all depending on the given system.

Besides these relationships, the workgroup has so far identified several other thema-thema and nomen-nomen relationships. Two nomens can, for example, be said to have an equivalence relationship, if they both are appellations of the same thema.

USER TASKS

The workgroup conducted two user studies in 2006 and 2007, and based on the results of these studies, four subject authority data user tasks were defined:

- *Find:* To find an entity (thema or nomen) or set of entities corresponding to stated criteria
- *Identify:* To identify an entity (thema or nomen) based on certain attributes/characteristics
- *Select:* To select an entity (thema or nomen)
- *Explore:* To explore any relationships between entities (thema or nomen), correlations to other subject vocabularies and structure of a subject domain

SEARCH FOR THE HIDDEN ROOTS OF CLASSIFICATION

SYNTAX OF FACETS

My wish is that in our search for hidden roots of classification, we should not stop with the postulates and principles at the near-seminal level. These form only a first approximation. What pleased me most was the announcement that this Seminar intended to dive deeper still, to find the very tip of the tap-root in the intellect, so to speak. In analytic synthetic classification, one of the vital steps is the determination of the helpful sequence of the facets of a subject. This means the Syntax of Facets. This in its turn means a harmonious sequence of the facets, that gives satisfaction to the human mind. Webster quotes the following passage to show the power of a good syntax:

"His mind moved in a rich erudite and complex Syntax
That turned all opposition into admiration".

The syntax of facets in classification based on the postulates and principles gives satisfaction to the majority of readers.

QUEST FOR THE REASON FOR SATISFACTION

What is the reason for the Syntax of Facets given by the postulates and principles being satisfactory to most people? The reason should be searched in the minds of the readers. This will lead us to the roots of classification hidden far deep in the intellect-in-action. In this behalf, a suggestion, that to help in the establishment of a fairly long-lived helpful scheme for classification, a team of epistemologists, psychologists, linguists, reference librarians, classificationists, and statisticians should investigate the way in which the human intellect works today that is, the Syntax of Facets that will give the greatest satisfaction to the greatest number of readers. Probably, the time was not then ripe for it.

ABSOLUTE SYNTAX

By 'Absolute Syntax' is meant the sequence in which the facet ideas of a subject arrange themselves in the minds of the majority of persons. Linguistic Syntax is the Syntax of Words that is, the sequence in which the words stand arranged in a sentence or in the name of a subject in a natural language. The Linguistic Syntax may vary with the language; often it does. The result in Step 5 in the steps in classifying a document corresponds to Absolute Syntax that is, Syntax of Facets.

In it, the kernel terms in the name of a subject stand rearranged according to the Syntactic Principles governing the sequence of the facets denoted by the respective kernel terms. On the other hand, the result in Step 3 corresponds to Linguistic Syntax. In it, the kernel terms stand arranged in the same sequence as the one in which these terms are found in the name of the subject in the natural language used.

Here is an example.

- Consider the Subject
- "The Heart of the Frog".

This is Step 0. the full title in Step 1 will be

- "The Heart of the Frog Zoology".

In Step 2, where only the kernel terms are retained, we shall have

- "Heart. Frog. Zoology".

This sequence is according to the Linguistic Syntax of the English language. According to the Linguistic Syntax of the Tamil language, the kernel terms will stand arranged in Step 2 as follows:

- "Zoology. Frog. Heart".

In step 5, the kernel terms will stand arranged as:

- "Zoology. Frog. Heart".

This represents the Syntax of Facets. It happens that the Linguistic Syntax of the English language differs from the Syntax of Facets; while the Linguistic Syntax of the Tamil language agrees with the Syntax of Facets.

There may be languages in which the Linguistic Syntax may give respectively

- "Zoology. Heart. Frog
- Frog. Heart. Zoology
- Frog. Zoology. Heart
- Heart. Zoology. Frog" respectively

The number of variations of Linguistic Syntax from the Syntax of Facets will increase with the number of the kernel terms in the name of the subject which is the same as the number of the facets in it.

ABSOLUTE SYNTAX AND FACET SYNTAX

In general, the number of Linguistic Syntaxes for the name of a subject, in the different natural languages all taken together, can become as great as factorial n, where n is the number of kernel terms in the name of the subject. But, there is only one Syntax of Facets for the subject. For this reason, it is conjectured that the Syntax of Facets is the same as the Absolute Syntax. This implies that the Absolute Syntax is the one conforming to the Postulates and Principles guiding the design of an Analytico-Synthetic Classification.

Problem for Investigation

The problem for investigation is, "Is there an Absolute Syntax governing the sequence of the facets of a subject, inherent in the human intellect-in-action as it is today?" This investigation should be made by a team of specialists in Epistemology, Psychology, Linguistics, Reference Service, Design of Classification, and Statistical Analysis.

Removal of Encrustation

It is not expected that the Absolute Syntax will be inherent in the minds of one and all the adults, without any exception. For, from childhood onwards the Linguistic Syntax of the mother tongue makes an incessant impact on the mind of a person. It is too much to expect that the encrustation formed by this incessant impact would not have become too hard and opaque for the inherent

Absolute Syntax to become operative. On the other hand, I only expect the Absolute Syntax will be operative with the majority of persons.

Frequency Study

While investigating the problem, the Team of Specialists would use the same assortment of subjects. They should examine a reliable random sample of persons drawn from each of most of the natural languages. Probably, it will be helpful to have three sets of random samples one for children, one for adolescents, and one for adults. The investigation may have to be done in five stages. In the first instance, without any suggestion whatever being made by the Team, the sequence of facets naturally preferred in the various facets by the different persons should be found out and recorded. Thereafter, an attempt should be made to break gently the encrustation of the Linguistic Syntax in the minds of the people. The degree of success in this work will throw the people into several groups. At the third stage, the sequence of facets in the subjects, preferred by each of the groups, should then be found out and recorded.

The work in the fourth stage will fall largely to the share of the Statisticians. They will have to construct the necessary and possible frequency tables and curves, and the correlation tables and curves and surfaces; and they should also furnish all the necessary statistical constants emerging from the study of the problem. In the fifth stage, it may be possible to find out, from the results tabulated by the Statisticians, whether there is an Absolute Syntax, and if so, what it is; and in particular, it can be verified whether the Syntax of Facets based on the Postulates and Principles for an Analytico-Synthetic Classification is the same as or at least a good approximation to the Absolute Syntax.

Help to Classificationist

The final findings of such a team of specialists will enable the classificationists to build schemes for classification on fairly firm foundations. At present, a good deal of professional energy and time get dissipated in discussing problems in classification guided solely by conjectures and conflicting opinions based on insufficient data. This wastage should be avoided. I wish that the deliberations of this Seminar leads to the solution of this problem along objective and scientific lines by Teams of Specialists, probing into the hidden roots of classification. The results will be of help in the study of absolute linguistics also. This piece of tiny research deserves to be provided for by a Foundation.

5

Library Cataloguing Strategies

A library catalogue (or library catalogue) is a register of all bibliographic items found in a library or group of libraries, such as a network of libraries at several locations. A bibliographic item can be any information entity (*e.g.*, books, computer files, graphics, realia, cartographic materials, etc.) that is considered library material (*e.g.*, a single novel in an anthology), or a group of library materials (*e.g.*, a trilogy), or linked from the catalogue (*e.g.*, a webpage) as far as it is relevant to the catalogue and to the users (patrons) of the library.

The card catalogue was a familiar sight to library users for generations, but it has been effectively replaced by the online public access catalogue (OPAC). Some still refer to the online catalogue as a "card catalogue". Some libraries with OPAC access still have card catalogues on site, but these are now strictly a secondary resource and are seldom updated.

Many of the libraries that have retained their physical card catalogue post a sign advising the last year that the card catalogue was updated. Some libraries have eliminated their card catalogue in favour of the OPAC for the purpose of saving space for other use, such as additional shelving.

GOAL

Charles Ammi Cutter made the first explicit statement regarding the objectives of a bibliographic system in his *Rules for a Printed Dictionary Catalogue* in 1876.

Those objectives were:

- To enable a person to find a book of which either (Identifying objective)
  - The author
  - The title
  - The subject
  - The category
- To show what the library has (Collocating objective)
  - By a given author
  - On a given subject

  - In a given kind of literature
- To assist in the choice of a book (Evaluating objective)
  - As to its edition (bibliographically)
  - As to its character (literary or topical)

These objectives can still be recognized in more modern definitions formulated throughout the 20th century. 1960/61 Cutter's objectives were revised by Lubetzky and the Conference on Cataloguing Principles (CCP) in Paris. The latest attempt to describe a library catalogue's goals and functions was made in 1998 with Functional Requirements for Bibliographic Records (FRBR) which defines four user tasks: find, identify, select, and obtain.

HISTORY OF CATALOGUING

Library catalogues originated as manuscript lists, arranged by format (folio, quarto, etc.) or in a rough alphabetical arrangement by author. Printed catalogues, sometimes called *dictionary catalogues*, began to be published in the early modern period and enabled scholars outside a library to gain an idea of its contents. Copies of these in the library itself would sometimes be interleaved with blank leaves on which additions could be recorded, or bound as *guardbooks* in which slips of paper were bound in for new entries.

Slips could also be kept loose in cardboard or tin boxes, stored on shelves. The first card catalogues appeared in the late 19th century after the standardization of the 5 in. x 3 in. card for personal filing systems, enabling much more flexibility, and towards the end of the 20th century the Online public access catalogue was developed.

These gradually became more common as some libraries progressively abandoned such other catalogue formats as paper slips (either loose or in sheaf catalogue form), and guardbooks. The beginning of the Library of Congress's catalogue card service in 1911 led to the use of these cards in the majority of American libraries. An equivalent scheme in the United Kingdom was operated by the British National Bibliography from 1956 and was subscribed to by many public and other libraries.

- *C. 245 BC:* Callimachus is considered the first bibliographer and is the one that organized the library by authors and subjects. The *Pinakes* was the first ever library catalogue. Variations on this system were used in libraries until the late 1800s when Melvil Dewey developed the Dewey Decimal Classification in 1876, which is still in use today.
- *C. 800:* Library catalogues are introduced in the House of Wisdom and other medieval Islamic libraries where books are organized into specific genres and categories.
- *1595: Nomenclator* of Leiden University Library appears, the first printed catalogue of an institutional library.

- *1674:* Thomas Hyde's catalogue for the Bodleian Library.
- *1791:* The French Cataloguing Code of 1791

More about the early history of library catalogues has been collected in 1956 by Strout.

CATALOGUING PROCESS

DESCRIPTIVE CATALOGUING

This embraces the description of the bibliographic or physical significance of the item except its subject content. The cataloguer also decides here which bibliographic elements should be used as access points for the item in the catalogue and determines the appropriate form of access points used. The description normally has many different elements arranged in standard formats.

The rules that should be followed for descriptive cataloguing in a medical library are the Anglo-American Cataloguing Rules, second edition (AACR2) and its revisions. As these rules are more or less the most used rules internationally in both manual and automated systems, using them will enable the user to see the same descriptive record format in any library he may use, and enable the library to use records produced in other libraries.

Defining the Subject Content

This is normally done using two types of tools which produce a subject description in a coded form or in the language(s) used in the catalogue, which is the only difference between using them, otherwise the processes are identical. The two processes are:

- *Classification*: Classification, through the notation of the classification scheme used, decides the general area in the collection where the item will be shelved. Most classification schemes lead to an arrangement of items based on their subject content. This allows the user to browse the shelves. Normally, a more specific shelving number or symbol must be added after the class number to give the item a unique place among other items in the same class. The resulting number is called " call number ".
- Standardization in classification, contrary to descriptive cataloguing, has not yet been achieved internationally. The library may choose a generalized scheme or a specialized one.

The general schemes most widely used in medical libraries are:

- Dewey Decimal Classification (DDC), which is now in its 21st edition and the second on CD-ROM.
- Library of Congress Classification (LCC), which is continuously subjected to revision.
- Universal Decimal Classification (UDC), which is widely used in Europe.

- Among the specialized schemes the most widely used one in medical libraries is NLM Classification.
- *Subject Cataloguing or Indexing*. The problem of this process is that it is language dependent and thus no standardization can possibly be achieved.

The process depends on two types of tools:

- *Lists of subject headings:* These may be general or specialized. Among the general ones, the most widely used list is Library of Congress List of Subject Headings (LCSH), while Medical Subject Headings (MeSH) is the most widely used list by medical libraries. It is now available in many languages.
- *Thesauri:* These are more recent than lists of subject headings and are more associated with automation in libraries. Most thesauri are specialized in their nature.

The choice between lists and subject headings and thesauri is mostly dictated by the indexing method, whether it is pre-coordinated or post-coordinated, as the former favours the lists while the latter adopts thesauri. Automation has introduced yet another way of indexing using free text search or selecting keywords as access points. Cataloguing may involve original cataloguing, that is the creation of cataloguing records in the library from scratch, or using existing records elsewhere which is known as copy cataloguing.

This may be carried out manually or automated. The sources for copy cataloguing may be:

- *Cataloguing-In-Publication (CIP)*: The data in CIP is created on the basis of prepublication galley proofs or preproduction information for the item. This data is usually given on the verso of the title page. CIP data has to be handled with care and should be compared carefully with the item itself when it is used as the basis for a cataloguing record, as it may have erroneous elements or is not in conformance with standards and rules adopted by the library.
- *Published Bibliographies*: Whether these bibliographies are catalogues of library holdings or published bibliographies, such as national bibliographies, they may be used for creating cataloguing records.
- *Machine-readable Records on Tape*: Some major libraries, such as NLM, may distribute their records on tapes in MARC format. The subscribing library may get such tapes, then use local computer system to select the records needed for the local catalogue. This approach requires significant local hardware and software. Recent development for this is the use of CD-ROM instead of tapes which is cost-effective.
- *Online Services*: Some files simply offer copies of cataloguing records, other online services allow user libraries to modify or

create cataloguing records in a variety of formats for incorporation into their local catalogues. Among these are OCLC, RLIN, WLN, UTLAS, and BCMP. NLM has three online files with cataloguing data: CATLINE (Catalogue-on-line) for printed materials, AVLINE (Audiovisualson-line) for audiovisuals since 1975, and NAF (Name Authority File) for name and series authority records.

- *Service Bureaus*: Several agencies and companies in some countries produce catalogue cards or other catalogue formats on demand. The cataloguing copy is provided in a form that is immediately usable in a local catalogue.
- *Book Suppliers*: Some book suppliers provide catalogue records (cards or otherwise) with the books they ship to their library customers.

Regardless of the source of the cataloguing copy, individual libraries may modify or augment cataloguing records they find in order to make them more useful in local catalogues.

Among such amendments the following are necessary:

- If the copy has subject headings and/or classification which the library does not use.
- If the edition of cataloguing rules used for the copy is different from the one applied by the library.
- If the library may wish to add further access points and explanatory notes to records to emphasize some local interest.

But if the cataloguer comes across an error in an access point or in another part of a cataloguing record, he should write to the appropriate institution and ask for clarification.

Other kinds of modifications are probably unnecessary, such as:

- Eliminating data to simplify records.
- Deleting data that the library feels does not assist users very much, such as ISBN or ISSN.

ORGANIZATION OF THE CATALOGUE

In a manual system, most library catalogues are divided into at least two parts:

Shelflist

The shelflist contains one record for each item in the collection. It is usually arranged by call number in exactly the same order of items on the shelf. It is useful for assigning individual shelving numbers, in making an inventory of the collection, provided it is annotated when the library has multiple copies in the same order. This shelflist may not be available for serials when they are not classified. A list of serials may replace it.

Main Catalogue

The main catalogue contains several copies of the record for each item in the collection. A copy of each record is entered: under the author's name, the names of any of the other persons or corporate bodies associated with the work described, its title, its series title, and various subject headings. It also includes cross-references, guiding users from unused forms of names and subject headings to those that have been used.

Many catalogues may also include guide or special heading to enable a user to determine quickly where in the overall sequence of records a particular catalogue file drawer, page of book catalogue, or part of a microform catalogue is located.

DICTIONARY VERSUS DIVIDED CATALOGUE

There are three major arrangements for manual main catalogues:

- *Dictionary catalogue*, in which author, title and subject access points are interfiled.
- *Divided catalogue*, in which subject access points are arranged in a separate sequence from author and title sequence. Some libraries divide even author and title access points as well.
- *Classified catalogue,* in which the call numbers serve as subject access points and are in a separate sequence from author and title access points. This arrangement usually requires a language subject index to class numbers used in the catalogue, although some libraries may be satisfied with the published index of the classification scheme used.

In an online catalogue there will be no need for such arrangements although the automated systems produce any arrangement as a by-product.

AUTHORITY FILES

The authority file is the file that contains the forms of names (of persons, corporate bodies or places), title, series, or subject headings and descriptors used in the bibliographic record, as well the required cross-references to and from these forms, and their relationship with other used forms. Authority records may be interfiled in the main catalogue, or may be kept in separate authority files, in a manual system. They must be accessible to cataloguing staff. In automated system, they are usually separate from the bibliographic records database but transparently interlinked with the number or symbol of the authority record.

The following is a brief description of the types of authority files:

- Name Authorities: A name authority record consists of:
  - The authoritative name form chosen for use in the catalogue.
  - Alternate forms of the name, and an indication as to whether cross-references from these forms are maintained in the catalogue.

- Any related names such as previous names of an institution.
- Source of the authoritative name.
- Any historical or biographical information about the name necessary to distinguish it from another name.
- An indication as to which set of cataloguing rules was used to establish the authoritative form.

Name authorities may be imported from cooperative ventures or from major libraries that have such files, such as NLM. They may be initiated also on cooperative basis particularly among libraries with a common language such as Arabic, because the forms of names may differ among the speakers of that language, and the library in the respective country is the best to verify them. With automated systems, it may be easier to use as a search tool as well if the file is constructed in a thesaurus form. These systems and the thesaurus structure will enable making the file multilingual.

- *Title Authorities*: These files will be particularly useful if the library uses uniform titles in its catalogue, or when variant titles exist among various editions of the same work.
- *Series Authorities*: A series authority record is required only for a monographic series, where individual works bear individual title and authorship information, in addition to an overall series title. This file should record the decision on how to handle series.
- *Subject Authorities*: The library may consider the list of subject headings or the thesaurus it applies as a subject authority, or restrict the file to the subject headings or descriptors it actually uses. This latter type has been eliminated when an automated system is used as it is going to do both purposes.

Catalogues of Special Collections

Some libraries maintain separate catalogue for special types of materials, such as audiovisuals, in addition to their inclusion in the main catalogue. In automated systems, such catalogues may be produced as by-product from the bibliographic database.

Filing Rules

Records in main catalogue in a manual system must be filed alphabetically according to standard filing rules, while those in the shelflist according to the filing order of the classification scheme in use. In an automated system, the system itself contains filing values for the elements of description that are considered in filing. These values are in fact interpretation of the filing rules adopted. As filing is always language dependent, the rules must cope with all languages represented in the catalogue, whether the characters are in roman or non-roman alphabets.

The major existing filing rules are:

- ALA filing rules/Filing committee, Resources and Technical Services Division, American Library Association. Chicago: ALA, 1980.
- Blaise filing rules/British Library Filing Rules Committee. London: British Library, 1980.
- BS 1749: 1985-British standard recommendations for alphabetical arrangement and filing order of numbers and symbols. London: BSI, 1985.
- ISO 7154-ISO bibliographic filing rules. Geneva: ISO, 1985. and ISO/TR 8393-1985, Exemplification of bibliographic filing principles in a model set of rules. Geneva: ISO, 1985.
- Library of Congress filing rules/prepared by John C. Rather and Susan C. Biebel. Washington, DC: Library of Congress, 1980.

The set of filing rules for Arab libraries discusses the agreement and disagreement of these filing rules and those used in some major libraries in the Arab region as well as standard rules for the region:

- ARIS-Net filing rules for catalogues, bibliographies and directories. Tunis: ALDOC, 1989.

The basic principles behind all these rules are:

- Filing is word by word rather than letter by letter.
- Filing must be strictly as is rather than as if which means that the word is filed as written not as it sounds or means, whether written in full or abbreviated form.
- A numeral files before the alphabet.
- Order of characters must be strictly adhered to.

This order is as follows:

  - Space, dash, hyphen and diagonal slash are given equal filing character and come first
  - Ampersand
  - Arabic numerals
  - Alphabet letters

- Different forms of the same letter have equal value and must be interfiled.
- All records in the same catalogue must be filed according to the same principles-the same rules.

SORTING OF CATALOGUING

In a title catalogue, one can distinguish two sort orders:

1. In the *grammatical* sort order (used mainly in older catalogues), the most important word of the title is the first sort term. The importance of a word is measured by grammatical rules. for example, the first noun may be defined to be the most important word.

2. In the *mechanical* sort order, the first word of the title is the first sort term. Most new catalogues use this scheme, but still include a trace of the grammatical sort order: they neglect an article (The, A, etc.) at the beginning of the title.

The grammatical sort order has the advantage that often, the most important word of the title is also a good keyword, and it is the word most users remember first when their memory is incomplete. However, it has the disadvantage that many elaborate grammatical rules are needed, so that only expert users may be able to search the catalogue without help from a librarian.

In some catalogues, person's names are standardized, i. e., the name of the person is always sorted in a standard form, even if it appears differently in the library material. This standardization is achieved by a process called authority control.

An advantage of the authority control is that it is easier to answer question (which works of some author does the library have?). On the other hand, it may be more difficult to answer question (does the library have some specific material?) if the material spells the author in a peculiar variant. For the cataloguer, it may incur (too) much work to check whether *Smith, J.* is *Smith, John* or *Smith, Jack*. For some works, even the title can be standardized. The technical term for this is *uniform title*. For example, translations and re-editions are sometimes sorted under their original title. In many catalogues, parts of the Bible are sorted under the standard name of the book(s) they contain. The plays of William Shake-speare are another frequently cited example of the role played by a *uniform title* in the library catalogue. Many complica-tions about alphabetic sorting of entries arise.

Some examples:

- Some languages know sorting conventions that differ from the language of the catalogue. For example, some Dutch catalogues sort *IJ* as *Y*. Should an English catalogue follow this suit? And should a Dutch catalogue sort non-Dutch words the same way?
- *Some Titles Contain Numbers, For Example 2001:* A Space Odyssey. Should they be sorted as numbers, or spelled out as *Two thousand and one*?
- *De Balzac, Honouré* or *Balzac, Honouré de*? *Ortega y Gasset, José* or *Gasset, José Ortega y*?

In a subject catalogue, one has to decide on which classification system to use. The cataloguer will select appropriate subject headings for the bibliographic item and a unique classification number (sometimes known as a "call number") which is used not only for identification but also for the purposes of shelving, placing items with similar subjects near one another, which aids in browsing by library users, who are thus often able to take advantage of serendipity in their search process.

'CATALOGUING PRINCIPLES'

In terms of descriptive cataloguing, 'principles' are regarded as underlying concepts for the design and develop-ment of cataloguing rules and the construction of library catalogues. Principles can also be Cataloguing principles do not necessarily mean that we must have a single standard for descriptive cataloguing, or that all cataloguing codes must be the same.

Cataloguing principles mean that we can have different, but compatible standards within the same framework. The Paris Conference was an international attempt to make national codes compatible. The Paris Principles are, in fact, an expansion of a few basic concepts developed over the last two centuries.

These concepts, which are repeated in various parts of the Statement of Principles are:

- The functions of the catalogue,
- The concept of multiple entries,
- The concept of uniformity in the choice and form of headings and entry words,
- The concept of functionality of entries and catalogues, and
- The concept of authorship, personal and corporate.

However, this chapter deals only with some of the principles that might be influenced by the new environment and that have been the subject of arguments among cataloguers for a long time, namely:

- The objectives and functions of the catalogue which influence all other principles,
- The structure of the catalogue and the kinds of entries and indexes, *i.e.*, main entries, added entries and references,
- Uniform headings for works and uniform headings for authors, and
- The form of personal headings and corporate headings.

The concept of main entry will be dealt with in detail, because it has been considered important in the literature on the impact of computerised catalogues on cataloguing principles.

There are other pre-existing principles, unstated or overlooked, in the Paris Principles, such as the general assumption that catalogued items are almost always stand-alone publications rather than 'dependent works'. This issue, and other related questions, such as the 'basic unit of description' and the 'edition' issue, will be discussed in the next chapter in relation to their treatment in the online environment, particularly in shared cataloguing systems.

In the extrapolation of cataloguing principles, it is necessary to be aware of the context within which they were originally meant to operate. The Paris Principles have been indirectly influenced by both the characteristics and the limitations of the manual catalogue. They were principles for a catalogue which had limited capabilities in providing access to bibliographic information. Those who contributed to the formulation and compilation of earlier cataloguing principles implicitly assumed that the physical form of the catalogue would be the card or printed book catalogue, either as individual catalogues or national bibliographies. On the whole, the Paris Principles were formulated at a time when there was little perception of approaches other than the traditional ones of author, title and subject.

Major Developments and Changes in Descriptive Cataloguing Since the Paris Conference

Nearly 35 years have passed since the Paris Conference and cataloguers have witnessed profound changes in many aspects of bibliographic control in general, and in descriptive cataloguing in particular, during this period of time. There has also been a considerable increase in unconventional forms of publications as well as various types of information sources and a considerable growth in different presentations of documents which demand increasing detail to retain precision in identification. Martin reviews some of the major issues which influence bibliographic control and access in the new environment.

The cataloguing world has also faced major challenges such as the increasing costs of cataloguing and the need for simplified cataloguing or *minimal level cataloguing* (MLC), the question of duplicate records in cooperative cataloguing systems and the potential danger that cataloguing principles and concepts might be de-emphasised by those coming from the new technology environment. The cataloguing community is now working in an environment totally different from that of the early 1960s. Given the influence of all these changes and developments in the world of cataloguing, a fundamental re-examination of cataloguing principles seems very necessary.

A Re-examination of Cataloguing Principles in an Online Environment

While current cataloguing principles deal with basic questions concerning the organisation of author/title catalogues, online catalogues have revolutionised access to bibliographic information beyond that approach. An important change in relation to providing access to bibliographic information in the online environment is that access is no longer controlled by cataloguing principles and rules to the same extent as previously but, to some extent, is now governed by various search/retrieval capabilities that were not available in the manual catalogue.

For example, access through keyword searching, truncation, Boolean searching, hypertext searching and, most importantly, access to the full text of items, lie outside of cataloguing rules. This is one of the most fundamental differences between an online system and a manual system that should be taken into consideration when re-examining cataloguing principles. Furthermore, while the boundary between description and access has faded in the online environment, cataloguing principles have traditionally placed little emphasis on description.

In the following parts some of the principles will be analysed with regard to the present and potential influences which the various capabilities of the new technologies might have upon them.

Objectives and Functions of the Catalogue in An Online Environment

In our re-examination of cataloguing principles, major consideration should be given to the objectives and functions of the catalogue. Most cataloguing principles, such as the basis for description, the structure of the catalogue and the choice and form of access points are, to a great extent, influenced by the objectives and functions of the catalogue.

The present cataloguing objectives, which were proposed by Lubetzky to the Paris Conference, have their origin in the work of Panizzi and Cutter dating from the nineteenth century. The traditional approach in the Paris Principles towards the functions of the catalogue has not been able to solve the controversies between the 'finding function' and the 'collocating function' of the catalogue. It is often stated that the first and second objectives are inherently in conflict, and to consider one as primary means to sacrifice the other. While the first function puts emphasis on the finding of specific items within a library collection, the second function focuses on collocation of the works of a particular author and the editions and manifestations of a particular work. These two different approaches influence the choice and form of main and added entries, references and the linking devices to connect related entities.

For example, in the finding function approach the focus of description and the basis for cataloguing data is the physical item in hand. Thus the main entry and added entries are provided according to the information on the title page because it is more familiar to readers. In this context, the relationship of the item to other works and its place in the bibliographic hierarchy is not identified and recorded. Wilson presents a well account of the conflict between the two objectives and their implications for the functions of the catalogue.

It is further stated that these objectives are not fully achieved in the manual environment because of its limitations in finding the actual location of items and the huge cost of making analytics and assembling all the works of a given author, *i.e.*, the collocating function.

A general question raised in the literature is whether the objectives and functions of the catalogue as set forth in the Paris Principles are still valid in the online environment. Another question which has to be addressed in this regard is: whether the catalogue in the online network environment should still maintain the same functions formulated for a pre-machine environment or should widen its scope to include new functions? While it is claimed by some writers that the current objectives and functions of the catalogue continue to be valid in the new environment and even that the new technology may help fulfil them more comprehensively and accurately others have challenged the validity and adequacy of the traditional objectives of the catalogue in the new environment.

Ayres states that the scope of the objectives must be expanded to include the impact that online catalogues have on the content of the catalogue. Buckland discusses the need to change our basic assumptions about the catalogue's purpose in order to design the catalogue of the future. He claims that we should pay more attention to bibliographic access and selection and should design the catalogue as a selecting aid. Heaney notes that library catalogues function not solely as descriptive lists of books but as elements of library management systems and as sophisticated information tools.

In addition to the finding and collocating functions, which are valid in any environment, the online catalogue helps to better identify and characterise entities in terms of their nature, scope and orientation through different data fields such as intellectual level, document type, genre, language code, geographic area code and additional notes. Similarly, a fuller description of the item helps the online catalogue to be used as a means for different users to choose one item over similar items. The locating of items is another function of the catalogue and, in this respect, online catalogues are far more capable of showing the location and status of the item(s) being sought.

In the following part, the functions of the catalogue will be analysed with regard to the impact of some of the major characteristics of the online environment.

These are:

- The integration of library operations,
- Developments in networking and in global access to catalogues,
- Access to other types of bibliographic databases, and
- Online search/retrieval/display capabilities.

Integration of Different Library Operations

The integrated online library system has made it possible for different library modules to use the same bibliographic records within the same database management system. Acquisitions librarians, cataloguers, circulation librarians, serial librarians and reference librarians all have access to the same database and use it for different purposes. In an integrated system, the end user may have access to parts of acquisition status, circulations and holdings information. It is therefore necessary for the online catalogue to fulfil the various bibliographic needs of different operations, from housekeeping functions to reference services. In this context, not only should the catalogue function as a finding tool as well as a collocating tool but it should also help in the choice between one work and others.

The combination of approaches to an integrated catalogue not only makes it necessary to expand the current objectives but also to put more emphasis on principles for the choice and form of access points as well as for description, *i.e.*, data elements beyond author/title information. For example, a reference librarian may need to find a specific item and at the same time identify different editions and manifestations related to that item to provide more help to the user.

Networking and Global Access to Catalogues

The fact that the resources and bibliographic information of hundreds of libraries participating in national and international networks are now accessible to any remote user calls for a reconsideration of the functions and objectives of the catalogue. The concept of 'catalogues on demand' extends the functions of the catalogue beyond providing access to a library's own collections.

With international access to individual catalogues, the question arises as to whether a catalogue should serve in the first place its local users, that is, to identify the holdings of a particular library, or to enable any user to access the collections of other libraries available through the network. Buckland asks: "What difference does it make that the catalogue now is concerned with the collectivity of collections rather than the local holdings of the individual library?" While catalogues should serve their local patrons well, they should also be useful to remote users. In such an environment, consideration should always be given to the fact that the item in hand for cataloguing may be a manifestation of another work known under a different title being held in another collection.

With respect to the network environment, there is some support for the precedence of the collocating function of the catalogue over its finding function. In a conceptual approach to a catalogue's functions as presented by Lubetzky to the Paris Principles, Wilson proposes that, with regard to the availability of different catalogues in an online network and with respect to the significance of 'work' over 'publication', priority should be given to the collocating objective. He proposes a redefinition of 'work' to be taken as the basic unit of cataloguing.

Dempsey points out that a lack of sufficient attention to the collocating objective of the catalogue has resulted in two problems in large shared databases: difficulty in authority control and an increase in duplicate records. Ayres supports a similar concept. In general, in a network, online environment and with regard to the needs of different users, we cannot give precedence to any function. Rather, all functions of the catalogue should equally be taken into consideration.

On the other hand, while in a large shared database the potential number of editions and manifestations of a work increases, it is more likely that access to a very specific bibliographic manifestation of a work, for example, a particular version, would be a common need for some users. The result of a study of

MELVYL at the University of California using transaction logs of remote users showed that known item searches constituted 40 per cent of searches. It is evident that in a shared system or network of catalogues there will be a good chance for the user to select those that suit his/her needs best among different representations of a work. Copy cataloguing through bibliographic utilities, which is usually a known-item search, is another example of such a user approach.

With the availability of catalogues to different remote users, it is hard to give absolute priority to either of the two traditional functions of the catalogue. A catalogue accessible to all types of users through a network will be expected to satisfy, as far as possible, different needs.

Availability of Different Types of Bibliographic Database

With respect to the accessibility of different types of online and/or on-disk bibliographic databases to various users, a combination of approaches in terms of the functions of the catalogue should be considered.

With access to book trade databases, the catalogue goes beyond providing holdings information and becomes a gateway to explore what is newly published, what is to be published and what is in print. In such an environment, emphasis is also put on other functions such as the crucial choice of one item over another. From a different point of view, the functions of the bibliographic database in the library world and book trade world are similar in many respects, such as the finding function, the selecting function and housekeeping function. Even the bringing together of works by a particular author and also collocation of series, are functions wanted by the two communities. A major difference is in the collocation of different editions and manifestations of a work, which libraries appear to consider important enough to control by rules of entry.

Online Search/Retrieval/Display and Functions of the Catalogue

All a catalogue's functions can be achieved more comprehensively through the search/retrieval/display capabilities of the online catalogue. An interesting aspect of the online catalogue which is duplicated from A&I services is the ability of the searcher to choose and/or combine a number of different searching options.

For example, keyword searching on place of publication, name of the publisher, date of publication, series information and ISBN or ISSN not only facilitates the finding function but it can also help in the choice of one item over another. Boolean searching can facilitate both the finding function and the collocating function. Hypertext searching on any term or a combination of terms can extend a known-item search to other items which may be unknown to the searcher but may have some kind of relationship with the item first found.

There is an important difference between the manual environment and the online environment in terms of search/retrieval/display capabilities of the catalogue and their influence on the two objectives. Whilst collocation in the manual catalogue is achieved through the physical pre-arrangement of records of related editions and manifestations of a work, in the online environment it can be achieved through the pre-coding and display of search results.

With many more data elements in MARC records, additional indexes and extensive search and retrieval capabilities, the online catalogue can be used as a selecting aid to choose specific items. This function, *i.e.*, the choosing function, which is of interest to different users such as acquisitions and reference librarians as well as the book trade, can be carried out more effectively. For example, combining key data elements, such as author or title with date of publication, country of publication, name of publisher and language of the item is a useful way to choose appropriate items.

Conclusion

The catalogue in the global online environment is supposed to satisfy all possible approaches. From the preceding paragraphs, it can be concluded that the functions of the online catalogue go beyond those laid down in the Paris Principles. The online catalogue with its extensive capabilities can widen the scope and content of the functions and fulfil new functions. It is therefore necessary that cataloguing principles for the online environment should cover all these different functions equally and should also take into consideration the influence of each function on other principles.

Structure of the catalogue and the concept of multiple entries

The structure of the catalogue has an important role in the fulfilment of its functions. Sections 3 (Structure of the Catalogue), 4 (Kinds of Entry), 5 (Use of Multiple Entries), 6 (Function of Different Kinds of Entry) and sub-sections 8.1, 9.1, 9.2, 9.5, 9.6 and also sections 10 and 11 of the Statement of Principles relate to the structure of the catalogue. The principles underlying the structure of the catalogue and choice of entries in the Paris Principles include statements concerning the determination and construction of necessary entries for a linear, alphabetical catalogue. Such a linear catalogue consists of main entries, added entries and references.

Online catalogues, on the other hand, go far beyond the linear author/title catalogue. they permit dynamic linking, merging and rearrangement of files. The structure of an online catalogue usually consists of bibliographic, authority and holdings records linked to one another, each of which is arranged in a given order. Multiple access points and related index files in an online system are not limited to traditional author/title headings. Since it is possible to specify more data elements in a record as access points, the structure of online catalogues may include other index files such as keywords, author/any keyword from title, standard numbers, language of the item, country of publication, date of publication, type of material, genre and readership level.

Cataloguing principles should take into consideration the complex structure of the online catalogue and provide principles for the construction of different files and also for the indexing of different fields and sub-fields concerning access to required elements in the record. They should also suit the structure of the catalogue including different indexes for searching and browsing. A possible approach would be to provide principles for the construction of browsable indexes which can help the searcher to get a clear idea of what sort of indexes are available for searching and retrieval. It is also useful to provide name authority files for browsing, like those offered by SIRSI and PALS systems and a uniform-title authority file for making the catalogue more effective in its collocating function. A possible development in the structure of the catalogue is through the concept of 'super records'.

The Concept of Main Entry

As a typical example of the impact of the online environment on cataloguing principles, it has been claimed that the concept of main entry has lost its value. It was indicated that with the advent of computerised catalogues the value of the main entry concept, which developed in the context of book and card catalogues, has been questioned, but no satisfactory and practical solution has emerged as to how its functions can be otherwise fulfilled.

Svenonius asks:

- "If the main entry were to be abandoned, what would replace its role in the construction of uniform headings? what would take its place in the structuring displays in online catalogs? how would abandoning the main entry affect single-entry and minimal-level catalogs"?

A review of the related literature of the last two decades shows a developing discussion in favour of abandoning the main entry concept in the online environment. Although before the advent of automated catalogues there were some proposals for the no-main-entry concept such as '*Description Independent System* (DIS)', 'alternative entry', and 'title main entry', developments in online catalogues of access to bibliographic information have given the issue a new dimension and the number of those who advocate the abandonment of the main entry concept has increased.

To many writers, the concept arose out of pre-machine systems and is said to be irrelevant in a developed online catalogue where the technology permits many more access points of equal value in the retrieving of bibliographic information. It is often also claimed that the process of determining main entries is one of the most complex, costly and time consuming processes in descriptive cataloguing.

In contrast to those supporting the simple abandonment of the main entry principle, others argue for its continued use in computerised catalogues. In a survey of the attitudes of cataloguers and cataloguing educators, Musavi found that more than half of the respondents disagreed with the abandonment of the main entry concept even in the online catalogue. The majority of respondents believed that online catalogues will not devalue the concept of main entry. Baughman and Svenonius assessed the implication of the possible abandonment of main entry in AACR2 and found that a number of problematic rules would result. Exploring the definitions and functions of main entry, Carpenter stated that some of the functions of main entry, particularly its collocating function, are still valid in the online environment.

The following part is an analysis of the main entry concept in terms of its functions in an online environment. The focus of this part is only on main entries for personal names.

Functions of Main Entry

Discussions of the main entry concept have been mostly concerned with the objectives and functions of the catalogue rather than merely its definitions.' Verona any consideration about the functions of the main entry has to be based on an evaluation of the general objectives and functions of the alphabetical catalogue. A similar idea comes from Carpenter who points out that: "If main entry is to have any function, it must be in the context of fulfilling an objective of a catalogue."

A major justification for the concept often lies in its collocating function, in bringing together both different editions of a work and the works of an author.

Carpenter states that other functions, *i.e.*:

- Naming a work,
- Providing credit to the principal author,
- Providing the only full entry, and
- Being the entry to which all others refer, are of historical interest.

Looking from a database perspective, Brooks and Bierbaum consider the uniform main entry as an essential device to link all the occurrences of a bibliographic mutation. Tillett emphasises the role of main entry in specifying the nature of the relationship between a work and the person associated with it. Heaney notes that the issue of the main entry is more complicated than its being only considered as a primary heading. it involves not the idea of "main" entry but also the adequate identification, within the record, of related works. As a collocating device, the concept of main entry has been retained not only in multiple-entry card catalogues but also with the same justification in automated catalogues.

In terms of collocation, main entry has two specific functions:

- Assembling and displaying works by an author, and
- Assembling and displaying different editions of a work.

Assembling and Displaying Works by an Author

Assembling of the works of an author can be achieved through a uniform heading for the author, whether recorded as the main entry heading or as an added entry. This function is thus not exclusively achieved by the main entry heading. Furthermore, the main entry heading alone cannot assemble all the works by an author. In many cases where an author is a joint author, editor, compiler or author of one part, his/her name may be presented as an added entry heading.

Assembling and Displaying Different Editions of a Work

While the most important justification for the main entry is in its role of assembling and displaying, in a meaningful and logical order, the various editions of a work, it has been a complex and debatable concept in the history of descriptive cataloguing. Although this function is attributed to main entry, it cannot be fully achieved through the main entry heading alone. In assembling the different editions of a work, the main entry heading is dependent upon a second collocating device: the uniform title.

Without the inclusion of a uniform title following the main entry heading in the record, the assembling function of the main entry is only partially achieved: it would be limited only to those works whose editions and manifestations have identical titles proper. Thus, neither of the two functions perceived for main entry in the Paris Principles can be fully achieved through the main entry heading alone.

As will be discussed further in this part, a combination of the author's uniform heading and the uniform title that is considered as a 'unifying mode of identifying' different editions of a work will fulfil the collocating function in a more comprehensive way.

CATALOGUING RULES

Cataloguing rules have been defined to allow for consistent cataloguing of various library materials across several persons of a cataloguing team and across time. Users can use them to clarify how to find an entry and how to interpret the data in an entry. Cataloguing rules prescribe which information about a bibliographic item is included in the entry and how this information is presented for the user. It may also aid to sort the entries in printing the catalogue.

The larger a collection, the more elaborate cataloguing rules are needed. Users cannot and do not want to examine hundreds of catalogue entries or even dozens of library items to find the one item they need. Currently, most cataloguing rules are similar to, or even based on, the International Standard Bibliographic Description (ISBD), a set of rules produced by the International Federation of Library Associations and Institutions (IFLA) to describe a wide range of library materials.

These rules organize the bibliographic description of an item in the following areas: title and statement of responsibility (author or editor), edition, material specific details (for example, the scale of a map), publication and distribution, physical description (for example, number of pages), series, notes, and standard number (ISBN). The most commonly used set of cataloguing rules in the English-speaking world are the Anglo-American Cataloguing Rules, 2nd Edition, or AACR2 for short.

AACR2 provides rules for *descriptive cataloguing* only and does not touch upon *subject cataloguing*. AACR2 has been translated into many languages, for use around the world. In the German-speaking world there is also the *Regeln für die alphabetische Katalogisierung* (RAK). Library items that are written in a foreign script are, in some cases, transliterated to the script of the catalogue.

ANGLO-AMERICAN CATALOGUING RULES

The Anglo-American Cataloguing Rules (AACR) were first published in 1967. AACR2 stands for the *Anglo-American Cataloguing Rules, Second Edition*. It is published jointly by the American Library Association, the Canadian Library Association, and the Chartered Institute of Library and Information Professionals in the UK. The editor is Michael Gorman, a British-born librarian living in the Chicago area and honoured by both the ALA and CILIP. AACR2 is designed for use in the construction of catalogues and other lists in general libraries of all sizes. The rules cover the description of, and the provision of access points for, all library materials commonly collected at the present time.

Despite the claim to be 'Anglo-American', the first edition of AACR was published in 1967 in somewhat distinct North American and British texts. The second edition of 1978 unified the two sets of rules (adopting the British spelling 'cataloguing') and brought them in line with the International Standard Bibliographic Description. Libraries wishing to migrate from the previous North American text were obliged to implement 'desuperimposition', a substantial change in the form of headings for corporate bodies.

AACR2 exists in several print versions, as well as an online version. Gorman has edited several revisions of AACR2 including a concise edition. Print versions are available from the publishers. The online version is available only via Cataloger's Desktop from the Library of Congress. Various translations are also available from other sources.

Principles of AACR include cataloguing from the item 'in hand' rather than inferring information from external sources and the concept of the 'chief source of information' which is preferred where conflicts exist.

Over the years AACR2 has been updated by occasional amendments, and was significantly revised in 1988 and 2002. The 2002 revision included substantial changes to parts for non-book materials. A schedule of annual updates began in 2003 and ceased with 2005.

AACR2 has been succeeded by Resource Description and Access (commonly referred to as RDA), which was released in June 2010. This new code is informed by the Functional Requirements for Bibliographic Records and was conceived to be a framework more flexible and suitable for use in a digital environment.

In the fall of 2010, the Library of Congress, National Library of Medicine, National Agricultural Library, and several other institutions and national libraries of other English-speaking countries performed a formal test of RDA, the results of which were released in June 2011.

OBJECTIVES AND FUNCTIONS OF THE CATALOGUE/DATABASE

Differences in the approaches of library cataloguing and A&I services towards creating bibliographic records are a result of different objectives which each of the two communities identifies for its bibliographic database. The major object of looking for an article's bibliographical citation in A&I databases is different from that of looking for bibliographic information in a library catalogue. While library cataloguing is traditionally concerned with the finding, identifying, collocating and organising of bibliographic entities, A&I services deal rather with the subject content of bibliographic entities and, to some extent only, the finding of works by a particular author.

In A&I databases, the assembling of all the works by a given author may be a common approach for some searchers, but there is usually no concept such as the assembling of all editions and manifestations of a work. Journal articles, patent documents, reports, dissertations and conference proceedings have fewer editions than books. Consequently, the concept of main entry, which is useful for bringing together different editions and manifestations of a work, has more justification in library catalogues than in A&I databases. A similar idea is present in the COSATI (the Committee on Scientific and Technical Information) standard with the policy of a main entry free environment: "The system works because only rarely are there technical reports that are about other technical reports and unrelated by contract number".

STRUCTURE OF THE CATALOGUE/DATABASE AND OF THE BIBLIOGRAPHIC RECORD

Because of the differences in their objectives and functions, library catalogues and A&I databases differ from one another in terms of the structure of the bibliographic record and the structure of the database. There is no concept such as multiple entries in A&I databases.

However, in terms of the structure of the record, there are similarities in some of the data fields which can potentially conform to the same standard: headings for persons and corporate bodies associated with an item, date of publication, title of analytic, title of monograph, title of collection or series, language of the item, ISBN/ISSN, conference identification information, abstract/ summary, country of publication, target audience and subject headings. These data fields can be treated similarly by the two communities by using identical terms/phrases. The searcher can approach the catalogue or the database with the same search string.

Choice and form of Access Points

This is one of the most important areas of possible reconciliation between cataloguing principles and indexing conventions. Because CD-ROM versions of A&I databases are becoming increasingly available to end users and have larger cumulations of citations in them, there is more need to reconcile variant names. Since there is usually no retrospective editing of headings when a CD-ROM is produced, such discrepancies are simply left alone.

Many A&I databases also include citations of monographs, such as conference proceedings, festschriften and books reviewed, that are duplicated in library catalogues. This also indicates the need for more consistency in name headings between library cataloguing and A&I practices.

In terms of the treatment of names for inclusion in the record for later retrieval, A&I conventions differ markedly both within themselves and from cataloguing conventions. In respect of the choice of names to be entered in the bibliographic record, A&I conventions usually provide author indexing in depth. They do not conform to principles such as main entry and the 'rule of three'. The names of persons associated with an item are entered as they appear on the item in hand.

For example, the UNISIST *Reference Manual* prescribes that the names of all individual authors associated with a given item are to be entered in the record, unless there is a clear indication on the original that the chief responsibility for authorship lies with choosing only one or less than all of the persons cited, in which case only those indicated as chief contributors are to be entered.

There are other similarities or differences:

- Since A&I databases are not searched through the exact titles of items, title is not as common an access point as in library catalogues. Instead, a title keyword index is provided for title as well as subject searching.
- As a first principle in the indexing of names, both communities invert names of persons to secure alphabetic arrangement by family names.
- A&I conventions regard the names of editors of collections as an essential element for the identification of monographs whereas cataloguing conventions put less emphasis on the role of such contributors, in that they no longer consider editors and compilers as main entries.

- In terms of the names of persons associated with a monograph, A&I conventions regard the form derived from the item as essential and other forms as optional.

Since A&I services do not normally use name authority files and do not maintain references, many of them prefer to include other forms of the name with initials immediately after the complete form:

- Wendt, Richard P. Wendt, R. P.
- Atkinson, H Craig Craig Atkinson, H

Library cataloguing, on the other hand, treats names with initials differently. For example, AACR2R has the following approach:

- Wendt, R.P. (Richard P.)
- Eliot, T.S. (Thomas Stearns)

One reason why many A&I services do not conform to the principle of uniform heading may be that they are usually discipline-oriented and, therefore, the chance of similarity between the forms of names within a given discipline is not great.

There are usually not many identical names with identical forenames or initials within a given A&I database. for example, there were only two authors with the surname 'Buckland' in the LISA database and three in ERIC but none with identical forename or initial.

- A&I conventions emphasise the addition to names of two other elements: 1) the 'role', *i.e.*, the type of intellectual responsibility, such as 'author', 'editor', 'compiler', 'translator', etc., and 2) the person's affiliation. Cataloguing rules, on the other hand, treat the role of persons in the statement of responsibility area and discard affiliations.
- With regard to corporate names, there are some similarities and differences between A&I conventions and cataloguing principles:
  - The full form of corporate names is entered by A&I services with the inclusion of an abbreviation or acronym of a corporate body as an optional element. AACR2R prescribes a similar approach without the optional inclusion of an abbreviation or acronym.
  - If the official or formal name of an organisation is usually quoted in the form of an acronym, this may be entered as the full form. AACR2R has the same approach.
  - The name of a corporate body should be entered in the language of the document, unless the name shown on the document is itself a translation, and the name in its original language is known, in which case the latter form should be entered if better known. AACR2R prescribes that the official language of the body should be used.

- Where several levels of an organisation are cited, they should be given in descending order of scale from the larger unit to the smaller. In terms of entering at the intermediate levels, if their inclusion does not add significant information to the entry, they may be omitted provided always that the most specific unit is cited and that the entry provides an unambiguous identification of the organisation. Similarly, AACR2R prescribes that a subordinate or related body should usually be entered as a subheading of the main body.

6

Academic Library System

An academic library is a library that is attached to academic institutions above the secondary level, serving the teaching and research needs of students and staff. These libraries serve two complementary purposes: to support the school's curriculum, and to support the research of the university faculty and students. The support of teaching requires material for class readings and for student papers. In the past, the material for class readings, intended to supplement lectures as prescribed by the instructor, has been called reserves. In the period before electronic resources became available, the reserves were supplied as actual books or as photocopies of appropriate journal articles.

Traditionally, one copy of a book was made available for each 10 students—this is practical for large classes only if paperback copies are available, and the books reused from term to term. Academic libraries must decide what focus they take in collecting materials since no single library can supply everything. When there are particular areas of specialization in academic libraries these are often referred to as niche collections. These collections are often the basis of a special collection department and may include original papers, artwork, and artifacts written or created by a single author or about a specific subject.

ACADEMIC LIBRARY STRUCTURES

Organisational structure can be defined as "one of the interrelated components that define any organisation referring to the definition of individual jobs and their relationship to each other as depicted in organisational charts and job descriptions." It clarifies how information is distributed, and jobs are organised. For decades the hierarchical structure of management was regarded as the most efficient way of managing an organisation. This system worked well in and environment where the future was predictable and librarians were in the driving seat. Hierarchies were not designed to foster creativity and lead workers to self-fulfilment.

It is therefore very difficult to introduce fundamental change within hierarchical structures which are naturally resistant to change. In an effort to bring about reorganisation within organisations institutions try to either modify the existing hierarchical structure or replace it with something else. Deming as cited by Mullins states that management systems still prevalent today have had a destructive impact on people. According to Deming "people are born with intrinsic motivation, self-esteem, dignity, curiosity to learn... " Qualities such as these are undermined by a management style that reward top achievers and punish those that do worse. Managers that exhibit such management styles use disapproval as a negative control measure. This approach leads to a climate where staff performance is primarily directed at pleasing their superiors and that inevitably lead to average performance.

According to researcher managers have a natural tendency to maintain the status quo. They would instinctively fall back on models and practices that worked in the past. The volatile nature and unpredictability of information services is forcing managers to adopt new management styles. It is beginning to dawn on people that the bureaucratic way of management is becoming outdated and that change will be more effectively achieved through education, sharing, motivation, teamwork and coaching.

Moran states that unprecedented change has forced managers to re-evaluate structures. Customary practices designed to maintain organisational stability are being questioned. To cope with change, organisations have started flattening structures to induce more flexibility within those organisations. These new structures being adopted have decreased levels of hierarchy, increased flexibility and resulted in diminishing boundaries between departments.

Issues to Consider when Introducing New Structures

Management theorists are very reluctant to prescribe to a particular structural model but advise that structure should rather be designed to meet organisational needs and goals. Organisations should try and learn as much as possible from others who have implemented organisational change. They should never introduce a structure simply because it is being used elsewhere but always to meet specific organisational needs. Of cardinal importance is to determine how people within the organisation will adopt the new structure. Researcher shares the following points learnt from a process of restructuring:

Before implementing a process of restructuring it is important to have clear vision, goals and objectives with the focus on service delivery. It is useful to establish a core team to lead the restructuring process. It is vitally important that senior management support the process, *e.g.*, a deputy vice-chancellor. It is important to involve the entire staff component, listen to their inputs and concerns since ownership by the staff is vital for successful change implementation. Staff development programmes should be part of the process to prepare staff for new functions or roles they may be involved in.

After implementation it is important to critically analise the performance of the academic library within the new structure. Managers often do not adapt easily to the flatter less bureaucratic structures that are generally being adopted. Even staff members at lower levels experience this problem. Generally it is very difficult to introduce change that goes against prevailing organisational culture. Proper planning is needed to take the organisation from the existing structure to the new one.

Employee input in developing such a strategy is crucial. Research indicates that organisational transformation had been most successful in scenarios where employees had maximum input. Finally evaluation is necessary after change implementa-tion to determine its success. In reorganised libraries structures are always flatter resulting in manager's roles reverting from directing to coordinating. The prime purpose of reorganisation is to create a more effective organisation. Reorganisation results in academic libraries becoming learning organisations.

The learning organisation is characterised by staff empowerment, is team based, decentralised, practices participative management and information sharing. In the learning organisation the person closest to a problem has the responsibility and authority to deal with it. Tom Wilson as cited by Moran states that the academic library is in bad need of reconstruction. To Wilson academic libraries were essentially designed to manage physical artifacts. The rise of the Internet has completely transformed the way information is created, distributed and accessed. The e-journal is a typical example. Johansen and Swigart as cited by Moran states "we had outlived the usefulness of models from the Industrial era but don't yet have robust organisational models for the information era". It is therefore of paramount importance that academic librarians continuously re-evaluate current structures and through an experimental process adopt new models. Moran states that for people who advocate restructuring there is good and bad news. The good news is that people understand that technological change will compel fundamental organisational change. The bad news is that there is a lack of urgency. Generally organisational change appears to be incremental rather than radical.

IMPACT OF ICT CHANGE ON ACADEMIC IBRARIES

The Internet has made information access and retrieval both simplistic and complex. Information retrieval systems are being designed to suit the needs of end users and therefore try to simplify the process. Simultaneously however the user is overwhelmed with so much information resources and choices that the process becomes complex. This creates a situation where the users need skills and knowledge in terms of search strategies and conceptualisation. Herrington is of the opinion that information literacy instruction at the point of need can be very effective. Wood and Walther is of the opinion that unlike popular believe the Internet will not completely replace the skills of professional librarians but rather make them indispensable.

Changes in the Job Description of Academic Librarians

An overview of the core competencies required by academic library and information workers gives one an idea of how dramatically information and communications technology has changed the library profession.

Cheng identifies the following core competencies needed by the future librarian:

- Good communication skills.
- Should be more than just computer literate and should have a good understanding of ICT and its relation to information resources.
- Should have an in-depth understanding of organisational and user needs that is research based and should organise library resources to satisfy those needs.
- Competent in Web publishing techniques.
- Skilled in manipulating metadata to organise digital information.
- Skilled in training users in the use of e-resources.
- Skilled in filtering, evaluating and appraising Internet information.

Researchers identifies another quality required, an in-depth understanding of what information resources are available on the Internet, as well as insight in terms of its reliability and scope.

The Changing Nature of the Academic Library

ICT is busy transforming the nature of academic libraries. A variety of terms such as hybrid, digital and virtual library are used to refer to the academic library. A digital library can be defined as "a managed collection of information, with associated services, where the information is stored in digital formats and accessible over a network".

The virtual library has been defined as "remote access to the contents and services of libraries and other information resources, combining an on-site collection of current and heavily used materials in both print and electronic form, with an electronic network which provides access to, and delivery from, external worldwide library and commercial information and knowledge sources". Hybrid libraries are libraries that provide access to both electronic resources and paper-based resources.

From the definitions it is clear that most of today's academic libraries fall in either the hybrid or virtual category. The library of the future is unlikely to be a physical entity as we know it but would probably be a Web portal providing access to information.

The emphasis will be on access to information rather than physical ownership. Akeroyd supports this view and states that as a physical space entity the library, as we know it is unlikely to prevail in a digital environment. One reason for this is that because of Web access the digital library is accessible from anywhere.

Changes in the Information Seeking Behaviour of Users

Academic librarians have a good understanding of the tremendous value of printed and electronic resources available to students at academic libraries. Academic library users do not necessarily share this insight. New generation academic library users have a preference for Web resources rather than visiting the library.

Research done on undergraduate engineering students in 2004 revealed that they would turn to the Internet as the primary resource for information for their projects. Moyo refers to a scenario where users were asked what they expect from an academic library service.

They responded as follows:

- All resources should be available in full text and be printable.
- The library service should be fast and easily accessible.
- 24/7 availability of a virtual reference service.
- Wish to do all library transactions online.
- Web resources that is easy to use and Web search engines that meet information needs.

What is clear is that new generation academic library users prefer the convenience of digital access above reliance on assistance from librarians. This preference for the Internet poses a serious challenge to the academic library which has to move from a paradigm of the library as a physical entity to a library where the users do not have to come to physically to make use of it's services.

Electronic access to information resources does have many advantages, *e.g.*:

- Multiple access which implies more that one user can access a resource simultaneously.
- Lots of resources are available in full text.
- 24/7 access which means users can access resources remotely, *e.g.*, from off campus or from dormitories.

One of the disadvantages of remote access from an academic library point of view is that users are not always aware of the fact that they are using library resources. One user stated: “No, I don't need to use the library, I use Internet resources”.

Despite the apparent preference for digital content the need for access to high quality digital content remains constant. Greater cooperation between library and faculty is necessary to develop ways to connect users and high quality digital materials.

IMPACT OF ICT ON COLLECTION MANAGEMENT

Collection development can be defined as the selection and acquisition of library materials based on current and potential user needs. Collection management goes beyond this. It is concerned with managing the utilisation, storage and accessibility of a collection. Collection development can thus be seen as a subdivision of collection management. Academic librarians find themselves in an era of unparalleled access to information.

The latest edition of Uhlrich's has indicated the availability of more than 1,72,000 journal titles. Although this appears to be a most ideal situation it is not because the financial resources available in acquisitions departments have not necessarily increased. The sheer volume of information available also makes selection of the most suitable information a complex task. The impact of electronic resources has made collection management a very complex and challenging task. There are budgetary constraints, numerous formats, ever changing user needs. Collection management implies involvement in tasks such as analysis of needs, negotiation of contracts and evaluation of resources. There was a time when the size of an academic library collection determined its stature. At that time the library's resources were generally adequate to meet most of its users needs. Since then the academic library has exchanged the ownership model for an access model where physical location becomes completely irrelevant.

Access versus Ownership

Information and communications technology has had a fundamental impact on library collection development policies. Academic libraries had traditionally applied an ownership or just-in-case approach to collection development. The premise was that users would need the material and make use of it. Having the material available in the library would also provide immediate access to it than having to borrow it from a third party. The cost of maintaining collections and increased demands for more information had forced academic libraries to reconsider the ownership model and adopt another model. Unparalleled price increases and shrinking budgets had ushered in a new model called access or just in time where the focus is to give the user the information that they need when they want it.

Cost

Technically it is more cost effective to produce an e-resource, for example an electronic journal, because the first copy costs are reduced. There is also savings in terms of packaging, delivery and storage. In practice these savings have not lead to reductions in the cost of e-journals. It has been suggested that the academic library adopts a pay-as-you-use approach. This make sense according to research done in 1997 that indicated that 22 per cent of science articles published in 1984 were never cited for the next 10 years. In the social sciences this figure goes up to 48 per cent.

Storage Space

With the access model there is no need for storage space, *e.g.*, back copies. Moahi cites Cooper who states that the storage cost per single copy is between

$25 and $40. Calculations to determine JStor pricing lead to the conclusion that the cost per single volume was between $24 and $41. When costs for re-shelving and maintenance were included, the estimated cost rose to $45 per title per year for a core journal and $180 per title per year for a large research library.

Enhanced Access to Information

One of the benefits of ICT is enhanced access to library services and resources. The academic library can expose its users to a much larger collection than it can house physically because users can access information remotely. With online access it is possible to accurately measure utilisation of e-resources and that is invaluable in determining which resources to purchase. It is easier to search e-resources and access speed is greatly enhanced. Other advantages are that users can simultaneously access the same resource, and there are no incidences of lost copies or mutilated issues. Singh is of the opinion that a paradigm shift is taking place within the academic library as more academic librarians are doing collection management rather that collection development. The focus is rather on interpretation of information rather than selection. Librarians are becoming knowledge managers rather than collection managers.

Digital Preservation of Data

One of the major costs facing the academic library is the cost related to the conversion and preservation of information in digital format. The cost of this process amounts to $1 per page. This does not include the cost relating to the annotation for indexing purposes and the cost of conversion of audio-visual material. One of the problems with converting records into digital image is the fact that the technology used to store these pages as a digital photograph results in large files which have storage implications and place demands on band-with. Funding allocated to preservation of digital material is generally inadequate. This has to do with expectations that the costs of digital preservation over length of time might be very high. It is also difficult to forecast cost in terms of how long to retain digital material in an archive and computer architectures needed to access material. Preservation of digital materials poses many challenges. It is further complicated by the fact that computer technology changes at an unprecedented rate.

There are concerns that changing interfaces, standards, formats and operating systems will render it impossible to read today's computer discs at some point in future. The implication of this is that one needs migration strategies to move data to new operating systems and structures or have scenarios where computers can simulate data structures and operating systems of previous eras. This scenario will make digital preservation prohibitively expensive. A great deal of current research into digital preservation is based on overcoming the technical issues to ensure long-term preservation of digital content. The issue of digital preservation initially came to the fore as an impending crisis. Fears were expressed that large portions of our cultural heritage were in danger of disappearing forever. Examples were cited of Web sites available today that might be gone to-morrow.

Although digital materials are more fragile by nature than analog materials the risk varies within different categories of digital materials. Although it is true that a Web site currently available may disappear overnight, the same does not apply to electronic journals. This realisation has transferred the focus from the immediate rescue notion to an approach that sees digital preservation as part of a carefully planned digital access management process. One way academic libraries can deal with digital preservation is through cooperation. Through cooperation various institutions can share costs. Another advantage would be that it would reduce redundancy. Because of the fragile nature of digital materials libraries cannot put off decisions to preserve digital information *ad infinitum*. Time is of the essence.

Unlike a book that can be repaired or rebound, once a digital file becomes corrupt it may be impossible or prohibitively expensive to restore the data. Another problem facing the academic library is the long-term preservation of digital information. There are questions concerning the long-term stability of digital information stored on disks and tapes. There is the potential of these media deteriorating over a period of time. Another way digital preservation is approached is by letting the vendors do the preservation. These days there are also escrow repositories, *e.g.* Elsevier has agreed to provide the National Library of Netherlands with a copy of Science Direct which the National Library will maintain and make available should Elsevier be unable to do so.

ELECTRONIC RESOURCES

ICT has fundamentally changed academic library collections. Forever gone is the era when an academic library's physical collection determined its stature. In the modern networked technological era the emphasis has shifted from ownership of physical resources to access to electronic resources that are globally accessible.

Internet Information

There are huge amounts of unedited information on the Internet. There are countless Web sites and no single listing of them all. There is also the phenomenon of Web sites disappearing overnight that create problems in terms of access.

The Invisible Web

Academic library users make use of search engines such as Google and Altavista to find information on the Web. As a result they are only exposed to a small portion of the Web called the 'Publicly Indexable Web' These students are only exposed to Web pages accessible via hyperlinks. Search engines do not index Web pages that requires authentication or Web pages behind search forms. The Web consists of two components namely the 'Publicly Indexable Web' also referred to as the visible Web and the invisible Web. The invisible Web refers to all those information resources available yet not indexed by conventional search engines yet accessible via the Web.

Masses of information available via the invisible Web are found in subject databases. Most of the databases that academic libraries make available to their users resort under the invisible Web, *e.g.* EbscoHost and Eric. Conventional search engines can find databases such as EbscoHost but cannot access them. Search engines can only find content that was indexed by their software called spiders or crawlers. The problem is that they only index Web content available in formats such as HTML and PDF. Michael K. Bergman in year 2000 in a paper on the invisible Web for an Internet Search Company called Bright Planet suggests that the invisible Web is 500 times larger that the visible Web with approximately 550 billion documents.

The Issue of Quality of Resources Available on the Visible Web

The Internet had become a very important research tool for academic endeauvour. Slaouti as cited by Stapleton notes that the relevance and importance of the Web as a research tool should not be underestimated. There is a stark contrast in the way resources are published on the Web versus traditional publishing. In the traditional print environment publishing generally was done by a publisher hence a controlled environment that impacted on quality as well as the scope of the audience being reached. The open nature of the Web, the development of sophisticated search engines, browsers, Web creation and publishing software and easy access to networks via low cost connectivity has developed the Web into a tool that can be easily utilised by the masses for publishing purposes, people who were formally shut out of the publishing process.

This has lead to a flood of Web publications of variable quality. During the 1990's library scholars recognised this dilemma and suggested criteria to evaluate Internet resources, *e.g.*, authority, purpose, coverage and objectivity and accessibility. These days a single search can yield hundreds of thousands of items. The unfiltered nature of Web resources has made evaluation of these resources essential. One often finds that unlike in traditional printed media, e-resources found on the Web often lack important criteria such as author or date. Web pages because of its non-linear textual nature has added new effects to the search process such as sound, videos and access to thousands of items by clicking a mouse. These new elements imply that new sets of skills are required on the part of the researcher.

Reference Works

According to Moyo reference statistics in academic libraries are plunging. At the same time electronic access of these resources are increasing. This tendency can be ascribed to the fact that users can access these resources remotely via the Internet. Internet connectivity and e-resources had become absolutely essential for the new reference service paradigm. One of the key elements of e-reference service success is that the service is available at the point of need. The tremendous growth in the use of online reference works has created a need within the academic library to develop services to support this type of service.

Academic libraries are turning to on-line real time reference tools also referred to as ORR to support students remotely. The Pen State University library has more than 300 databases that students may access. On-line real time reference support is used to assist students at the point of need. E-reference works share all the benefits of e-resources, *e.g.*, 24/7 remote accessibility, concurrent access for multiple users and the potential for online updating to keep content up to date. Electronic communication had become the primary mode of communication in e-reference services. Online chat had become the method of choice. Some e-reference application providers have added *Voice over IP* (VOIP) to their products which enable voice dialogue with the library user.

E-reference services have many advantages, *e.g.*:

- Availability via the Internet.
- Service at the point of need.
- Easy for people who are unable to come to the academic library, *e.g.*, the physically disabled.
- 24/7 availability.

Moyo cites Stormont who states that online real time reference support is very labour intensive. In order to cope academic libraries have adopted a distributed staffing model where the load of the service is shared among various libraries.

E-Journals

The e-journal can be defined as "a version of the traditional print or paper-based journal which is disseminated electronically in some form or other directly to the end user." Although e-journals had been in existence since 1976 it became prominent during the 1990's. Since it's inception in 1665 the printed journal remained the primary vehicle for communication among academics and researchers. The advent of the Internet transformed publishing radically as it made it possible to publish cheaply. Internet also made access universally available. Because of the Internet academics and researchers became more creative and productive.

Cost Factors

There had been major increases in the cost of journal subscriptions during the last two decades. According to researcher between 1986 and 1996 the average increase per journal subscription had been a whopping 147 per cent. This state of affairs had been laid at the door of the commercial publishers. Moahi states that simultaneously there had been a significant increase in the number of science and engineering journals published. Because of ever decreasing budgets academic libraries are unable to purchase the titles they deem necessary. Falk cites McCabe of Georgia Institute of Technology stating that publishers offer libraries bundled packages of e-journals under the pretense that it is cheaper but these deals actually inflate prices.

Moahi is of the opinion that a consequence of these bundled deals is that academic libraries end up with titles they do not want or need. Despite the fact that publishers have substantial cost savings on first copy production of e-journals and also save on distribution costs, these savings are not passed onto their customers. Cost of e-journals tend to be similar or higher that their printed counterparts. What further complicate matters are the fact that provision has to be made for connectivity and desktops, which means additional costs. Aggregate publishers also tend to drop titles without prior consultation with academic librarians.

Academic Library's Response to Publishers

Despite general expectations that e-journals should be cheaper than printed versions publishers maintain the status quo by maximizing profits. Publisher's attitudes have forced academic institutions to take a tougher stance against them. Recently the Senate of the University of California instructed the library to sever all ties with Elsevier, *e.g.*, cancel subscriptions and cease submission of research papers if negotiations with them fail to obtain a reduction in the price of subscriptions. Harvard University has cancelled their Elsevier subscriptions of bundled journals. The Senate of North Carolina State University urged that excessive prices from publishers be resisted.

Four North Carolina universities had signed a deal for a bundle of 1300 journals in 2003 with the proviso that no titles are dropped. When these institutions wanted to renew subscription for 2004 the price was so exorbitant that they all cancelled the deal. Cornell University and the University of Missouri also cancelled subscription with Elsevier for the same reasons. Three North Carolina universities have drafted policies to only forward research to publishers whose journals are reasonably priced and widely accessible.

In the event of this not being possible they will include an "authorisation to publish' clause in contracts that empower the author to retain copyright to reproduce research for academic and research purposes. Kansas University includes a clause in their contracts that give them permission to use their research for teaching and research purposes and retain the right to make it available on public accessible Web sites.

Open Access Journals

The open access initiative is aimed at making scholarly research freely available via the Internet. Open access journals are journals available on the Internet for academics, researchers and the general public. The open access journal philosophy received a tremendous stimulus with the birth of the *Public Library of Science* (PLoS). At its conception 30,000 scientists promised their support in terms of submitting research. The first open access journal to emerge was PLoS Biology in the year 2003 which was received with great enthusiasm. In the publishing arena the Biomed Central publishing house embarked on free access to peer-reviewed journals. Recently the *Directory of Open Access Journals* (DOAJ) made open access journals available covering different languages and subjects.

Open Access Archives

Many leading universities are setting up electronic archives as depositories for their research output and are granting access to it. There are plans in progress to use theses archives as a platform to provide open access journals. The *Massachusetts Institute of Technology* (MIT) has made software freely available for managing electronic archives. Currently there are approximately 140 universities that have established open access archives. The number of journals held in these archives have increased from 20,000 in 2001 to 1.3 million in 2003. Although this is still fairly insignificant compared to the 2 million peer reviewed journals printed annually it nevertheless sends out a clear warning signal to commercial publishers of what is to come. In Europe the Open Archives Forum was established. The goal of this forum is to establish electronic archives and make it globally available.

e-Books

There are various definitions for e-books but e-books are essentially published books and reference materials that were digitised and are distributed electronically. In the year 2000 e-books were heralded as the new publishing revolution. One market research company predicted that by 2005 there would be 1.9 million users. Forrester Research predicted that income generated from e-book sales would increase from $9 million in 2000 to $414 million in 2004.

Unfortunately e-book popularity never rose to expected heights. Despite the negativity surrounding e-books it had not demised completely. There are still some companies dealing with e-books that are profitable and experiencing growth. One of the first commercial e-book services, NetLibrary, was established by OCLC in 1998. The NetLibrary collection has since grown to over 400 000 titles. The shortcoming in the NetLibrary system is the fact that an e-book can only be used by one user at a time. Questia, another commercial e-book service went live in 2001. Their target market was students and they employed librarians to manage collection development. By 2003 Questia had more than 400 000 titles from more than 200 publishers.

Advantages of e-Books

E-books have numerous advantages. There are no printing, storage, warehousing and shipping costs. Consequently e-books can be published at costs much lower than conventional books. Additional advantages are online availability, keyword-searching capability, cross-referencing, adjustable fonts, electronic bookmarks and imbedded audio. Updating e-books will be easier than re-editing conventional books. From an academic library point of view benefits would include cost savings in terms of shelving, binding, circulation, overdue notices and management of fines.

All needed would be a person to maintain the collection and a person to manage user accounts. Print collections in academic libraries are very expensive to acquire and maintain. E-books are also environmentally friendly in the sense that no tree pulping is necessary to for its production. The flaws in current e-book technology will be overcome. When that day dawns e-books being much cheaper to produce and publish than printed books as well as economies of scale will tip the balance in favour of e-books.

Disadvantages

The devices needed to read e-books are relatively expensive, *e.g.*, hand held devices, PC's and laptops. In order to minimize piracy publishers use proprietary hardware devices and software platforms. This lack of universal standards is a problem. The question many ask is whether e-books pose a threat to libraries. Can it eventually put libraries out of business. Although e-books did not take off as well as expected within the public domain, the use of e-books at schools, colleges and universities are rapidly increasing.

Use of e-Books

Falk refers to research done by Forrester that indicated that 4 million e-books were sold at campus stores in year 2000. Forrester forecasted that by year 2005 e-book sales should have increased to 140 million. Research indicates that students are developing a preference for e-books above printed books. At the University of Rochester Rush Rhees Library course reserve section students were exposed to printed books and their e-book equivalents. Statistics compiled on a weekly base indicated a three to one preference in favour of the e-books.

SOME OF THE PROBLEMS RELATING TO ELECTRONIC RESOURCES

Online full text implies availability of articles rather that the entire content of a particular journal. The complete contents of a publication are seldom put into a full text database. This implies that an author one might have seen in a physical publication may not be traceable in electronic format. This predicament also applies to archiving where there is uncertainty about the percentage of a journals content that is archived in digital format.

Another concern is that the academic library in a sense has lost control over the resources it make available to its users. When academic libraries subscribe to aggregator databases, *e.g.* EbscoHost or ProQuest they subscribe to a service, a list of titles bundled together of which many are useful and many not so useful. One of the problems is that aggregators sometimes drop titles. Typically this would happen when publishers withdraw all their titles.

The Chronicle of Higher Education has reported in 2003 that Elsevier has been removing articles from aggregator files because of various reasons, *e.g.*, scientific misconduct, plagiarism and errors. On the Web there are masses of information available. With search engines, *e.g.* Google or Yahoo one may find useful information and record the URL or title. There is however no guarantee when one wants to revisit the site that it may still be available. Sites on the Web sometimes disappear overnight. An organisation may have merged with another one or the host server might have become dysfunctional.

The quality of information available on the Web is also sometimes questionable. Any individual with access to the Web and basic hardware and software can publish on the Web regardless of whether the person's views are factually correct. On the Web are more than an estimated billion Web pages and this create problems for users of the academic library to distinguish between what is useful or not.

Another problem is that search engines cover only a small portion of what is what is available on the Web. There are lots of information behind firewalls and thus inaccessible. Many crawlers of search engines only focus on html and ignore graphics. Generally ASCII files will not be found. To assist users academic library services should try and inform users when sites have relocated or are no longer available.

CHANGES IN THE EDUCATIONAL ENVIRONMENT

ICT have changed every fibre of society including education. Lifelong learning has become essential. A very competitive working environment has influenced this. Even educational methodologies have changed. Greater interaction between learner, educator and material is becoming the norm. Learners have greater choices in terms of curricula. The 24 hour networked classroom became reality leading to the birth of the virtual library.

Network technologies and new educational methodologies have empowered learners, given them a greater measure of control and participation in the learning process and enabled network interaction with both fellow students and lecturers. Change in institutions of higher education will compel academic libraries to change accordingly. The most dramatic change according to visionaries will take place in distance education. This was a direct influence of the Internet. When the day dawns when distance education becomes the norm, universities the way we know them may vanish and virtual libraries may become a reality. Recently an author warned that the railroad managers overlooked the fact that they were in the transport business. He noted that universities must remember they are in the education business and not the campus business. If campuses disappear libraries will disappear.

There are already examples of cyberspace universities, *e.g.* Phoenix. If academics should fail to restructure their institutions' external forces will do it. Of cardinal importance is to focus on what education wants to achieve and how one can fulfill it. Survival of the academic library will depend on its ability to continuously reshape and reorganise.

Distance Education

New technologies driven by ICT innovation have enhanced the virtual delivery of academic programmes and stimulated unparalleled growth of distance education at institutions of higher learning. The phenomenal growth in distance education technologies has lead to an escalation in the availability of online academic programmes and a tremendous increase in remote users. In order to support these programmes academic librarians have developed excellent portfolios and programmes for remote students. One aspect that is neglected is evaluation of these programmes.

What is of critical importance is to establish how these programmes are used, which ones are used more frequently than others and why. Monash University library in Australia provides online curriculum content to their students all over the world. The university library provides online access to more than 440 online databases, 140,000 e-books and 20,000 e-journal subscriptions. Apart from full text databases and e-books the university library also provides digital audio recordings of lectures that become available minutes after conclusion of lectures.

According to Ho Monash University library has made a paradigm shift to a complete new service module that utilises e-commerce technologies. Moyo is of the opinion that the transformation in distance education has created a need for distance librarianship.

Changes in Scholarly Communication

The rising of the Internet and subsequent Web during the 1990's has resulted in the decline of the printed journal as the principal medium of scholarly publication. The costs of journals have increased dramatically driven by commercial publishers trying to control research content. This resulted in depriving many researchers of access to needed resources. The Web has also made fast and easy electronic publication possible and has increased direct communication between researchers.

Publishers immediately started making electronic versions of printed journals available on the Web. This was however seen as perpetuating the status quo in a new medium. Scholars started seeing in the new technology the potential to develop a new model for publishing research and an opportunity to return ownership of scholarly output to the rightful owners of the research.

These sentiments were driven by shortcomings in existing scholarly journal publishing which were:

- The time to publish an article was to too long.
- The existing model demanded transfer of copyright to the publishers.
- A too rigid peer review system that tends to favour publication of authors from the more prestigious institutions.
- Journal prices had become unaffordable.

One of the outcomes of this dissatisfaction was the birth of the e-print which is essentially an electronic version of a research paper. E-prints lead to the development of e-print repositories that are an archive of e-prints accessible to the public. Some of the advantages of e-print repositories are the reduction of publishing barriers, increased visibility of research and rapid dissemination of research results to a wide audience.

Consortia Collaboration

Initially libraries got involved in consortia in order to reduce costs particularly with regard to the acquisition of e-resources. Consortia development is thus an attempt to maximize limited resources through co-operation and resource sharing. In the consortia scenario the emphasis is on access to information rather than ownership. Consortia collaboration provides more power when it comes to negotiating contracts. It also provides a platform for libraries to co-operate in terms of services. Nowadays libraries also turn to consortia to provide advice and guidance in complex decision-making. The input of consortia is also valuable in terms of evaluating e-resources in terms of quality, different options, *e.g.*, whether to subscribe to journals or pay article-by-article.

The South African Scenario

In terms of network infrastructure South Africa is not on par with first world countries where consortia cooperation is very effective. For the establishment of an information society in South Africa proper connectivity infrastructure is an absolute prerequisite. There is an uneven distribution of telecommuni-cations infrastructure across South Africa stemming from the political ideologies of the apartheid government. This inequity is also prevalent in South African academic libraries. Institutions for the privileged white people were well financed and resourced under the apartheid regime. Institutions for blacks were under funded and thus under resourced; hence the distinction between advantaged and historically disadvantaged institutions. Because of this there are great differences in wealth and the collections of academic libraries.

In South Africa there are five academic library consortia.:

1. CALICO (Cape Library Cooperative) based in Cape Town.
2. ESAL (Eastern Seaboard Association of Libraries based in Kwazulu-Natal.
3. FRELICO (Free State Libraries and Information Consortium) based in Free State.
4. Gaelic (Gauteng and Environs Library Consortium) based in Gauteng.
5. SEALS (South Eastern Academic Libraries System in the Eastern Cape.

Essential for the development of successful consortia is low cost tariffs coupled with high bandwith connectivity. Academic institutions constantly engaged with government agencies to achieve this ideal. Library consortia can also be invaluable in assisting member libraries with change management because "An organisation needs external coaches to catalyse, guide and facilitate a change process", the reason being that people within the academic library are sometimes to closely involved with daily activities to see things objectively. An outside view often helps to see things in the right perspective.

ICT MANAGEMENT ISSUES

Libraries are caught midstream between print versus a digital setup. To navigate the transition from print to digital remains enormously challenging. Rapid ICT development had resulted in lots of incompatible systems being used within libraries. To manage ICT is a complex and daunting task. To select the right ICT technologies is a major management issue. It is very difficult in a world where hardware and software changes at a phenomenal rate.

The shift in the academic library from printed resources to electronic resources that are accessible via campus networks or remotely and the fact that users can even request services via the network has lead to a decline in users visiting the library. The growing electronic nature of the academic library is resulting in it becoming less visible as a physical entity to its users.

What is also disturbing is the fact that users are often oblivious to the fact that they are using library resources because of the seamlessness of access. Users are not aware of the fact that to make those resources available are costly in terms of subscriptions, infrastructure and staff. Academic libraries need to find a way to reverse this scenario of the library loosing its visibility. Hooper suggests that the academic library should use ICT to stimulate interaction between user and the library. It should be done in such a way that the user could identify with the academic library providing the service and experience a sense of ownership.

As a starting point the academic library can interact with the user relating to loans, database searches and other services available. It is also important to create an environment where the user can provide feedback relating to service shortcomings and suggestions that could lead to improvement. Stakeholder relationships are also very important. It is of vital importance for the academic library to ensure that their operations dovetail with the strategic goals of the university it supports. In these days where accountability is becoming the norm it is essential to run operations in such a way that the academic library at any point is in a position to provide proof of the value of its services as a return on investment made by the university authority.

THE FUTURE ROLE OF THE ACADEMIC LIBRARIAN

INTRODUCTION

In 2005, the decision of the University of Wales at Bangor to make all of its subject librarians redundant caused shock and terror throughout the academic library world, both in the United Kingdom and beyond. Was this an aberration, or was it a straw in the wind? The future of the liaison librarian in the university is an issue that currently occupies many minds. It is naturally of prime concern to the liaison librarians themselves, but it is also a significant issue for library managers. There is an interesting range of opinions on the subject, all claiming to plot emerging trends by extrapolating from current observations, and all pleasantly unhindered by empirical data. One study, at least, is candid enough to admit that "the future is difficult to predict".

It is normal now to find comments in the press along these lines: "with users switching to electronic access to resources instead of books, and using search engines instead of librarians to track down information, libraries face a struggle to remain relevant". Not surprisingly, the library profession's view of the future is largely positive, with rallying cries such as: "there are no limits for academic librarians in the 21st century, there are, however, endless opportunities". We can only polish our crystal balls and guess at what the future may hold. It is nonetheless interesting to see what the profession has to say about its future, and this survey will review some of the recent writing on the subject.

INFORMATION LITERACY

As many traditional library roles began to disappear in the early 1990s, the profession seized upon information literacy as its salvation. Academic librarians began the often painful process of reinventing themselves as teachers who would guide students through the complex process of information discovery and evaluation. To many, this is still seen as a key role. Rader, for example, in describing the work of liaison librarians, says that "above all, they strive to ensure that all students learn appropriate information skills to help them achieve information fluency and become productive members of the information society." But do the students want to be taught? A recent survey of undergraduate students in the United States found that "respondents generally say they have 'good' to 'very good' skills for... the university's online library system."

However the researchers warn that "this response is likely overstated, considering that the literature on self-assessment of skills finds that students overrate their skills in general, men more so than women". There seems no reason to think that this will change. As Reyes puts it, "students want to be self-sufficient and have unmediated, immediate access to information. The very changes in our information technologies have changed this information seeking behaviour, giving the control that once belonged to libraries over to the users."

Perhaps the more important question is: how do academic staff view the role of the librarian in educating students to find and evaluate information? A recent survey in the United Kingdom found that "the great majority of librarians see teaching information literacy and offering subject-based expertise as core roles for them, and central to what they do; researchers are generally supportive, but more equivocal about whether these are core as distinct from ancillary roles for librarians". A 2000 survey of academics and librarians in Canada found that "in the area of teaching/instruction, there was a sharp contrast between the librarians' willingness to collaborate and the faculty's lack of interest". Could it be that the material we are presenting in our classes is too elementary to meet the needs of our students? As Reyes remarks, "it is no longer sufficient to teach the mechanics of a single database. We can now move on to make correlations between keyword searching and rhetorical analysis in order to illustrate the use of language in scholarship." But are we really ready to move on? Asher argues that

- what a librarian can't do... is teach students to extract information from resources, theorise, or locate meaning. Teaching students to analyse data, evaluate ideas, and develop a philosophical understanding framed within a subject discipline are elements of information literacy that lie outside the expertise of most librarians. Universities hire academics to do that.

REFERENCE WORK

Many university libraries have reported a steady decline in enquiries at their reference desks, presumably because many students are now independently finding enough information for their needs. As Markey concluded "although research findings demonstrate that end users are not conducting sophisticated online searches, the vast majority are satisfied with their searches. In fact, percentages of users who express satisfaction with the results of their searches reach into the high seventies and beyond."

The consultation report that led to the redundancy of liaison librarians at the University of Wales at Bangor put it more bluntly "the process of literature searches is substantially de-skilled by online bibliographic resources". The recent literature repeatedly calls for more flexible delivery of information services.

For example, a report from the United States asserted that "future librarians will increasingly need to take their skills to the clients that need assistance. That model, sometimes referred to as 'place as library,' could be virtual or in person in remote site classrooms or offices, but the organisational model will change to accommodate the 'traveling' staff model". One American librarian has gone so far as to suggest that "librarians could even be assigned to live in dorms, in exchange for room and board, so that they are truly available, visible, and a part of the college student's world".

Presumably only young, single librarians need apply for these positions, and this also suggests that there may be problems in recruiting staff to provide these innovative outreach services. When the library at George Mason University in Virginia opened a new information commons, it specially recruited staff to work in this very different environment. Even so, some staff were dissatisfied, especially because of the long opening hours. The manager suggested "perhaps we should begin to look to the retail environment for our recruits". Clearly she has a point: to refugees from Wal-Mart, any library must look like a pleasant work environment.

It remains to be seen whether the refugees from Wal-Mart will make good librarians. The previously cited IMLS Task Force report suggests that virtual reference services could be outsourced. In a similar vein, the director of the Law Library at the University of Colorado at Boulder has suggested that in the future faculty can expect round-the-clock reference and research assistance. However, they should not be surprised if their midnight reference questions are answered by someone on the other side of the world. Computer tech support has already moved overseas, pioneering the way for other services to follow. Why shouldn't libraries form worldwide consortia to provide 24/7 research assistance, for practical and for financial reasons?

This could be a boon when you have a request in the wee hours of the morning that calls for a straightforward answer, such as the identification of the source of a quotation, but it could mean less quality or less precision in responses requiring more complex research. A university librarian in England has argued that university libraries have not put sufficient staff resources into dealing with enquiries. He has developed plans for providing increased support for users, but admits that his plans are "not fully funded".

RESEARCH SUPPORT

If undergraduates are now finding much of the information they need via Google and Wikipedia, surely there is still a need for experienced librarians to meet the more advanced information needs of researchers? A recent survey of researchers at Deakin University in Victoria reported that "a recurring theme of the interviews was the need for research assistants to undertake information seeking, in particular library-related information seeking. While this was commonplace with many senior researchers, it was a very attractive proposition to those without such assistance and/or those with limited research funding". Funding is indeed the key issue here and many libraries will be unable to afford to provide experienced, highly qualified librarians to provide in-depth research assistance to all postgraduate students and academic staff. Brookman and her colleagues discussed the advantages of having an "informationist" attached to clinical teams in a UK hospital trust, but concluded that "funding is not available for the full implementation of the informationist model". On the other hand, there are areas where funding is more generous, and in these situations it may be possible to provide high level research assistance. Bintliff sees her law library providing such services in the future:

- Faculty can expect more customized information coming from the library, more information that is tailored to support an individual's specific scholarship and teaching. Faculty will find more information 'pushed' at them even before they ask for it, as librarians use 'faculty interest databases' to track and anticipate faculty requests. Librarians will capitalise on the ever-faster ability to receive, assemble, and disseminate information via electronic communications. In addition, librarians will work with faculty to compile an array of information and sources adapted to their specific needs.

Even where funding is available, there is still the question of the level of disciplinary knowledge required to provide research support at an advanced level. The study of clinical librarians conducted by Brookman and her colleagues looked at the possibility of librarians going beyond information retrieval to evaluation and appraisal and found that "those who argued against having the C[linical] L[ibrarian] evaluating the literature, put forward the argument that to critically appraise the sources it is necessary to have a clinical background and real knowledge of the context of the work."

Pagel reports that, for liaison librarians at Emory University in Georgia, "subject expertise is becoming the norm." Advanced subject expertise, probably at doctoral level, will be necessary if liaison librarians are to convince academics that a librarian can be a real partner in the research process. When Ducas and

Michaud- Oystryk surveyed academics at the University of Manitoba, they found that, on the question of collaboration with librarians on research projects, "performing a literature search... was [an] area where both groups saw potential for collaboration. In all other areas, faculty were much less receptive to collaboration with librarians."

A recent survey of academics and librarians in the UK found that both groups agreed in not seeing a core role for librarians as "subject-based experts embedded in departments or research groups".

INFORMATION TECHNOLOGY

- Librarians and library staff have to be very tech savvy, especially given the popularity of information commons and the ubiquity of information workstations... The major challenge will be retraining the staff member who prefers to keep doing what he/she has been doing in the same way it has been done, who sees their value to students and researchers as one shared with their traditional mode rather than be attuned to actual values perceived by the younger generation of students and faculty who have been educated within a technological environment.

There is general agreement in the literature that liaison librarians of the future will need sophisticated IT skills. A survey of an international group of senior academic librarians revealed that, with regard to skills of future academic librarians, "IT and communication skills remain at the top". That is not to say that liaison librarians will need degrees in information technology, but they will need to be highly skilled at keeping abreast of developments which will be of use to them and their clients:

- University libraries, both in teaching and in research institutions, can no longer provide core services without assistance from and cooperation with central Information Systems departments... Learning to work with those cultures and seeking collaboration at every turn is essential. Learning to evaluate technology and make technology-based decisions is critical for the university library staff in every functional area.

Burnett and Bonnici have examined some of the questions that this raises for the training and accreditation of librarians. They argue that "the future of librarianship is seriously implicated... by the demonstrated inability of the discipline of information studies... to establish its claim to a unique body of abstract knowledge."

These concerns are perhaps vindicated by Ducas and Michaud-Oystryk, whose survey of librarians and academics at the University of Manitoba found that "in the area of information technology, both librarians (49 per cent) and faculty (43 per cent) ranked assistance with retrieving an electronic document the highest." If retrieving an electronic document is the acme of their IT skills (real or perceived), liaison librarians definitely have cause for concern.

OTHER ROLES

There are a range of other tasks that are seen as being important for the liaison librarian of the future. A UK study reported that:

- There are... a number of additional roles that librarians are interested in developing: providing specialist advice in copyright and I[ntellectual] P[roperty] R[ights] issues; managing non-technical metadata issues; acting as technology specialists in facilitating access to electronic resources; and – most importantly – managing institutional repositories of digital information. With respect to copyright advice, some libraries already employ specialist lawyers; others told us that they had taken the role into the library from other places (*e.g.* the registry) where it had previously resided".

A recent American report on the top ten assumptions for the future of academic libraries stated that "there will be an increased emphasis on digitising collections, preserving digital archives, and improving methods of data storage and retrieval... Librarians should collaborate with disciplinary colleagues in the curation of data as part of the research process". The same report predicted that "distance learning will be an increasingly more common option in higher education", and a recent UK study found that many librarians saw the facilitation of e-learning as a core role for the future, although academics did not appear to share that opinion.

The recent literature has surprisingly little to say about collection development, but at least one study maintains "that the importance of research library collections only continues to increase".

Phipps however is less certain: "will we continue to 'build' collections? Oh, I know, there will always be books. And for at least five more years the dominant form will be print. Then what?" Some academic library managers have forecast a more extreme scenario where "libraries may be replaced altogether by a single net collection operated by government or other institution". This latter scenario may not be far-fetched: in Germany the federal government has already negotiated nation-wide licences for databases from Emerald and Springer. Barry makes an interesting point about career structure:

- A challenge for the profession is the need to create job structures so that the only way to progress financially in the field is not through management positions. Administrative work takes time away from the continued skill development needed to stay current with the rapidly evolving information environment. Placing high performers in these positions often does nothing but waste the time and energy required for maintaining currency and effectiveness in their positions.

CONCLUSION

From reading the literature, a composite picture emerges of the liaison librarian of the future. It shows a young, outgoing professional who is comfortable hanging out in campus cafes and student halls of residence and able to communicate easily with undergraduate students. At the same time, he or she will be a subject expert, with advanced knowledge of the literature of one or more disciplines and able to work closely with academic staff and postgraduate students. On top of this, our liaison librarian will be extremely proficient with technology and an expert with various software packages used for teaching and research. Clearly there is nobody who fits this Identikit picture. It is easy to see why so many of our current liaison librarians feel under stress. We cannot go on pretending that liaison librarians can provide such an impossibly wide range of services. So what will become of the liaison librarian's role? Perhaps it will split into a variety of roles, each re-aligning itself with other roles to create a new range of professionals. In the university of the future, we may see a group of Learning Support staff, who provide undergraduate students with training and support in a range of study, information and writing skills. We may see another group of Research Support staff, who combine an information specialist role with a more conventional research assistant role and are attached to academic or research units throughout the university. And we will certainly find IT staff who specialise in applications used in teaching, elearning and research, probably as part of the university's central IT support infrastructure. The final word belongs to a reference librarian at Queen's University in Ontario:

- For librarians, two scenarios loom on the horizon. The optimistic or allencompassing future demands that librarians be enthusiastic and flexible enough to create a dynamic learning environment. These librarians will be adept at creating an intellectual landscape densely populated with electronic information sources and rich with a variety of services tailored to shifting needs. The pessimistic future is a passive one where our services and spaces are underused and irrelevant to students and faculty. This future is likely to evolve unless librarians respond creatively to the impact of electronic resources in academic libraries. Administrators who fail to make the transition will see their institutions fall far behind their counterparts. Librarians who cannot or will not make the transition will witness the loss of their workplace as they know it and lose their roles in it.

THE IMPACT OF INFORMATION TECHNOLOGY ON ACADEMIC LIBRARIES

In the 1990s, academic libraries are undergoing unprecedented change deriving from a combination of accelerating prices of library materials and space, an enormous increase in the amount and types of materials available, and rapid development in electronic technologies. Whatever the local differences in academic librarianship in the countries today, there is no question that information technology is transforming research, scholarship, teaching and learning, and with it, the role of libraries and librarians. Day strongly believes we are already seeing a shift from measuring library services in terms of size and comprehensiveness of collections to one of measuring the quality of service delivery: delivery of documents irrespective of origin, increasingly in electronic form, with access to the electronic library from the users' desktop.

THE EMERGENCE OF DIGITAL LIBRARIES

Definition of Digital Library

A working definition of digital libraries provided by Waters are: "Organisations that provide the resources, including specialised staff, to select, structure, offer intellectual access to, distribute, preserve the integrity of, and ensure the persistence over time of collections of digital works so that they are readily and economically available for use by a defined community or set of communities."

Digital Libraries Concepts

The digital library concepts requires librarians to be information architects in order to build effective, scalable Web sites to serve the digital demands of patrons. 'Just in time", a method introduced in the early '80s to manage inventory, is now an expectation of consumers for any business providing online. 'Just in time' applied to libraries is information delivered "where you need it, when you need it, and in a format that is useful. This strategy requires libraries increasingly to adopt 24/365 service to keep up with the demands of their patrons for core services, and to offer services through what is often called the digital, electronic, or virtual library or reference desk.

Technical Requirements of a Digital Library

The United States National Information Infrastructure programme has identified a number of critical technical challenges that need to be resolved if usage of electronic networking is to be both simple and efficient.

The listing of them below illustrates that all are important for the proper running of a digital library:

- Network components that can handle voice, and text simultaneously, and can operate seamlessly
- Information appliances and services that can provide access and services in a scalable, efficient and inter-operable way
- Information access techniques that can enable efficient searches of large distributed information repositories, making the myriad of information resources understandable

- Multimedia information technologies that can, for example, synchronise and integrate real-time delivery of voice, and can support search and retrieval based on image content
- Infrastructure for application development that can provide common solutions
- Technologies that are dependable and manageable
- Technologies that are easy to use and services that are accessible by users with widely varying skills, experiences, abilities and backgrounds
- Inter-operability among heterogeneous systems will be required on an unprecedented scale
- Security and privacy technologies that are easy to use and provide appropriate levels of security to suit the requirements, cost constraints and convenience of the end user
- Technologies and services that provide portability, mobility and ubiquity.

The Roles of Digital Libraries in the Academic Environment

Researcher provide a comprehensive remarks of the roles of digital libraries in teaching and learning. A library is fundamentally an organised set of resources, which include human services as well as the entire spectrum of media. Libraries have physical components such as space, equipment, and storage media; intellectual components such as collection policies that determine what materials will be included and organisational schemes that determine how the collection is accessed; and people who manage the physical and intellectual components and interact with users to solve information problems.

Libraries serve at least four roles in learning:

1. *First, they serve a practical role in sharing expensive resources:* Physical resources such as books and periodicals, films and videos, software and electronic databases, and specialised tools such as projectors, graphics equipment and cameras are shared by a community of users. Human resources—librarians support instructional programmes by responding to the requests of academicians and students and by initiating activities for teachers and students. Responsive services include maintaining reserve materials, answering reference questions, providing bibliographic instruction, developing media packages, recommending books or films, and teaching users how to use materials. Proactive services include selective dissemination of information to faculty and students, initiating thematic events, collaborating with instructors to plan instruction, and introducing new instructional methods and tools. In these ways, libraries serve to allow instructors and students to share expensive materials and expertise.

2. *Second, libraries serve a cultural role in preserving and organising artifacts and ideas:* Great works of literature, art, and science must be preserved and made accessible to future learners. Libraries preserve objects through careful storage procedures, policies of borrowing and use, and repair and maintenance as needed. In addition to preservation, libraries ensure access to materials through indexes, catalogs, and other finding aids that allow learners to locate items appropriate to their needs.
3. Third, libraries serve social and intellectual roles in bringing together people and ideas: This is distinct from the practical role of sharing resources in that libraries provide a physical place for academicians and learners to meet outside the structure of the classroom, thus allowing people with different perspectives to interact in a knowledge space that is both larger and more general than that shared by any single discipline or affinity group. Browsing a catalouge in a library provides a global view for people engaged in specialised study and offers opportunities for serendipitous insights or alternative views. In many respects, libraries serve as centers of inter-disciplinarily—places shared by learners from all disciplines. Digital libraries extend such inter-disciplinarity by making diverse information resources available beyond the physical space shared by groups of learners. One of the greatest benefits of digital libraries is bringing together people with formal, informal, and professional learning missions.

- Formal learning is systematic and guided by instruction. Formal learning takes place in courses offered at schools of various kinds and in training courses or programmes on the job. The important roles that libraries serve in formal learning are illustrated by their physical prominence on university campuses and the number of courses that make direct use of library services and materials. By making the broad range of information resources, digital libraries open new learning opportunities for global rather than strictly local communities.

Much learning in life is informal—opportunistic and strictly under the control of the learner. Learners take advantage of other people, mass media, and the immediate environment during informal learning. The public library system that developed in the U.S., in the late nineteenth century has been called the 'free university', since public libraries were created to provide free access to the world's knowledge.

Public libraries provide classic non-fiction books, a wide range of periodicals, reference sources, and audio and video tapes so that patrons can learn about topics of their own choosing at their own pace and style. Just as computing technology and world-wide telecommunications networks are beginning to change what is possible in formal classrooms, they are changing how individuals pursue personal learning missions. Professional learning refers to the on going learning adults engage in to do their work and to improve their work-related knowledge and skills. In fact, for many professionals, learning is the central aspect of their work. Like informal learning, it is mainly self-directed, but unlike formal or informal learning, it is focused on a specific field closely linked to job performance, aims to be comprehensive, and is acquired and applied longitudinally. Since professional learning affects job performance, corporations and government agencies support libraries with information resources specific to the goals of the organisation.

The main information resources for professional learning, however, are personal collections of books, reports, and files; subscriptions to journals; and the human networks of colleagues nurtured through professional meetings and various communications. Many of the data sets and computational tools of digital libraries were originally developed to enhance professional learning. The information resources—both physical and human—that support these types of learning are customised for specific missions and have traditionally been physically separated, although common technologies such as printing, photography, and computing are found across all settings. This situation, is depicted in fig.

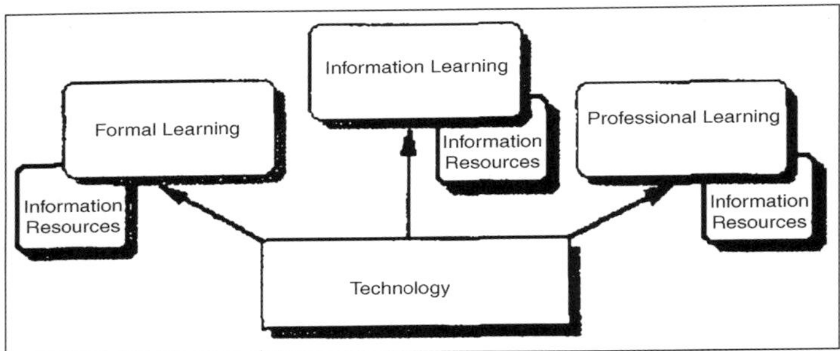

Fig. Current Models of Technological Support for Types of Learning

Digital libraries combine technology and information resources to allow remote access, breaking down the physical barriers between resources. Although these resources will remain specialised to meet the needs of specific communities of learners, digital libraries will allow teachers and students to take advantage of wider ranges of materials and communicate with people outside the formal learning environment. This will allow more integration of the different types of learning, as depicted in fig.

Although not all students or academicians in formal learning settings will use information resources beyond their circumscribed curriculum and not all professionals will want to interact even occasionally with novices, digital libraries will allow learners of all types to share resources, time and energy, and expertise to their mutual benefits.

Characteristics of Digital Libraries

A few of the now familiar characteristics that should distinguish digital libraries from traditional libraries.

The Evolving DL Faces Many Unknowns

For all of its problems and challenges, the print-on-paper environment is well known to us and largely understood. We know how to manage it; we are painfully aware of its costs; and we are familiar with its benefits and its limitations. Our digital library future, by contrast, is full of unknowns and unsolved problems. The list of these is too long and too well rehearsed to need reciting. In addition, the underlying digital technology continues to change. So, even if we could discover the unknowns and solve the problems today, we could not freeze our solutions. Consequently, we are faced with the prospect of creating organisations that are flexible and that accommodate changes, including large changes, easily and regularly.

The DL will Offer Ubiquitous Access

Digital libraries will be designed to support a great range of users at a distance rather than being limited to those on the premises. In other words, unless we create restraints, any and everyone with the necessary hardware can use our digital libraries. This characteristic means both that we should expect a larger variation in the types of users and that as suggested, be responsible to determine whether and what sort of limits will we place on access.

The DL will Host Remote Users

Since digital library users will ordinarily be off the premises, anew, entirely different set of challenges will arise with regard to what we have known as reference and other help services. Our experience with help services has largely been face to face and interpersonal, and efforts to create sophisticated, remote help services are still rudimentary today.

The DL will be more Fully Technology Based

From the creation of metadata to the provision of information services and training, digital libraries will be predominantly technology based. This stands in stark contrast to the essential character of traditional, residential libraries. This is problematical not only because librarians are reluctant to design systems that are technology as opposed to people based but also because often librarians do not possess the necessary expertise to do so. Yet we are not eager to let the process out of our hands. On the positive side, much of the cost of traditional libraries has resided in the manual processes and procedures. While no one supposes that digital libraries will be inexpensive, we should design them in so far as possible to avoid many of these costly manual procedures.

The DL will be open and Customisable and a Part of a Much Larger Information Smorgasbord

Though the qualifications of a digital library can be conveniently limited by definition, they cannot be so conveniently limited by practice. There is a debate over whether or not the Internet is a library. An approach to this question is rather more pragmatic: if growing millions of individuals use the Internet regularly as the source for information on all subjects, it is a library. For all its limitations, it may be a very poor library but it is one nevertheless. For this reason, it is unlikely that our digital libraries will monopolise the library activities of our constituencies in the same way that our traditional libraries have. Digital users today have already sampled the smorgasbord information world of the Internet and have correspondingly broadened their appetites. In addition, it is increasingly common for information users to desire to customise information retrieval, a desire that reduces patience with our more inflexible information systems.

The DL will Offer Distinctive Functions

As surely as digital libraries will discard functions common in traditional libraries, they will necessarily concern themselves with new functions. Commonly named among these are such activities as intellectual property management and database creation and management, the latter being normally associated with administrative computing and data processing. In terms of functionality, therefore, digital libraries will differ markedly from traditional libraries.

Radically Altered Job Descriptions for Information Professionals Will Evolve

To the degree that digital libraries are the business of librarians, this means the incorporation of radically changed or new functions in the librarians portfolios. Digital libraries ignore old boundaries and fall across lines currently marking divisions between libraries, computing organisations, and telephony/ networking departments. Therefore, that digital libraries are not solely the province of librarians and that the new constellation of functions inherent in digital libraries will require the evolution of new information professionals with job descriptions that are as yet unspecified.

Such new job descriptions will reflect new combinations of skills represented in these currently distinct agencies along with those from other areas, such as intellectual property law and business.

As Suggested, See New Focuson Original Materials

In the rapidly passing era of traditional libraries, most of our resources and energies were expended on acquiring, organising, managing, and explaining commercially published materials. Because of the slow but steady movement of commercial publishing into the Internet environment, it is likely in the future that access to commercially published digital resources will increasingly be provided directly by publishers.

The role of libraries as gateways to commercial academic materials, therefore, will diminish. At the same time, however, because of the capabilities of technology, digital libraries will increasingly focus on providing access to original materials, both those born digitally and those converted from analog formats. The effect of this will be to enrich vastly the research potential of our resources and to provide new opportunities for our institutions to benefit from the potential commercial value of such holdings. The new content paradigm for digital libraries will be raw, source materials.

The DL will have Commercial Characteristics

As a result of the shift in digital libraries to original materials, as suggested, find the means to exploit the commercial value of such materials to a degree never before possible. Digital libraries, therefore, must from the outset be designed to support commercial activities. Correspondingly, support for digital libraries will likely include business plans, replete with market assessments, commercial partnerships, and new concerns for cost-effectiveness and year-end financial performance. In other words, because of the value of their data, digital libraries will have an imperative to function in a more business-like, for-profit manner.

As Suggested, Experience New Competition

We must be increasingly aware that, as representatives of primarily traditional, not-for-profit institutions, we do not enjoy sole ownership of the future of digital libraries. Even as we gather here, a host of new competitors for the business of education and the distribution of knowledge and information resources is assembling.

For this reason, we must not presume that the digital library world will evolve to our specifications, especially if we work on digital libraries as a closed community of librarians. Just as the world-wide-web swept over us and, with unbelievable swiftness, changed the nature of our communication environment, so too may we be over-washed by some new inescapable digital library model from unanticipated sources.

Custom, User-Built Digital Libraries

Apart from large commercial interests, some user-built, highly focused information storage and retrieval services, such as the NASA Astrophysics Data System or the on-line journal of high energy physics, suggest that elements of the digital library may best be developed by the users. Creating these technically customised data and information retrieval systems requires intimate familiarity with the subject matter, jargon, and academic habits of the user communities and likely could not be accomplished by librarians. Clearly we must ponder the implications of these examples for our assumptions and methodologies.

WORKPLACE ENVIRONMENT IN THE DIGITAL ERA

What might we expect of the workplace environment in the new millennium academic library?

Libraries will take Over Campus Computer Centers

Academic libraries will pursue bolder organisational experimentation. This will include focusing on the information and services needs of users. There will be wider distribution of administrative responsibility and authority, as hierarchical structures are broken down and key activities and operations are integrated. We can expect more fluid and flexible structures, enhancement of team and small group processes, and more collegial and collaborative working relationships. Continuing a trend that is already taking root, the academic library will assume administrative control of campus academic computing services. With the expanding mandate for accountability, there will be a greater focus on data collection and analysis. This will entail a rethinking of standards and benchmarks for assessment and more creative approaches to defining output measures and quality impact.

Academic Library Funding will Remain Stable

Responsibility-center budget models will expand across higher education, embracing the library. This relatively new system of distributed financial authority places libraries into a more rigourous fiscal relationship with academic programmes. Units will be taxed to support library operations, requiting intensified communication and accountability. Library funding will remain stable. The greatest growth will continue to be in collection and information access programmes.

The library budget as a percentage of total campus budget will not change substantially. Library development and fundraising activities will accelerate, as more colleges and universities pursue external funding from private, corporate, and foundation sources.

This will involve a greater focus on endowments rather than on raisin funds for specified capital projects. Library budgets will increasingly fund research and development, infrastructure upgrade and replacement capabilities, and risk capital for innovation and advancement. The trend towards outsourcing of library operations and services will accelerate. We have already seen substantial success with serials jobbers, approval plans, binding, photocopy services, building maintenance, and security. This will lead to further experi-mentation in cataloging, collection maintenance, document delivery, and preservation.

Digital Acquisitions Budgets will Quadruple, and more, Eating up 40-50 Per cent of Acquisition Budgets

Print-based collections will remain dominant over the next decade. However, substantial resources will be allocated to the acquisition of electronic information, as reference sources and scholarly journals become computer-based and the economic feasibility of the scholarly monograph is increasingly questioned.

The percentage of investment in digital information will grow from the current 5-10 per cent of acquisitions budgets to 40-50 per cent. There will be an ongoing need for investment in local collection building, however, because what has not been acquired and preserved cannot be made available to users and other libraries. Even as collections continue to expand, the gap between what is being published and what we can afford to acquire will continue to grow. As a result, there will be a dramatic decline in ownership: new information accessible through libraries will plunge dramatically.

Nevertheless, the role of the academic library as a depository and gateway for government information will expand, as traditional print-based distribution models are eliminated.

The academic library will expand its role in scholarly publishing and communication. Project Muse at Johns Hopkins and High wire at Stanford, and the Journal Storage Project spawned by Mellon are examples of the library's central involvement in the management of current and retrospective electronic publications. More than 50 per cent of reference transactions will take place over campus networks

Patron-initiated and Controlled Services will Expand Rapidly

Libraries are already beginning to employ self-circulation, computer renewals and recalls, direct interlibrary loan, and document delivery. Full-text databases are becoming commonplace. The role of library staff as interpreters and mediators of user information transactions outside of local collections and services will decrease. Inside the university, the librarians' role as instructor will be formalised in a separate college department focusing on information and network literacy.

The technology of the World Wide Web that is evolving rapidly and unpredictable with the World Wide Web Consortium co-ordinates many activities in the areas of user interface, technology and society. The World Wide Web which was first announced by CERN in 1991, 2-3 years ago most people had not heard of it but by the end of 1996, there were 300,000 Web sites. Libraries are creating Web sites to help students to distinguish between relevant and irrelevant information.

The Web is likely to have a profound impact on education, communication and research activities of the universities.

Examples:

- *The Web empowers individuals:* They can easily reach a worldwide audience. Anyone can publish material that would never have been published in the past, and it is instantly available to millions of people.
- *The Web offers us the best of both worlds. Anyone can publish:* Their views cannot easily be suppressed, for good or ill. And anyone can comment, validate and offer judgement or advice.

The E-mail for example is extremely valuable for communication between the library and its users. Users Borrowers are expected to return their books within about two weeks. Very many do without reminders, but for those who need reminding, for some reason e-mail is a more effective spur than other methods. Online catalogs will increasingly define accessibility and not just local ownership. Thus the links between the local collection, the bibliography of a discipline, and the text of the publications/sources will become blurred. Remote use of online catalogs and databases is increasing rapidly at most colleges and universities.

An example, at Carnegie Mellon, already 75 per cent of catalouge use is remote. Remote access to information necessitates new instructional efforts. Levels of all traditional collection circulation activity - general and reserve borrowing and interlibrary loan - will decline significantly. They will fall prey to the rapid growth in options for electronic document delivery and the implementation of electronic reserve systems. The new electronic journals already offer facilities unavailable to users of paper.

These include:

- The ability to search for particular content within a paper or a complete journal;
- The ability to move easily between the table of contents of a journal and the abstract.
- Facilities to annotate articles to create a personal virtual filing cabinet and
- The ability to move quickly from the article you are reading to one which it cites in its references, and that includes forward citing, example the ability to go to articles that cited the one you have just been reading but which were published later.

An example, the American Astronomical Society has digitised into electronic form all the articles in the last 20 years of its journal which can now be accessed. Academic libraries will house and manage campus usability laboratories focusing on the needs of the user and will involve users as part of the design team.

Reference assistance to users will be electronic-based, with more than 50 per cent of transactions taking place over campus networks in batched or real-time communication, up from the current neglible levels. User profiles linked to SDI-type services will ensure delivery of relevant, cur-rent information to faculty and students on a scheduled basis. Academic librarians will increasingly pursue service goals as part of multiple consortia-based relationships. There will be joint investment in commercial services and acquisition of materials, in the purchase and use of technology, and in the hiring and development of staff.

Librarians will be Key Players in Developing Technological Innovations

Technology is currently poised to transform the fundamental nature of operations and services. From the early days of automation in the 1970s, academic libraries have moved to the cur-rent distribution and individualisation of technology and digital conversion and production. The challenge of the next decade will be the application of intelligence to the searching and retrieval capabilities of library systems.

The library will play a central role in the future development of the campus information environment. Rather than reacting to campus technology decisions, library staff will be integrally involved in determining what the next innovations will be. In the new world of the desktop workstation, academic libraries have a mandate to integrate high-speed access both to scholarly and institutional information. They need to provide tools for filtering, analysing, and manipulating information.

The predominant mainframe-based library management systems will be completely replaced by client-server technologies and applications that include robust full-text content and intelligent links to network-based sources. Automatic language translation software will be introduced, contributing to the development of a renewed global acquisitions programme for both based and digital sources. Campus network infrastructures will extend to all student, faculty, and staff work and living areas.

This will provide dependable connectivity for a growing array of applications, including distance learning. Wireless technology will be introduced and will receive its initial testing in library services. The retrospective digitising of library collections, particularly unique materials, will evolve as a central activity in academic libraries. Newly formed digital knowledge centers will manage the operations and partner with academic departments, publishers, and other libraries.

The Number of Librarians Working in Academic Libraries will Decrease

Libraries will increasingly view staff development as an integral and essential component of organisational success. With retooling of skills emerging as a three-to-five year cycle, participation in training courses will be mandated for all employee groups. As technology programmes advance and dominate library collection and service activities, technical staff as a percentage of total staff will increase significantly. This will produce a net reduction in the number of librarians employed in academic libraries.

It will also promote more effective working relationships between librarians and technologists, improving current conditions marred by distrust, inadequate communication, and lack of shared investment in planning. Academic libraries have not responded effectively to demographic cultural, racial, and ethnic shifts. They will collectively enter the next century still recognising the important trends producing a more pluralistic society but without well-developed and well-coordinated strategic directions for the role and contributions of the library. Telecommuting, which is increasingly commonplace in commercial settings, will become a viable and acceptable option for *academic* library employees.

An expanding array of library operations and services will be performed from home, enabling improved competitiveness for the recruitment and retention of talented staff. Academic libraries and library education programmes will collaborate on the development of internship and certification programmes for new professionals. This will be necessitated by the anticipated rapid increase in retirements in the next 15 years, as well as by the need to develop new approaches to the preparation and orientation of the next generation of academic librarians. An example of a university library, De Montfort University in the UK that has been developing a digital library environment for some years past.

The lessons they claim to have learnt might be summarised under the following headings:

- The digital library will develop more quickly than people think;
- The digital library is still a complex, unstable entity for which little theoretical structure exists.
- Because of this inherent instability, investment and implementation are still high risk.
- Digital libraries operate in a global environment: new products and services can become *de facto* standards very quickly.
- Co-operation is therefore a key factor for maintaining competitiveness.
- The content of the digital library will become the dominant factor.
- Copyright issues will be resolved or side-stepped because the market will demand it.
- The economics of the digital library are not yet well understood.
- Library jobs and roles will change very rapidly.

7

Online Cataloguing Library and e-Readers

INTRODUCTION

Online cataloguing, such as Dynix, has greatly enhanced the usability of catalogues, thanks to the rise of *MA*chine *R*eadable *C*ataloguing = MARC standards in the 1960s. Rules governing the creation of catalogue MARC records include not only formal cataloguing rul lges like AACR2 but also special rules specific to MARC, available from the Library of Congress and also OCLC. MARC was originally used to automate the creation of physical catalogue cards; Now the MARC computer files are accessed directly in the search process.

OPACs have enhanced usability over traditional card formats because:

- The online catalogue does not need to be sorted statically; the user can choose author, title, keyword, or systematic order dynamically.
- Most online catalogues offer a search facility for any word of the title; the goal of the grammatic word order (provide an entry on the word that most users would look for) is reached even better.
- Many online catalogues allow links between several variants of an author name. So, authors can be found both under the original and the standardised name (if entered properly by the cataloguer).
- The elimination of paper cards has made the information more accessible to many people with disabilities, such as the visually impaired, wheelchair users, and those who suffer from mold allergies.

ONLINE CATALOGUE USER EDUCATION ISSUES

The central question that directed this study, "What might be the components of a model programme to instruct users of an online catalogue?" challenges a commonly held view within the field of librarianship and information science. This view is that an effective "user friendly" inter-active computer system-such as an online catalogue-should not require instruction at all. While such a view is not universally held, it is common especially among system developers and others who are steeped in the use of computers in libraries and elsewhere.

A frequently articulated design specification for end user oriented systems is that all system use instruction should be provided as part of its interface-through such things as introductory help screens, user prompts, and labeling conventions-and should be all that even the most naive user needs to know to be able to effectively use that system. A corollary of this view is that efforts to develop an instructional programme for the online catalogue suggest that the catalogue is not fulfilling its purpose and that its design is flawed. With this logic, any effort to provide instruction in online catalogue use by public services staffs might be viewed as wasted effort at the least, and provide implicit criticism of the designers as well.

Though the project from its inception questioned this view of the incompatibility of "user friendly" online systems and instruction pro-grams, it did not simply embrace the contrary view that formalized instruction must be given to all online catalogue users. Interactive systems for the general public are simply too new and untested for us to assume either of these positions without a period of considerable experimentation and practical examination of what works and what doesn't work for our users.

A certain amount of curiosity, fascination, or mystique naturally accompanies technological evolution. At this early stage of online catalogue implementation, learning from the practical experiences of others, as well as from more formal research findings, is essential if we are to move beyond these phases in our programme development. Baker and Nielsen review much of the early literature on the debate about the value of online catalogue user education, pointing out particularly the sampling bias in the widely cited CLR *Online Public Access Catalogue* (OPAC) studies, a bias which caused users who experienced difficulties in using online catalogues to be underrepresented in the findings.

We became interested in creating a model programme for educating online catalogue users for a variety of reasons:

- There was (and is) wide recognition that the perfect online catalogue simply does not (yet) exist.
- There was (and is) a perception by many librarians that the online user interface may not accommodate all user needs at present and may never do so.
- "User friendly" systems are not indeed friendly to all, judging from the experiences of many reference librarians who have worked with users trying to master such systems.
- The pace of change in interface improvements can seem painfully slow once any online catalogue system "works" in the sense that it meets managerial (not necessarily user) criteria for "satisfying."
- A general training programme that conveyed infor-mation retrieval concepts might aid users as they moved on to other automated systems both within and beyond the library setting.
- The numerous online catalogue instructional prog-rammes that had

been initiated in various settings-particularly in academic libraries-suggested that making an effort for consistency in instructional planning was worthwhile and beneficial.

METHOD OF ONLINE BIBLIOGRAPHIC DATABASE SERVICES

The online bibliogtapic database services are different. Local holdings generally are not an issue, but what is important is the for-pay access these services provide for a myriad of databases. Mainframe computers are used also for maintenance of, access to, and searching of such online bibliographic database services as DIALOG, ORBIT, BRS, WilsOnline, and others.

Such data bases are searched by users from all over the world, typically gaining access via some form of telecommunication device and a local terminal or computer. Some pros and cons need to be indicated here, and can be elaborated upon later. Even though these databases are online, they are not online in real time the way OCLC and the others are. The individual databases serviced by DIALOG, for example, are updated monthly, quarterly, or even more slowly than that. OCLC is updated instantaneously. When a library enters a holding to the database, it is immediately made available to all 6,000 users. For want of a better definition, this notion of instant updating and record availability is a way of understanding "real time".

A second major deficiency of DIALOG, ORBIT and BRS is that the various databases to which they provide access, all have different search rules (protocols is the fancy word for rules). This means that someone who knows how to speedily and effectively search ERIC may not have any idea how to search Predicasts. On the other hand WilsOnline, being a service offered by a single company for all of its databases-a couple of exceptions notwithstanding-does not require a different set of protocols for each of its databases. This is an important issue and points to a major direction for the future, that is, the normalisation of databases. Lets continue with technology review.

Minicomputers are smaller, but still quite powerful computing devices which have been quite effectively used in local library or regional automation efforts. They have been especially effective in such applications as online circulation control systems for individual libraries (as with many college and university libraries, plus some public libraries), and libraries in combination (*e.g.* public libraries with many service outlets; regional public library systems consisting in many individual public libraries; and consortia, *i.e.* several libraries in combination, sharing a single minicomputer.)

For almost twenty years the MINICOMPUTER has been successfully used to maintain control of all of the books (and other library materials) held by all of the libraries participating in the system. It indicates where they are located (*i.e.* on the shelf, in circulation, or any other status), who has them, reserves or holds them for use by library patrons when they are not immediately accessible;

it maintains a complete record of all of the registered library users which includes their name, address and other appropriate information so that the user can be notified if he or she has overdue books, a reserved book is available, or for other information pertaining to library service; it also keeps track of the amount of money owed by individuals who returned their books late.

Individual suppliers of these minicomputer based systems have addressed such applications as online acquisitions; online catalogs [confusingly referred to as PACs (Public Access Catalogs)]; serials acquisitions, cataloging and check-in; film control and booking; and special collection control (an important application for libraries which have special collections such as videos which may circulate only for one or two days at a time).

More and more libraries are using these minicomputer-based systems for full public access catalogue use and complete circulation control. Note well that the precondition for such applications to run on the minicomputer is the creation of a machine readable database of the library's holdings.

The conversion of library holdings to machine readable form has been the biggest obstacle to the complete and successful automation of libraries. Invariably the conversion of the data to a form manipulable by the computer is the most problematic, difficult, and expensive part of automation.

MARC FORMAT

Things would be a hell of a lot worse if there were no standardised format, the MARC format. Because of MARC everyone can use and share the same data for conversion purposes. Of equal importance is that a competitive market exists of automation purveyors, all of whose systems are predicated on MARC-based databases. All of the software for these minicomputer systems is written to operate on MARC records. There is no way to adequately explain within the time constraints how incredibly important this standardisation of cataloging data, the MARC format, is. Let's move on to the most exciting and fun machines to use.

MICROCOMPUTERS are used primarily in single library and single function applications. There are a variety of microcomputers available and in use by U.S., libraries. Microcomputers are being used in such administrative applications as fund accounting, word processing, and data base management. The kinds of microcomputers used to perform these functions typically are based on the Intel chips, that is, the 8088, and the 80286 - 80486 chips which are on the IBM PC, XT, AT, and compatibles; and the Macintosh, which is based on the Motorola 60000 series of chips. From smart toys and hobbyists' enthusiasms, micros have evolved to become devices with as much as 16 to 64 million bytes of random access memory, and which store over 600 million bytes of data on a single hard disc drive. Devices of such monstrous capacity (and smaller ones, too) can support sophisticated local area networks of PCs and/or terminals. Microcomputers are being used to perform such library functions as acquisitions, cataloging, serials control, and circulation control. In the last couple of years they have been used, too, as public access catalogs and sophisticated database storage and searching devices. Typically, most micro based systems do not accept, process or output cataloging data in conformity with library standards, that is, the MARC record. However, there are exceptions, and definitely more are coming along.

What has made the big difference in capacity for micros is the storage medium, CD-ROM. CD-ROM stands for Compact Disk - Read Only Memory. The CD-ROM platter is capable of storing over 16,000 pages of information, and is approximately 511 wide.

The combination of the PC, a CD-ROM reading device, and a CD-ROM disk with a database on it, have made possible unprecedented extensions of automation, and more specifically have made possible the distribution of databases on to PCs which heretofore could only be stored on mainframe computers with massive disk storage.

With all of the equipment required to use a CD-ROM now costing less than $2,000, a library now has the hardware for storing and accessing the entire U.S. MARC format database. The compaction of data, the relative inexpense of the CD-ROM storage medium, and the reduction in unit cost for data processing as represented by the PC have made it possible to provide the most sophisticated applications to operate wholly self -sufficiently in the most remote and tiny locations. The only requirement is a stable power source compatible with the equipment.

CD-ROM is the extremely powerful solution to the tremendous costs of remote site online telecommunication charges to a host computer. With CD-ROM the database sits out there in Timbuktu. With terminals online, we have to pay the phone company for providing the connection between the terminal where we are and the computer at some remote site. Many public libraries have several databases that are on CD-ROM at their disposal: Books In Print Plus and Ulrich's from R.R. Bowker, Dissertation Abstracts, WilsOnline, InfoTrac, etc

In addition to such bibliographic databases, companies such as the Library Corporation of America make the MARC database available on CD-ROM as well as software to search it and prepare catalogue cards and labels from the MARC records. This particular product is called Bibliophile and it has been very successful in as a source or medium for inexpensively capturing Library of Congress cataloging data.

Bibliophile also provides for the printing of catalogue cards and labels from the Library of Congress catalogue record. No more typing catalogue cards and labels. Through Bibliophile a database of MARC records could be created for the books cataloged. Library Corporation will take the records created locally from its Bibliophile product and create a CD-ROM catalogue of the library's holdings. Public and other libraries all over the country have availed themselves of this service.

AN ONLINE DATABASE WITH KEYWORD ACCESS

KEYWORD SEARCHING

In an online database with keyword access, it is possible to retrieve a record through keywords, whether in main entries, added entries or any other significant word indexed from the text of the record. A major characteristic of keywords is that they are not controlled by cataloguing rules and they are not subject to authority control. Therefore, keyword searching on names will retrieve only those records that match the term(s) keyed in by the searcher. Keyword searching capability cannot replace the main entry in terms of its collocating function. It can, however, facilitate the collocating function: once access to one or more specific items has been provided through keywords, the searcher can extend the search by keying the exact form of the author heading or the uniform title found on the retrieved record(s) to search for related editions with the same terms only.

Boolean Searching

Boolean search is another capability for bringing together different editions of a work. This can be done by keying in two or more data elements such as the author heading and the title proper or the uniform title, by using the 'AND' operator. Since the title proper of different editions of a work may vary, titles proper in conjunction with author heading cannot be a useful element for the collocating function. The 'author/title' search key, which many systems provide, is an implicit Boolean search which has the same limitation. Instead, a Boolean search on the author uniform heading and the uniform title, including relevant qualifiers, can achieve the collocating function more effectively. This approach is another justification for the main entry concept.

Index Browsing

The browsing capability removes the burden of entering the exact search terms and enables the searcher to gain an overview of an index containing an alphabetical list of all headings. Browsing, for example, the author index will display together all the works by an author irrespective of his/her type of contribution. Nevertheless, for the uniform citation and display of entries in the browsable author index we need to identify the primary author. To link works, however, the primary author's name should be in a uniform heading. This is again another justification for the concept of main entry in an online environment.

It can be seen that, even with browsing capability, a useful collocation of different editions of a work is not possible with the present structure of entries.

Browsable indexes could help solve the collocation problem if the author and the title indexes are pre-coordinated for meaningful arrangement and display of related entities.

ONLINE DISPLAY AND THE CONCEPT OF MAIN ENTRY

Since the display format in online catalogues is independent of the storage format, when a number of records are displayed in response to a query, the retrieved titles need to be displayed in conjunction with a second primary identifier such as the author heading.

Otherwise, not only is the identification of the retrieved items not complete, but different works by an author are also not distinguished and assembled. This primary element is necessary in online displays of related works. Carpenter states that the primary key provides a unique identification of the record. He also points out that: "Discussions about main entry have changed focus from records to useful displays". Online displays, for instance, default listings in brief displays, require that, in addition to titles proper, another principal element must be displayed.

The following example may help to make this idea clearer:

- As the convention now exists in many OPACs, when there is an editor or a compiler for a work and the work goes under title main entry or a corporate heading and the editor or the compiler is given an added entry as opposed to main entry, his/her/its name would still need to be displayed in conjunction with the title proper in the brief display to uniquely identify the work and to differentiate between works with identical titles. From another perspective, that of the catalogue user who does not understand what main entry is, an editor or a compiler may seem to be the primary identifier or access point which should be displayed in conjunction with the title in brief displays and in single entry listings.

As a concept, the main entry relates rather to the nature of relationships between entities than to the physical medium through which those entities are to be described. Many works, particularly in the fields of literature, law and music, require such a uniform construct for identification and collocation. Even if technology provides catalogues with sophisticated devices to link two or more related entities to one another, it would not help the user if catalogues do not show him/her the nature of these relationships. Without such a concept the catalogue, whether manual or computerised, would lose its integrity and usefulness.

From the preceding discussions concerning the possible influence of different online search/retrieval/display capabilities, it can be concluded that online catalogues still need a construct to carry out some specific functions which cannot be fulfilled thoroughly through other devices. Of great concern is the fact that the main entry concept is not meant to be a single function element but rather a concept that is essential to fulfil some basic functions. Thus it is in need of a re-definition that will focus on its multiple functions.

Main entry is a uniform construct for the naming and identifying of works and also for the useful collocation and arrangement/display of the different editions and manifestations of a work. In addition to the identification of the primary author, the concept of uniform citation is dependent on two key identifying elements: uniform titles for works and uniform headings for authors.

FORM OF HEADINGS IN AN ONLINE ENVIRONMENT

In addition to the principle of uniform headings, which is essential to the integrity and the collocating function of the catalogue, the form of names in headings, as emphasised by IFLA/Unesco in 1961 should be agreed upon both nationally and internationally. This principle needs to be examined with respect to searchers' expectations and also to the searching/retrieval/display capabilities of the online catalogue. The form of personal and corporate names will be discussed with respect to the possible influence of the online environment.

FORM OF CORPORATE HEADINGS

The issue of corporate headings was one of the problems on which there was no international consensus at the Paris Conference. Even today different national codes have different approaches towards the form of headings.

Searching, retrieval and display of corporate names in online systems are often frustrating to the user. Many of the problems concerning the searching of corporate bodies' publications relate to the form of headings for these bodies.

Little has been written on the form of corporate headings in an online environment. Some of the implications of searching corporate names in online systems have been briefly addressed by Arlene Taylor, Brunt and more fully by Greig. The result of a study by Henty, concerning unsuccessful keyword searching, indicates that the reasons for the users' search failures are, to some extent, due to the implications of variant forms of corporate names.

Some of the problems concerning the searching, retrieval and display of corporate headings in online systems are:

- It is particularly difficult to search under the exact form of corporate headings in online catalogues because the user has to key in the search string. How much of the heading should be keyed in by the searcher to initiate the search, since corporate names are usually long, often similar to one another and appear in different forms such as acronyms, initials and subordinations?
- In some cases, headings for subordinate bodies associated with the same parent body do not follow a uniform approach. While the 'World

Health Organization' appears as the heading for this body, a number of subordinate bodies incorporating the acronym 'WHO' are treated as headings in the catalogue. for example, 'WHO Collaborating Centre on Environmental Pollution Control', 'WHO Commission on Health and Environment', 'WHO Expert Group on Pesticide Residues'. The same problem exists with the 'Food and Agriculture Organization of United Nations' and some of its subordinate bodies beginning with 'FAO'.

- Entering corporate bodies under the name of the higher body would often cause inconvenience for the searcher, especially in large catalogues and shared systems. The use of indirect corporate headings is not innate and could appear meaningless to catalogue users. They "can be considerably distorted because of re-arrangement of the elements of the name and, in many codes, by translating the name of the jurisdiction".
- The addition of a geographic name to the heading for corporate bodies often does not make sense in the online environment. Exact searching and truncation on headings beginning with the name of the jurisdiction often result in too many hits. Headings like 'Australia. Australian Parliamentary Observer Group', 'Canada. Canadian High Commission' and 'Canada. Canadian Armed Forces' which are problematic for searching could be more straightforward if 'Australia' and 'Canada', were omitted from the heading.
- Truncation on the name of the parent body will usually retrieve too many records that are not easy to distinguish from one another, especially in brief displays where, because of screen limitation, the name of the parent body alone may fill the allotted space.
- Clustering of all the publications of different departments and divisions of a corporate body is not usually sought by searchers. Also, it does not make sense in brief displays where, because of screen limitation, only the first few elements of the heading are displayed thus obscuring the name of the actual issuing body. Consider, for example, how frustrating the retrieval of publications of different subordinates bodies of the United Nations would be in an online catalogue.

FORM OF PERSONAL NAME HEADINGS

The form of a name is an important factor in searching and retrieval, particularly in online systems in which the searcher has to key in the name as the search string. In online catalogues with many search/retrieval capabilities it is important to see whether this principle needs a rather different approach. In a manual environment, a problem with the form of heading is that searches for works of authors must be in the exact form and order of their name headings.

This requirement is no longer totally necessary since cross references in authority records and keyword searching allow for the searching of names in different ways. If the searcher is not sure as to which part of the name forms the surname for efficient searching, for example, Jean De La Fountaine, Walter De La Mare, Dante Alighieri, cross references or keyword access offers the possibility to search names in any order. Keyword searching capability also reduces the need for complete "surname+initials+(full forenames)+dates" headings as in AACR2R.

Truncation of headings, especially automatic right-hand truncation, can help retrieve works by authors whose complete heading is not known to the searcher. Variations in the fullness of forenames seem unimportant in systems with a truncation capability. Using 'Price, H H' and 'Grossman, Allen R.' as examples, Arlene Taylor proposes that an online catalogue with keyword searching of headings and automatic right-hand truncation needs rather different rules for the formulation of headings and references.

Wajenberg claims that, with keyword searching, the inversion of surnames and rules for the choice of entry-element in compound surnames and names with prefixes become unnecessary. Using the heading 'Mozart, Wolfgang Amadeus' as an example, he points out that the most useful form of name is the fullest form. Kilgour on the other hand, proposes that for a single-screen miniature catalogue author entries can be reduced to surnames alone. His survey of two online catalogues in the North Carolina State University, containing approximately 3.4 million entries, showed that surname searches produced mini catalogues of one screen 12.6 per cent of the time, two screens 22.5 per cent, and three screens 30.1 per cent.

He claims that his finding, that nearly two-fifths of the cataloguing of books in a large university library produces entries that will be displayed in mini catalogues of one screen, demands revision and simplification of cataloguing practices in large research libraries For example, he proposes that with keyword search function no added author fields will be necessary for multiple surnames.

There are other factors, such as the need for default listings of the works of an author and the needs of the book world, citation traditions and international exchange of bibliographic data, which require the standard order of 'surname, forename' in full form for personal headings. There is at present no consensus on the form of headings among the different creators of bibliographic records. There are, however, to some extent similarities between library cataloguing and the book world: both tend to use the best known form of name with library cataloguing more inclined to use the complete form.

E-READERS

e-BOOK FORMATS

eBooks come in a variety of formats. Some publishers and sellers also place DRM protection on the books so they cannot be copied, viewed on multiple devices, or restricted to specific readers. There is no consistent licensing as each licence is an agreement between author, publisher and seller:

- ePUB is an open source format and continues to develop. ePUB books can contain video and active links which make the books dynamic. ePUB is the most versatile of all eBook formats. Textbooks developers are looking to this format as it will allow for content and media rich books, moving away from what can be done with traditional text and print media. ePub can be read by most popular devices except Amazon's Kindle. Amazon currently offers an e-mail service that lets you convert ePUB documents and books into the AZW format for a fee, though formaang and interactivity may be lost.
- MOBI also known as MobiPocket is owned by Amazon and is similar to the AZW format for Kindle. The MOBI format can be read by most of the popular readers except the Nook. MOBI was once the most popular format but is losing ground to ePUB.
- PDF is a format that is commonly used to publish documents and images. PDFs are essentially images of pages and therefore do not allow text to flow between pages or to fit the screen size. PDFs are best read on larger computer screens and not mobile devices. PDFs can be viewed in most readers except the first edition Kindle.
- Plain Text formaang allows for a very small file size, allowing large books such as the Bible to be distributed in this format. Plain text is read by major readers except Nook.
- HTML is the markup language for web pages and most eBooks that use HTML can be read in a web browser. Some other eBook formats include HTML in their packaging of books.
- Kindle/ AZW is a version of MOBI and is exclusive to Amazon Kindle. It can be read on a variety of mobile devices with the Kindle App. It cannot be read on other readers such as the Nook or Sony reader.
- eReader was originally developed for Palm. This format supports hyperlinks and images. The Nook can read pdb files while the Kindle cannot.

WHERE TO FIND e-BOOKS

Before you go out and make a purchase for a dedicated reader it might be worth your while to explore what books are available in eBook format. Take some time to read a few books on the devices you already have access to such as your computer or smart phone if you have one. eBooks are not quite the same as print. Some eBooks contain images and some do not. Some free versions were entered by volunteers and may contain a typo or two.

Let's explore a few places to find eBooks:

- Google eBooks puts the power of the Google search engine to work scouring the web for eBooks. Some books are hosted by Google, others from major publishers and distributors. If you are not tied to a particular reader Google books is a good place to start to find the books in a variety of formats. You can find many free books from the public domain, as well as books for purchase.

- Project Gutenberg has a large collection of books in the public domain. Currently there are over 33,000 free eBooks available. The eBooks on Project Gutenberg are found in 3 main formats plain text, ePUB, and MOBI.
- eBooks.com has a wide range of eBooks for purchase including many academic titles for colleges. eBooks.com sells books in PDF, for computer based reading; ePUB, Mobi and MicrosoV reader for mobile devices. eBooks has an eReader app for iPod/iPad/iPhone devices. eBooks from eBooks.com can also be read on a computer
- Amazon Kindle eBooks Books sold at Amazon for the Kindle are primarily in the AZW format, though some may be in MOBI depending on agreements with the publisher. AZW format is proprietary to Amazon and includes DRM protection. Amazon also offers some free ebooks that are in the public domain. Amazon offers the Kindle app for iPod/iPad/iPhone and other mobile devices.
- Barnes and Noble eBook store sells NookBooks formaXed for the Nook. They currently have over 2 million eBooks available. NookBooks are in the ePUB format, eReader and some PDF, though most books have DRM protection on them. Barnes and Noble offers an app called the Barnes and Noble e-Reader for iPod/iPad/iPhone and other mobile devices.
- Borders has adopted the ePUB, PDF and Mobile format for its books; most have DRM protections. Like other book sellers, they also have free books in the public domain. Unlike Amazon and Barnes and Noble, Borders does not sell its own reader but recommends seven different readers on its web site. These are described in the last section on eReaders. Borders also offers a free eReader app for many mobile devices.

The Apple iBookstore currently sells books for reading only on Apple mobile devices, through the iTunes interface. Rumours persist that Apple will release its iBooks app for the Mac and PC in the future but there are always rumours surrounding Apple. Apple prefers the tactile sensation of 'turning pages' with the touch screen on its mobile devices that current desktop and laptops do not have. Apple iBooks are in the ePUB format and allow for interactivity such as viewing embedded video and active web links. Apple also sells fully illustrated books and magazines because of the colour planorm provided by its devices.

e-READERS

Reading eBooks can be done on a variety of devices with a range of apps and programmes. As suggested, begin with a look at reading on computers and multifunctional devices and end with a look at some of the major dedicated readers.

e-READING SOFTWARE FOR COMPUTERS

If you own a computer you can read almost anything though you may need more than one programme to do so. Reading on your computer is not as comfy as reading a book curled up on the couch or siang in your back yard, but you do have access to a vast library of books. Each of the major eBook sellers provides a version of their reader for your computer. If you use a Windows based PC you can choose from Kindle for PC, Adobe Digital Editions, Nook for PC, or Borders eReader for PC. If you are a Mac user you have a similar selection of choices Kindle for Mac, Adobe Digital Editions, Nook for Mac, or Borders eReader for Mac.

EREADING ON MULTIFUNCTIONAL MOBILE DEVICES: iPODS, iPADS, AND MOBILE PHONES

Multifunctional mobile devices are just small computers, some with an added phone. These include iPods, iPads, iPhones, Android Phones, Blackberries and an increasing number of small tablets. Most of these mobile devices have LCD screens which make reading in bright light a bit of a challenge; most are colour and many have touch screens and support the interactivity of the ePUB format. Velocity Micro offers Android based tablets, Borders recommends two, these are described later on.

The device that offers the richest media content support for eBooks is currently the iPad. If you already have a number of gadgets in your bag you may wish for a multifunctional device so you have fewer devices to deal with. Similar to the computer, the devices can have a variety of e-reader apps installed so they can handle a large variety of book formats and work with all the major eBook distributors. Kindle Reading Apps, Nook Apps and Borders eReader Apps are available for mobile devices including apps for iPods/iPads/iPhone, Android and Blackberry phones. Adobe Digital Editions which reads PDF and ePUB can be used on a variety of mobile devices.

DEDICATED e-READERS

When it comes to dedicated eReaders the ones that get the most coverage are the Amazon Kindle and the Barnes and Noble Nook. These two major book sellers have developed their own eReaders. Borders has taken a more open approach and does not market to a particular eReader allowing the reader greater choice. As suggested, begin with a brief summary of the Kindle and

Nook readers currently available and then look at the 7 that Borders recommends. Amazon currently offers the Kindle 3 and Kindle DX. The two models each come in two flavours—wifi or wifi and 3G. 3G is provided free allowing you to purchase books and download them whereever you are.

The more recent release of the Kindles uses pearl e-ink which allows for crisper images and text, and reading in bright light. The screens are not touch screens, navigation is carried out via a keyboard and side buXons. The kindle 3 has a 6 inch screen and the DX 9.7 inch screen. Kindle supports; AZW, PDF, MOBI, TEXT formats. It does not support ePub, but a programme called Calibre can convert epub to MOBI. Amazon currently offers an e-mail service for a fee to convert files. The Barnes and Noble Nook now comes in two models the original in black and white and the new Nook Colour. Both have two flavour; wifi or wifi and 3G.

As with the Kindle the 3G is free. Both devices use e-ink and can be read in bright light. Nook Colour has a touch screen and designed for those who love reading magazines. The traditional black and white e-ink did not do justice to the visual images found in many magazines. Nook colour also has extras including some web browsing, e-mail access and games. It is clearly aimed at the iPad, though the Nook colour is not yet a true multifunctional device. The Nooks support the following formats: EPUB, PDB, PDF, MP3, JPG, GIF, PNG, PMB. It does not read Mobi, AMZ, LRX/LEZ, or Text

There are other eReaders on the market that are not tied to a specific vendor. Borders offers a comparison chart for a variety of readers it recommends.

Below is a brief summary of each:

- Aluratek Libre Pro supports books in the ePub, PDF, TXT, RTF, FB2, MOBI, PRC formats. It can play mp3 files and uses an LCD screen that is black and white.
- Kobo Wireless eReader support eReader, ePUB and PDF formats. It uses e-ink and has a 6 inch screen.
- Sony offers 3 models of eReader; the Pocket edition, Touch edition and the Daily Edition. The Sony models all have touch screen navigation and use e-ink. The pocket edition is not wireless and requires a computer to sync books to. They support ePub, PDF, TXT, RTF, and BBeB formats. Sony also has its own eBook store.

Finally rounding out our look at eReaders the Cruz reader and Tablet from Velocity Micro. The Cruz Reader is not a standalone eReader, it more a multifunctional device. It is a colour eReader with 7" screen that also browses the web, plays mp3 files, watch movies, play games and has some productivity apps. The Cruz Tablet is a true multifunctional Android colour tablet. There are two versions of this device—one with Borders eReader and the other with Amazon's Kindle soVware.

There is a great deal of variety in this very fluid technology. It is apparent that eBooks are here and are gaining more and more ground. eBook readers continue to improve as time goes on. Just as with computers, change is inevitable. Reading is a very personal experience therefore each person should make the choice that works for them. It is clearly not a one size fits all experience. Do your research and make the choice that works for you.

e-BOOKS AND e-AUDIOBOOKS FROM THE LIBRARY

Medicine Hat Public Library pays a company called OverDrive to provide access to copyrightprotected eBooks and eAudiobooks for Library patrons. Anyone with a valid library membership and a PIN number can access these resources from home.

Currently, patrons can have up to 5 electronic titles checked out at once and each title can be kept for a maximum of 3 weeks. At the end of the lending period, each title will automatically expire. There are no late fees! While the file will still be visible on your computer or portable device, you will not be able to open it and it can be deleted. Due to restrictions imposed by book publishers, only one person may have an electronic title checked out at once. So when someone checks out The 9th Confession by James Patterson, that book is unavailable to everyone else until it is returned.

A FEW THINGS TO KNOW ABOUT e-BOOKS

Library eBooks come in two formats: ePub and PDF. The main difference between the two formats is that ePub books have reflowable text: as you increase the text size, the words automatically shuffle to fit your screen. PDF books do not have this feature, so when you increase the text size you may need to scroll from left to right to read everything on the page. Both formats are compatible with PCs, Macs, and most portable eReaders like the Sony Reader, Kobo and Nook. The iPad, iPhone and iPod Touch are also compatible with ePub files when downloaded directly to the device using the OverDrive Media Console App. In order to read an eBook on your computer or to transfer it to an applicable eReader, you must first install Adobe Digital Editions which is freely available from the Library to Go web site.

A FEW THINGS TO KNOW ABOUT e-AUDIOBOOKS

eAudiobooks from the Library come in two formats: MP3 and WMA. Both formats will work on PCs and most portable audio devices. Unfortunately, WMA files are not compatible with Mac computers. Depending on the type of software your Apple device is running you may be able to transfer a WMA file through a PC. In order to download an eAudiobook and transfer to a portable device, you must first install OverDrive Media Console which is freely available from the Library to Go web site.

LIBRARY TO GO

Library to Go is the library's catalogue for finding and downloading eBooks and eAudiobooks.

BEFORE YOU START BROWSING: DOWNLOAD THE REQUIRED SOFTWARE

In order to read and transfer eBooks you must first download the Adobe Digital Editions software. For eAudiobooks you must first download OverDrive Media Console.

Both are freely available on the Library to Go web site below the green menu on the left-side of the page:

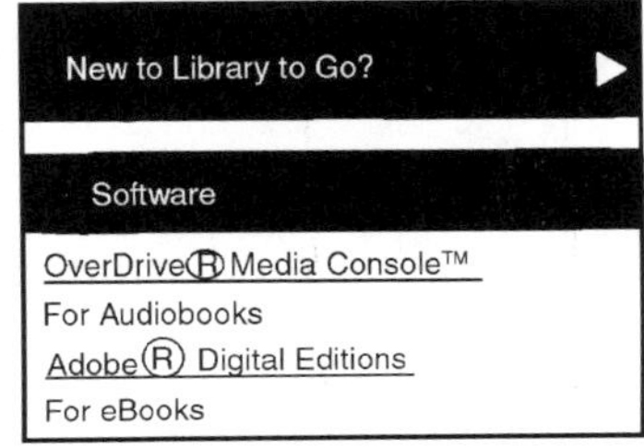

ACTIVATING THE SOFTWARE

After you have installed the software, you need to take steps to activate it before downloading digital materials.

Adobe Digital Editions Requires Activation

You must create an Adobe ID in order to transfer eBooks from a computer to an eReader. When you open Digital Editions for the first time click 'Get an Adobe ID online' and follow the prompts to create your Adobe ID. You can then enter your Adobe ID and password in the relevant boxes in Digital Editions to activate.

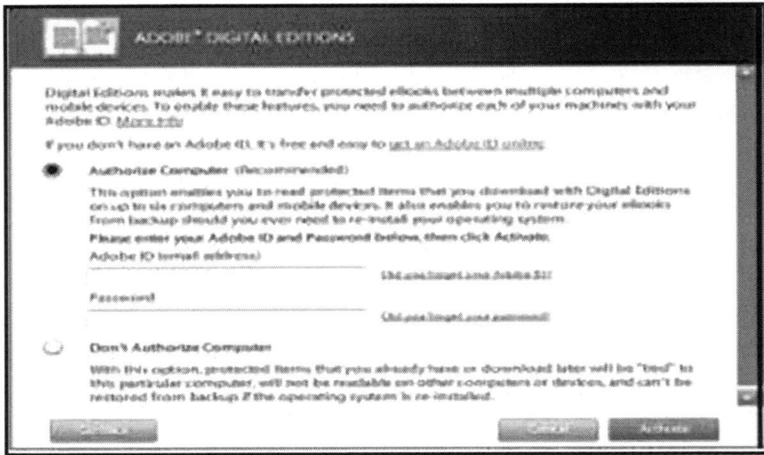

OverDrive Media Console Requires a Security Update

The first time you open an eAudiobook with OverDrive Media Console, a message will appear saying that a security upgrade must be performed before the file can be opened. Simply follow the on-screen instructions to perform the quick upgrade.

FINDING TITLES USING LIBRARY TO GO

You can search for a particular title or author using the 'Quick Search' box near the top of the Library to Go page.

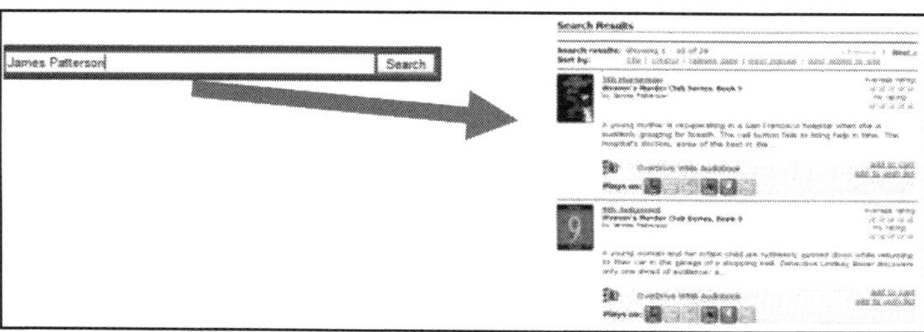

The 'Advanced Search' option to the right of the 'Quick Search' box can be used to perform a more specific search. You can also browse for titles using the green menu on the left side of the page or the categories in the centre of the main Library to Go page.

DOWNLOADING AN e-BOOK

When you have found an eBook that interests you, simply click on its title for more information:

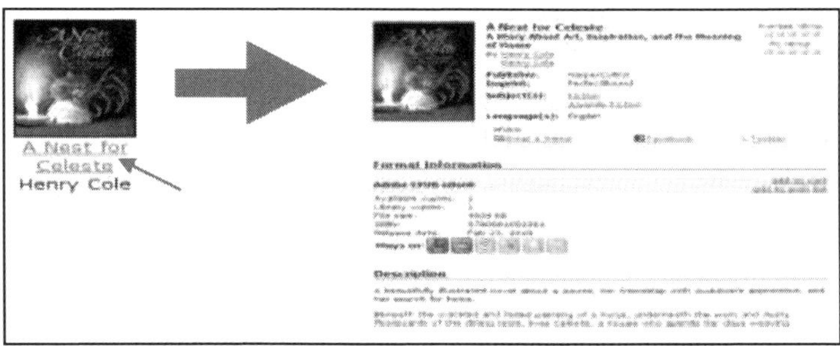

If the 'Add to Cart' option is visible in the grey bar under 'Format Information', then the book is available to download and you can click to move to the next step. If you see 'Place a Hold' instead, then the item is checked out by someone else and you can click to enter your e-mail address and receive notification when the item is available. Once the item is available for download, you will have three days to complete the checkout. After you click 'Add to Cart' you are given the option to 'Continue Browsing' or 'Proceed to Checkout'- if you 'Continue Browsing', your items will stay in your cart for 45 minutes.

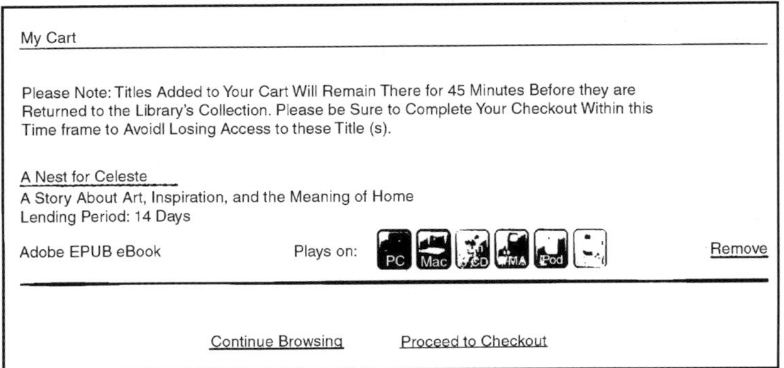

Clicking 'Proceed to Checkout' brings you to a screen asking for your Library card number and PIN number.

When you have entered this information, you will be brought to the Check Out screen:

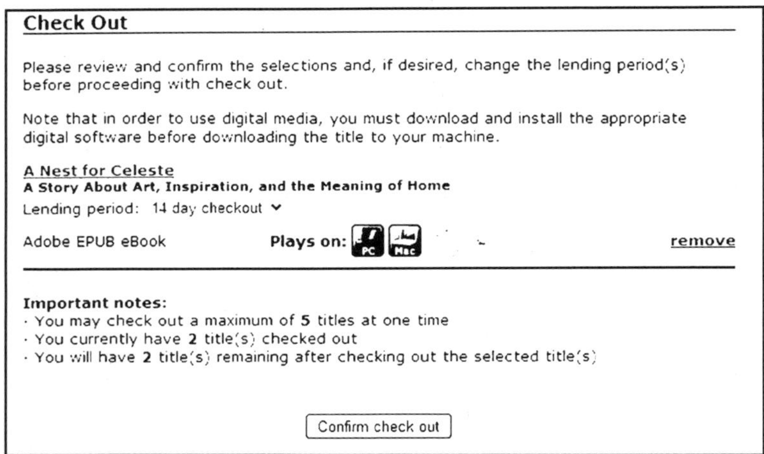

From here you can choose your lending period and see how close you are to your 5 item limit. When you're ready to download, click 'Confirm Checkout' and then the 'Download' button on the next screen that appears.

**If this is the very first time you have downloaded an eBook from the Library, you will need to tell your computer which programme it should use to open the file.

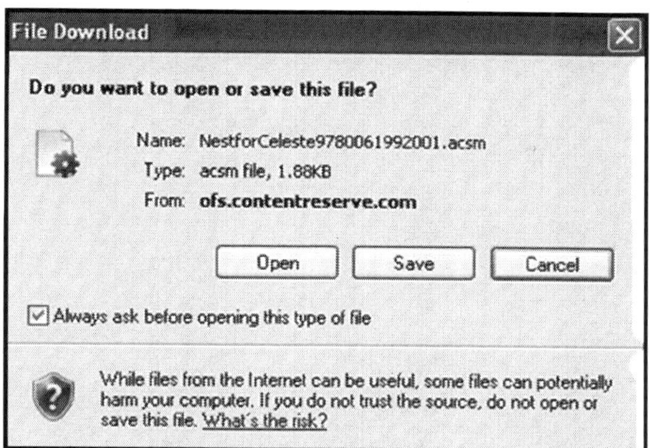

To select the programme to open eBook files, you must click the 'Save' button, choose 'Desktop' as the destination and then click save.

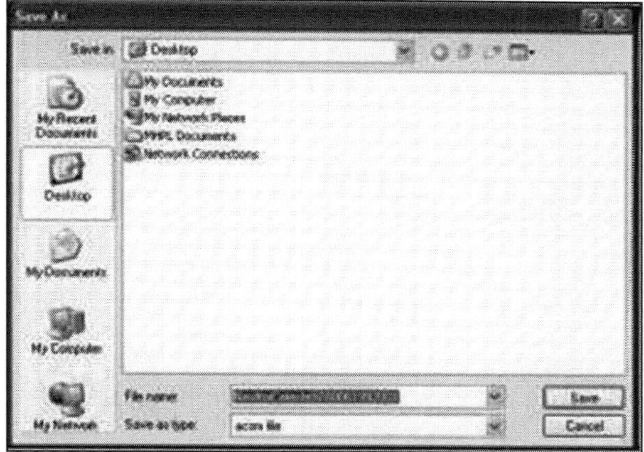

Next, find the file on the Desktop, right-click the icon, go to 'Open With' and click 'Choose Programme'.

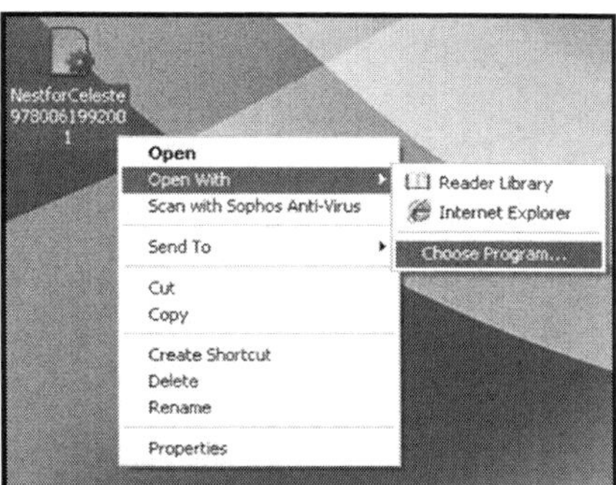

Choose Adobe Digital Editions from the list of programmes, click the box next to "Always use the selected programme to open this kind of file' and click 'OK'.

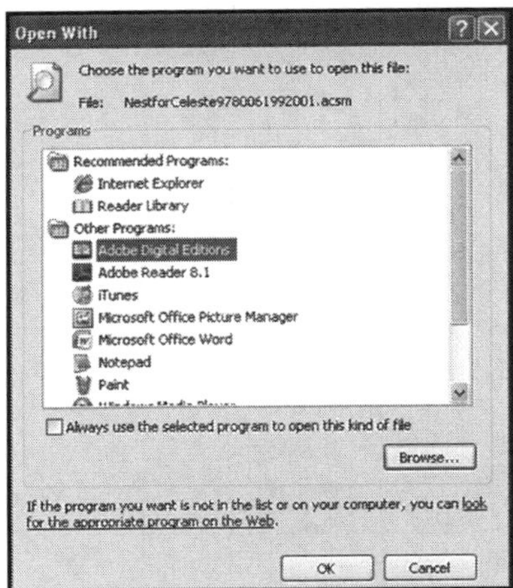

If Digital Editions does not appear in the list of programmes, you will need to find it using the 'Browse' button. Usually, it is saved under Programme Files \ Adobe \ Adobe Digital Editions \ digitaleditions.

TRANSFERRING AN e-BOOK TO AN e-READER

To transfer an eBook from Digital Editions to an eReader such as the Kobo Touch, you must first connect your eReader to your computer. If a window opens asking what Windows should do with the connected device choose 'Take No Action'. Then open Digital Editions and follow the steps to authorise your reader if you are using it for the first time. Click on the icon for Library View in the top-left corner of the screen.

Your eReader should appear at the bottom of the Bookshelves area on the left side of the screen. Simply drag and drop the title you wish to transfer onto your eReader.

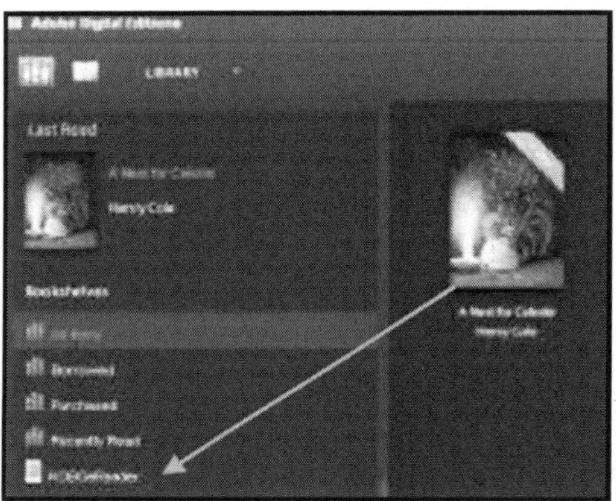

If your eReader does not appear in Digital Editions after you have plugged it in, you may need to download your eReader's software before your computer will recognise it.

RETURNING YOUR e-BOOKS EARLY

Any eBooks you borrow through the library system will automatically return themselves at the end of your borrowing period but if you finish an eBook early, you can also return it yourself. In the Adobe Digital Editions software on your computer, click the 'Go to Library View' button in the top left corner:

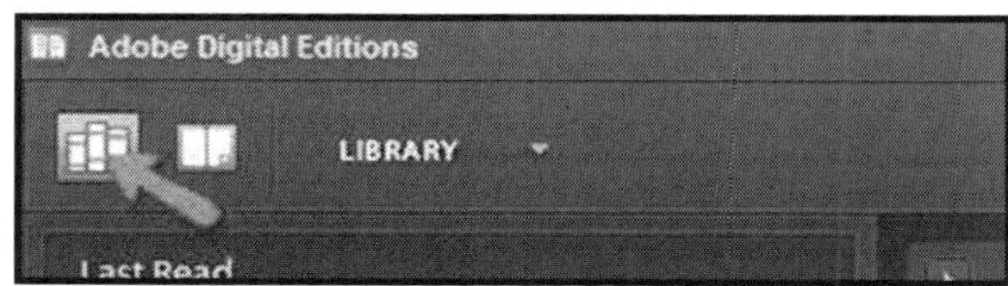

Next, click the 'Item Options' button for the book you wish to return:

Finally, click the 'Return Borrowed Item' in the Item Options menu:

DOWNLOADING AN e-BOOK DIRECTLY TO A SONY WIFI e-READER

The Sony WiFi eReader will allow you to borrow eBooks from the library directly on your device without the use of Adobe Digital Editions or any external applications.

To download books onto your device, use the following procedure:

- Turn on your device.
- Go to page 2 and select the 'Public Library' icon.
- If you are asked to set up an account in the Sony eReader store, follow the prompts to do so. This will authorize your eReader to open the library books you borrow.

- In the 'Public Library' section, select the option to 'Discover More' or 'Find a Library'.
- Type in 'Medicine Hat' into the search area and press the small magnifying next to it.
- Select the 'Medicine Hat Public Library System' and then select the 'Library to Go' option—this will take you to the Library to Go homepage where you can login, search for, and download your eBooks.

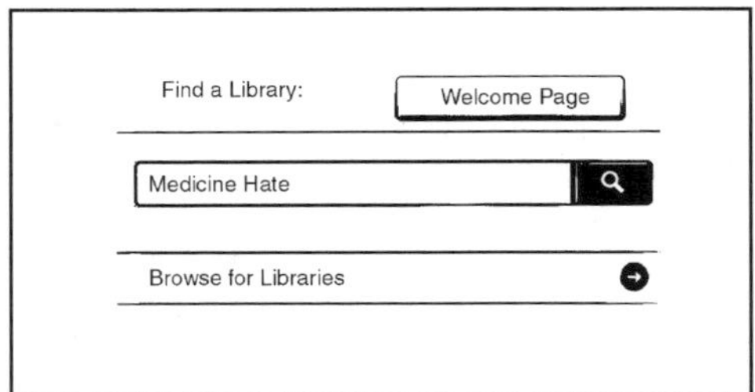

RETURNING e-BOOKS DIRECTLY ON A SONY WIFI e-READER

To return your eBooks directly from your Sony Wifi eReader use the following procedure:

- Select the 'Books' icon on your eReader screen.
- Press the Menu button.
- Select 'Return Books.'
- Select which books you'd like to return by checking the appropriate boxes.
- Press 'Done'.

Overdrive Media Console Mobile is a free app available for most iPad/ iPhone/iPod Touch, Android, Blackberry and Windows Mobile devices. This app allows you to download titles directly to your device over Wi-Fi or 3g. However, not all file formats are currently compatible. Apple devices, for example, only support eBooks in ePub format and eAudiobooks in MP3 format. You can download the app from the app store for your device or the Library to Go web site. You must register your Adobe ID with the Overdrive Media Console Mobile app and you will be prompted for your library card number and PIN before you can download an eBook or eAudiobook.

HOW TO DOWNLOAD e-BOOKS AND e-AUDIOBOOKS WITH OVERDRIVE MEDIA CONSOLE MOBILE

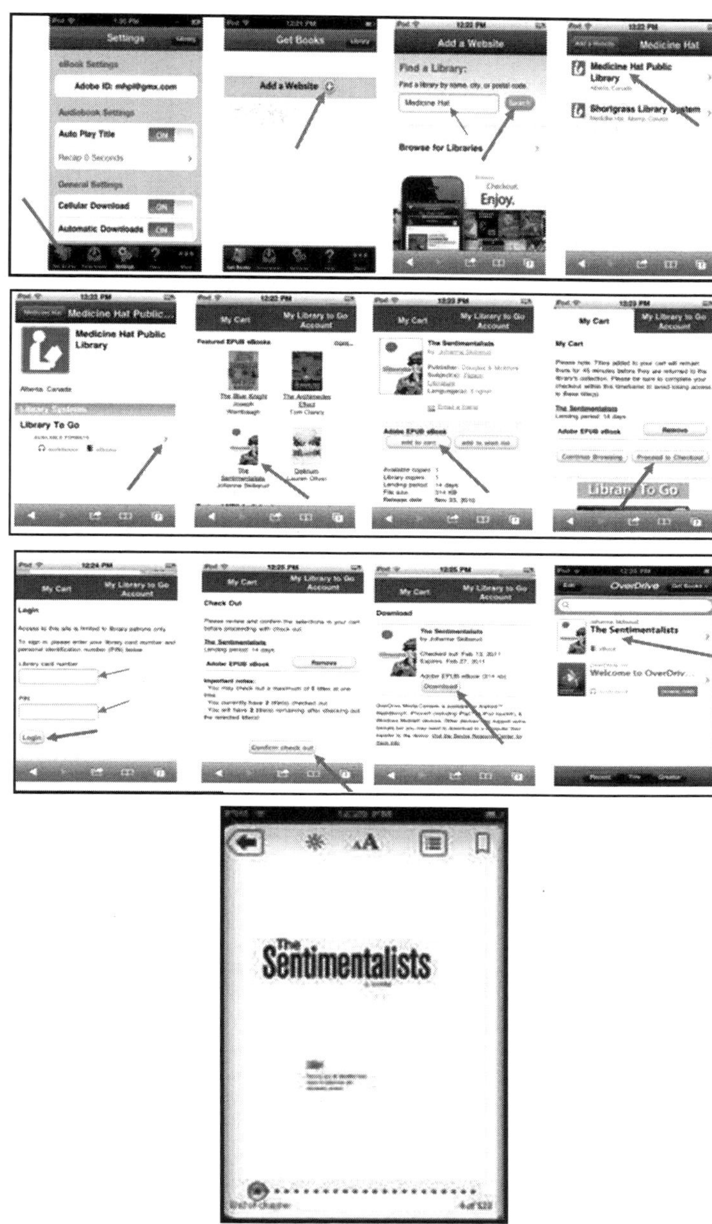

Note

Library books borrowed through the OverDrive Media Console app will always be found by opening that app on your device. For example, if you downloaded a title on your Kobo Vox using OverDrive, the next time you wanted to go and read it, you would open the app instead of looking for the title in your library.

RETURNING e-BOOKS DIRECTLY FROM YOUR PORTABLE DEVICE

You can also return your eBooks directly from your portable device by using the OverDrive Media Console app. By swiping your finger across the title on the main page you will be shown a button to delete the book. When you click that button, you will then be given the option to delete only, or delete and return the book. Deleting the book only will free up space on your device, while deleting and returning the book will also free up space for another title in your Library to Go account.

Each device is different but most do offer you the option to return items early. To find out if your device has this feature, try to delete the item and see if you are asked whether you want to return the item as well. If you are not given the option, then look in the settings section for each borrowed item.

DOWNLOADING AN e-AUDIOBOOK TO YOUR COMPUTER

The process for finding and checking out titles is the same for eAudiobooks and eBooks. After checking out an eAudiobook click Open in the File Download window.

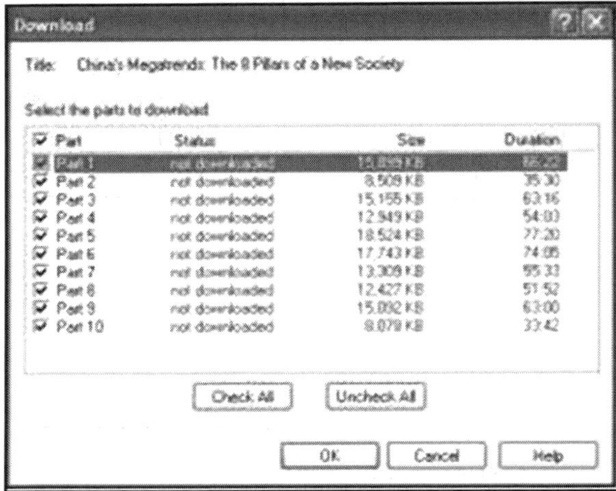

Overdrive Media Console will open automatically. eAudiobooks are divided into parts to facilitate faster download times. You will need to tell Overdrive Media Console which parts to download by checking the boxes beside the parts you want. The default option is to download all parts. Once you have checked the parts you want, you can click the 'OK' button to download.

It could take a while to download depending on the speed of your Internet connection and how many parts you choose to download at once After the eAudiobook has downloaded, it will appear in Overdrive Media Console.

From here, you can click the 'Play' button in the top-left corner to listen to the eAudiobook on your computer. The 'Download' button lets you download any parts of the eAudiobook that you missed.

TRANSFERRING AN e-AUDIOBOOK TO A MOBILE DEVICE

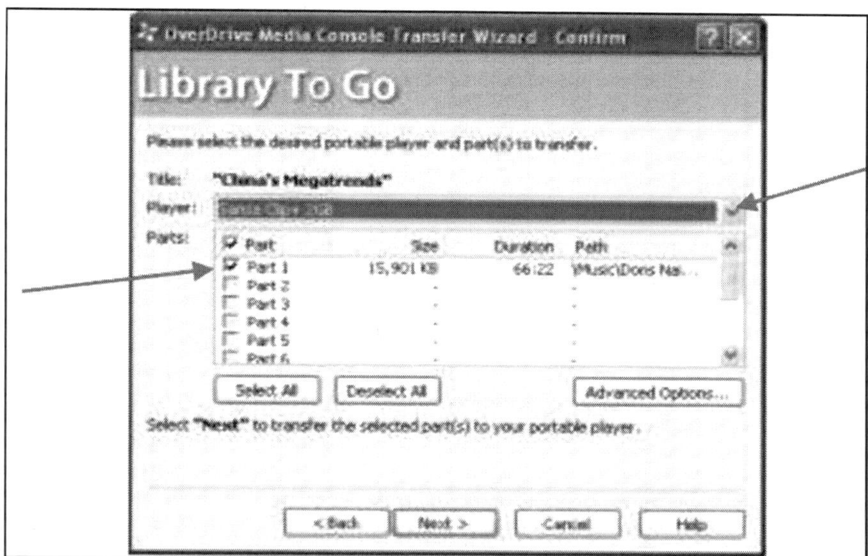

- Connect the device to your PC.
- Open Overdrive Media Console.
- Click the title of the eAudiobook you wish to transfer and click the 'Transfer' button in the topleft corner of the screen.
- Select your player and which parts of the eAudiobook you wish to transfer and click 'Next' to begin the transfer.
- Click 'Finish' and remove your player from the PC.

Special Considerations if Transferring to an iPod

- Some titles are not compatible with Apple devices st have iTunes v9.1 installed on your PC to transfer to an iPod.
- The iTunes setting 'Manually manage music...' must be enabled for Apple devices. Adjust this setting as follows.
  - Connect the device to your computer.
  - Open iTunes.
  - In iTunes, locate the device in the left vertical navigation panel and click the device.
  - If it is not already checked, place a checkmark next to the option 'Manually manage music...'and
  - Click the 'Apply' button.

Please note that at this time transferring WMA audiobooks to an Apple device running iOS 5 is not recommended due to compatibility issues between OverDrive Media Console and Apple iTunes. If you do attempt to transfer WMA files to an Apple device then please be sure to back up your files before starting the process. If you are still experiencing difficulty transferring an eAudiobook to your Apple device, please consult the Help section on the Library to Go web site for other possible solutions.

8

Information Technology in Library Science

ELECTRONIC INFORMATION SYSTEMS

Some clues about how authors and readers might behave in digital libraries and hypertext publishing systems can be perceived by looking at how people currently use computer bulletin boards, computer data bases, and other information services and electronic mail systems. Instead of viewing these systems as technical precedents, it is instructive to consider them as experiments in developing appropriate models for intellectual property and reader/user/author behaviour that might be adapted for more ambitious applications such as Xanadu.

PRODIGY AND CompuServe

Prodigy and CompuServe are commercial services that provide a variety of bulletin boards, electronic mail, infor-mation services, and entertainment. They embody significantly different models of user behaviour, and their pricing strategies are markedly different. Prodigy targets the consumer and home markets, and treats its users as relatively passive information consumers who do not interact much with each other. Prodigy offers users access to many different kinds of information, as well as bulletin boards, electronic mail, and some entertainment. Its services are made available for a fixed monthly fee.

Usage-insensitive pricing is made possible by the paid advertising that Prodigy presents along with nearly every screen of information displayed to users. When Prodigy imposed a usage-pricing scheme for sending electronic mail, many users felt that their contract with Prodigy, as well as their "free speech fights," had been violated. In contrast, CompuServe has been oriented towards business and professional users and always had usage-based pricing based on connect time.

CompuServe information services are specifically focused, organized into a complex hierarchy of bulletin boards and data bases, many of which are moderated by an expert, who in some circumstances is compensated by CompuServe. This finer-grained categorization enables CompuServe to impose sur-charges for supposedly more timely or valuable information, but its user population is presumably used to paying for information according to its value. Users engage in heated electronic dialogues with one another on bulletin boards, commenting on and criticizing one another's postings. Both Prodigy and CompuServe place some limits on user downloading.Some materials, such as shareware or public domain software from both sources, can be downloaded without restriction, but other materials are restricted. The two systems differ, however, in the locus of restrictions. Prodigy is a centralized service which means it sets and enforces the downloading policy. CompuServe, by contrast, has a more decentralized policy because it is essentially an umbrella organization for a number of information services, and these services often have their own downloading policies. Quite recently, however, both Prodigy and CompuServe have expanded user opportunities to download materials, although this adds to the cost of the service.

THE INTERNET

The Internet is a vast network of networks that inter-connect thousands of computing sites in government, industry, and academia. The Intermit has evolved from primarily providing electronic mail services to become the infrastructure for significantly broader services of information exchange and collaborative work. Like CompuServe, the heart of the Internet is a vast collection of newsgroups in which participants from around the world post and comment on messages. Some people take on the role of newsgroup moderators, but the overwhelming majority of newsgroups are unmediated. Author and reader behaviour on the Internet are largely governed by norms or "netiquette" that have evolved over time and that are enforced both by system administrators and by the informal but effective sanctions of "flames" (critical messages) directed at violators. Included in these norms are rules about selecting newsgroups in which to post messages, sensitivity to authors of posted messages when citing or responding to them, and other matters that affect both authors and readers. Users of the Internet vary greatly in their perception of intellectual property laws as they apply to this new kind of publishing system. Some users, especially new users who are college students, act as if the Internet services and the information that can be had by exploring the Internet are completely free.

In fact, each host machine that serves as an Internet site has to pay a fee for the privilege. Institutions recoup these fees as well as other costs associated with use of host machines by passing them on, even if the costs are not immediately evident because they may be borne by a particular unit of the institution, rather than directly by those who use the machine for Internet services. Those who post information not authored by them on Intermit bulletin boards or in electronic newsletters delivered by Internet sometimes do so with a conspicuous notice that it is being posted without copyright permission, thereby asserting the poster's view of an appropriate scope of fair use.

But some who post materials on the Internet explicitly assert copyrights on the messages that they post. And it has become increasingly common for electronic journals distributed on the Internet to contain a notice that those who contribute items to the journals are responsible for obtaining whatever copyright permissions might be needed. Although "net" users generally regard it as fair to download items from the bulletin board for one's personal use, and even to send a copy to a friend who might otherwise not see the item, it is considered bad manners (or worse) to redistribute more widely someone else's posting without its author's permission.

Still, it is worth noting that because "the net" is so vast and the number of its users so large, it can be extremely difficult to police it for copyright purposes. Authors who distribute works on the Internet are generally not paid to publish, and receive no royalties. Nor do readers generally have to pay to read items on the Internet. But it is fair to state that many Interact activities are being paid for (or at least subsidized) by Interact participants' employers.

Hence, it can be argued that anything posted on the Internet that is work-related is the intellectual property of the employer who provides access to the Internet by paying for the computers and telecommunications infrastructure.

Employers may feel that the value of the information their employees glean from the Internet outweighs the costs of the time to obtain it, but it is unlikely that many employers explicitly make this analysis. In addition to electronic mail and newsgroups, the Internet now supports several innovative services that enable it to function as a distributed digital library with vast holdings. If an Internet site chooses to make some of its information publicly available, a user on another site can use the anonymous FTP (file transfer protocol) mechanism to retrieve it. Other experimental services, some with fanciful names like Archie, Gopher, and World Wide Web, build upon FTP to provide users with a worldwide index so that they can find sites that offer the information they seek.

The WWW service allows users to retrieve what they want even if they cannot directly connect to the site that stores it. These new services are being enthusiastically embraced in the academic and research communities of the Internet, but they pose even more problems for intellectual property rights because they erode the boundaries between public and commercial information sources.

LEXIS ARM WESTLAW

Lawyers have had access to digital libraries of legal materials for well over a decade, thanks initially to the farsightedness of a paper manufacturer, which perceived a market opportunity for providing electronic access to judicial opinions, statutes, regulations, and other legal materials. This manufacturer formed Mead Data Central, whose Lexis data base lawyers use regularly. Like so many other print publishers, the major legal print publisher, West Publishing, did not see the market opportunity for electronic information services until after Lexis had become a major success.

Although a late entrant to the business, West has succeeded in designing a digital library of legal materials that offers some services, particularly the key numbering system that West had long used in print, that give it some competitive advantage. The initial pricing scheme employed by Lexis and by West was similar to that used by CompuServe: usage-based pricing based on connect-time. This pricing strategy worked particularly well because lawyers could typically pass these charges on to clients. Over time, both services developed pricing strategies for institutions, such as law schools, where connect-time charges could not be passed on.

Both services also now permit downloading of electronic versions of legal materials as well as printouts of selected materials. No special charges seem to be levied for these services, although usage-based charging would absorb the costs through connect-time, and institutional subscription pricing would be based on a predicted quantum of such uses. There is no technical reason why these two digital libraries could not become hypertext publishing systems. Their considerable financial success might suggest that this extension would be a natural one, and indeed, at least one author has tried to make them become so.

Professor Peter Martin of the Comell Law School sought to bring about this kind of expansion of legal data base functions by creating a hypertext treatise on Social Security Law on the Lexis system. Because Lexis had no particular incentive to promote its use, Martin eventually negotiated an arrangement by which he could "port" the treatise to a CD-ROM so it could be commercialized. Professor Henry Perritt of Villanova Law School has also proposed hypertext publishing systems built on top of digital libraries of legal materials as a way to produce electronic casebooks. But except for the work of a few pioneers, such as Professors William Andersen of the University of Washington Law School, William Boyd of the University of Arizona Law School, and Ronald Staudt of the Chicago-Kent Law School, hypertext has yet to come to the field of law. The richly inter textual nature of law makes it a natural field for hypertext applications, and perhaps ways can be found to create them on top of a digital library of legal materials such as Lexis or Westlaw, and make them commercially viable.

THE EVOLUTION OF INFORMATION TECHNOLOGY

Researcher provide a comprehensive remarks of the evolution of IT where he claimed that during the 1950s, computer systems were used mainly for scientific applications, with scientists the primary users and custodians of these systems. Business use of computers for mainly functional applications, such as accounting, began in the 1960s. The era of the 60s is known for the birth of *Data Processing (DP)* or *Electronic Data Processing (EDP),* which created a whole new profession.

During this period:

- The computer was perceived as a number crunching tool.
- Attention was focused on the power of these modem tools to compute, with much less emphasis placed on the overall value of information as a resource.

In the 1970s, more organisations moved towards the use of computers to provide management with information. This concept soon became known as *Management Information Systems (MIS).* Although MIS concepts were considered to be a major breakthrough in the use of computer systems to process information, organisations still emphasised the computer itself rather than focusing on the data and information as major components of the systems.

Many other concepts evolved during this period, examples:

- Database Management Systems (DBMS).
- Decision Support Systems (DSS).

The domination of mainframe computer systems gave way to the introduction of *minicomputers.* This new generation of computers became instrumental in the development of *Distributed Systems (DS).* The introduction of personal computers or microcomputers was another landmark development of this period. The technological advancements of the 1970s paved the way for a new era in the 1980s, which became known as the *Information Age.*

The significant phenomena of this era include the greater recognition of information as a major organisational asset and its importance in a competitive world economy. Another important characteristic of this era is the emphasis on the management of information and related resources utilised to maintain information resources. Furthermore, greater participation by users of information services became a major fact of this age.

The new generation of end users are more knowledgeable than their counterparts of a few decades earlier, and they created many networks of information systems sharing the vast powers of computers, data, information, and knowledge. In addition, technological advancements in telecommuni-cations allowed information users to exchange information more freely than ever. The old dream of developing computer systems that could think intelligently, learn, and make recommendations to decision makers carne closer to reality through many new applications of *Artificial Intelligent (AI)* and its component Expert Systems (ES).

NEW INFORMATION TECHNOLOGY RESOURCES

There are several developments which have lead to a new perception and assessment of the use and management of information technology resources.

These include:

- Recognition of information as a major organisational resource.
- Greater emphasis on utilisation of information as a major driving force in achieving effective strategies.
- New integration of telecommunications and information processing systems.
- A vast array of components comprising information technology resources.

Today, information technology resources consists of all types of information, representing various *functional entities* of organisations. Organisational information now can appear in all forms, which are processed by a conglomeration of computer machinery, examples:

- Mainframe,
- Minicomputers,
- Microcomputers,
- Reprographics, and
- Video discs.

It is communicated through the use of communication systems. The information is generated through the use of many information processing and management systems in diverse organisational structures. In addition to mechanical, procedural, and technical components of information technology resources, one must also consider the human elements.

These human elements can be divided into three categories:

1. Those individuals who are involved in different activities of generating information.
2. Those who are the primary users of information.
3. The management team responsible for the overall management planning functions of information technology resources.

One can argue that the role of the information technology resources management team has become more important to the overall success and growth of many organisations. In addition, the task of managing these resources is far more complex and sophisticated in the information age. Information technology resources are no longer viewed by many organisations as number crunching 'black boxes,' but rather as vital resources for identifying new opportunities and developing strategies.

Information Management in the 1990s

The cost of computing has dropped drastically in the past two decades. There is considerably more advanced information and communication devices available. AB a result, organisations of all sizes and types have been employing this technology to increase their competitive advantages. With the rapid evolution in information technology, the effectiveness of the traditional management techniques to the management of this technology has been the subject of much speculation by both researchers and practicing managers.

Clearly, this changing technology is in need of an evolution in its management as well:

- A management approach that is as dynamic as the technology itself,
- Keeping pace in its methods and strategies as the technology matures,
- Making drastic shifts in direction when necessary, and
- Always providing new opportunities for growth, is the essential ingredient for strategic management of information technology resources.

As information technology resources become more important to the overall success of the organisation, its management may not only be limited by technical planning and execution as was true in the past. With the current number of end users and their demands for information technology services, successful organisations will utilise the expertise of their information technology personnel to provide needed support for the end user in order to obtain the necessary competitive edge.

COMPONENTS OF INFORMATION TECHNOLOGY RESOURCES

Processing Hardware:

- Mainframe-based Systems.
- Mini-based Systems.
- Micro-based Systems.
- Word Processing.
- Micrographics.
- Reprographics.
- Video Disks Processor.
- Desktop Publishing Systems.

Telecommunications:

- Private Branch Exchange (PBX).
- Broadcasting Systems.
- Local Area Networks.
- Telecommunication Access.
- Systems.
- Facsimile Systems.
- Satellite Communications.
- On-Line Processing Systems.

Information:

- Marketing.
- Production.
- Personnel.

- Financial.
- Strategic.
- Intelligent.
- Accounting.
- Legal.
- Economy.
- Government.
- Trade.
- Publication.
- Public.

Office Automation:

- Text Management Systems.
- Electronic Mail.
- Teleconferencing.
- Computer Conferencing.
- Video Conferencing.
- Intelligent Copies.
- Intelligent Printers.
- Dictating Systems.

Systems Professionals:

- Chief Information Officer (ClO).
- Systems Managers.
- Systems Security.
- Administrators.
- System Analysts.
- Database Designers.
- Programmers.
- Computer Operators.
- Data Entry Personnel.
- User Support Personnel.

Processing Software:

- Operating Systems.
- Database Management Systems.
- Procedural Programming Languages.
- Fourth Generation Languages.
- Word Processing Software.
- Electronic Spreadsheet Software.
- Communications Software.
- Graphics and Desktop Publishing Systems.
- Project Management Software.
- Miscellaneous Software.

Management Structures:

- Centralised vs. Decentralised Structures.
- Departmental Computing Structure.
- Information Center Structure.
- End-User Computing Structure.
- Chargeback Processing Structure.

Information Systems:

- Data Processing Systems.
- Management Information Systems.
- Decision Support Systems.
- Transaction Processing Systems.
- Expert and Knowledge-Based Systems.
- Database Processing Systems.
- Executive Information Systems.
- Distributed Processing Systems.

End Users:

- Strategic Planners.
- Financial Managers.
- Marketing Managers.
- Inventory Managers.
- Production Managers.
- Personnel Managers.
- General Managers.
- Accountants.
- Legal Advisors.
- Economics.
- Publication Personnel.
- Training Personnel.
- Public Relations Personnel.
- Clerical Staff.
- Technical Specialists.

NEW INFORMATION TECHNOLOGY (IT) PRODUCTS

MOST IMPORTANT PRODUCTS OF THE '90S

The 1990s was a decade of rapid technological advances. Client-server architecture evolved into a viable alternative to mainframe computing. Enterprise applications such as groupware, inventory control, supply chain, and systems management emerged as platforms for the evolution of business systems. The PC became a Ubiquitous and increasingly powerful desktop tool. And the Internet was embraced as a communication medium, consumer platform, and business conduit. Here are 10 of the most important and influential products introduced in this decade.

1. *Sun Microsystems' Java:* The brave little embedded operating system

started out as a platform for write-once-run-anywhere computing and ended up as the Web's favourite tool.

2. *Nets Cape Navigator:* There's probably no greater development in the history of IT than the emergence of the Internet and World Wide Web. By the time Marc Andreessen and Jim Clark launched their graphical Web browser, Navigator 1.0, in 1994, there were more than 1 million Internet hosts. While Mosaic was the first widely distributed browser, Navigator set the standard in terms of look and functionality. And in the process, it shook Microsoft to its core—no small feat.
3. *Lotus Notes:* Lotus Development Corp. licensed Notes, the product most commonly associated with the term groupware, from Iris Associates in 1989. By the time IBM bought Lotus in 1995 for $3.5 billion—primarily to acquire the groupware technology—Notes had an installed base of almost 2 million seats. Lotus made a successful effort to integrate Notes with the Internet when it introduced Domino in 1996.
4. *Microsoft Office:* Microsoft didn't come up with the idea to bundle a spreadsheet, word processor, and graphics package into a productivity suite, but it made the most of the concept-and created a business computing standard. Microsoft has continued to enhance the bundle, including links to the Internet.
5. *Oracle's Relational Database:* The original work on relational database technology was done by Edgar Codd when he was at IBM in the early 1970s. However, Oracle took the relational model and established it as a database standard, through both rapid technological advance and aggressive marketing. In the 1990s, Oracle continued to enhance the basic architecture to incorporate symmetric multiprocessing and object extensions.
6. *Sun Microsystems' Enterprise 10000 Server:* Sun made believers out of many of those who had been skeptical about the scalability of symmetric multiprocessing servers when it shipped the 64-node E-I0000 in May 1997.
7. *SAP Rl3:* The third version of SAP's suite of enterprise applications, introduced in 1992, integrated and automated back-office systems and convinced many companies to re-engineer their business processes to accommodate the software.
8. *Computer Associates' Unicenter:* Introduced in 1993, CA's systems management software unified a disparate set of products and processes, and provided a comprehensive view of IT systems. CA continued to strengthen the product with the introduction of the graphical, object-oriented TNG version in 1997 and the three dimensional TND version in 1998.
9. *Intel's X86 Architecture:* Intel led the PC industry on a price/

performance curve that mirrored Moore's Law-and then some. When Intel launched the 66-MHz Pentium processor in 1993, it set the stage for a quantum leap in desktop processing, making possible powerful personal productivity applications and eventually online commerce.

10. *Microsoft Windows:* In the spring of 1990, Microsoft CEO Bill Gates introduced the latest iteration of the company's graphical front end, Windows 3.1 and it was an instant hit with the public. Since then, billions of copies of the operating system have been sold, and, along with its siblings, Windows NT and Windows CE, Windows has proved to be one of the highest-impact products in IT.

WELCOME TO THE INFORMATION SUPERDORM

Malone regard that "we are now at the threshold of a new era, driven this time not by the technologies of production and transportation, but by the technologies of information, communication and coordination." An extraordinary array of information technologies is providing not only powerful new tools for dealing with these changes, but also a promising framework for creating entirely new opportunities. Advances in computers, software, telecommunications, networking, and electronic media are vastly increasing the quantity, quality, and accessibility of all forms of information.

Internet

Internet as a "bunch of communications protocols that enables millions of computers to talk with each other. It is already replacing overnight mail and faxes as a way to communicate quickly and over long distances. Begun as a research project of the US Defence Department in the 1970s, it has become the:

- Technological trend in academic libraries of the '90s with dial up databases such as CompuServe, small corporate and university databases that are interconnected via the Internet.
- Thousands of companies have started to promote and sell products over the Net and at the same time, businesses are discovering that they can streamline operations and increased productivity by connecting their in-house networks to the Internet.

Almost overnight, the net grows from an academic resource into an ocean of capitalist dream.

World Wide Web

Subscribing to the Internet opens the door to many different types of information and communication possibilities. The World Wide Web, a *subset* of the Internet and one of the Internet's most popular and employs simpler computer applications, such as Windows, and more transparent commands then the internet.

By using browser software and fast modems, a subscriber can easily:

- View individuals' and organisations' home pages.
- Graphical tables of contents to more-detailed files contained within.
- Best of all, a user need not be a computer pro or a rocket scientist to surf the Net.

With the attributes such as multimedia, hyper linked, dispersed, dynamic, versatile and multi platform, the reason for Web popularity is the ability it affords to send and receive graphics, photographs, movies, and sound along with text. Several factors have contributed to this rapid growth, "most notably, technological advances in software, hardware, and communications that have made connections more economical".

Electronic Mail (E-Mail)

A way for computer users to exchange messages in completely different offices, locations, organisations, cities, countries, even continents using the e-mail programme available through the *Internet Service Provider* (ISP) to create, read, and manage the e-mail messages. Educationally, e-mail has continue to grow more important. It has also become easier to exchange not only textual messages but a variety of files, including graphics, software programmes, spreadsheets, and databases. Ingram believe that e-mail will become part of a total distance-education system that might include elements of videoconferencing, interactive multimedia, and other learning tools.

Lotus Notes

A complete 'environment' or 'platform' for several computer applications and can be used:

- to send electronic mail,
- As an electronic calendaring system,
- As a scheduling system.
- As a bulletin board.
- As a publishing system for the web,
- As an automated workflow system and
- As a group ware system.

Intranets

James view Intranet as a network that lets people within an organisation share the kind of information one's can experience—and create—with Netscape Communicator Professional such as:

- Pages full of text, graphics, sound, and video;
- Fill-out form;
- e-mail with pictures;
- Specialised newsgroup and interactive conferences;
- Directories full of files one's can download; and

- A broad range of custom-tailored resources for research, education, or business.

Thus by using a standardised methods, or protocols for moving information from one computer to another, an entire office, or even a corporation with many physically remote sites, can communicate without worrying about specific hardware or software.

Multimedia

Multimedia tools enable us to express ideas that are more difficult to describe with words than they are to demonstrate in some way. For those who are aural or tactile learners, for example, multimedia provides a fresh new means of comprehending something.

Videoconferencing

Ingram claim that videoconferencing is increasingly used for individual and group meetings as well as to deliver education and training at a distance. Brown University Computing and Information Services view videoconferencing as an interactive audio/visual meeting channel to sites worldwide via high speed telephone lines. Thus, videoconferencing combines the benefits of face-to-face interaction with the power of telecommunications.

As claimed by Littman, the videoconferencing rationales are as follows:

- Enhance the quality and intensity of communications.
- Engender a sense of responsibility and involvement among individuals who could not otherwise meet with each other.
- Lead to the articulation of policy, goals, and objectives through consensual decision making.
- Enable academic librarians to hold interactive sessions regardless of location on such topics as Internet access and use, intellectual freedom and copyright.
- High school students can be introduced to resources in an academic library, thus saving field trip and liability insurance costs.

Virtual Reality

Virtual reality has captured most organisations. It benefits an organisation, by gathering information on customers/users, competitors, and potential markets.

Cavanaugh describes the creation of 'virtual offices' that has enable:

- Communications between employees and vendors.
- Advertise products and services globally.
- Deliver new products or packages of services.

CD-ROMs

Rogers view that the advent of CD-ROMs in libraries was the introduction to the world of high-tech ware for many librarians. CD-ROMs are found in every library today and are loaded on most business networks but are often simply presented to end users, from car mechanics to astronauts. This technology is revolutionising the way students and professionals can assemble and access information.

Being fixed systems:

- The *content* on CD-ROMs is finite, although the amount of information on a disc is still impressive.
- The *functionality* of CD-ROMs and the number of tricks they can perform is finite.

Amendments to the software, indexing, and content are done at the will of the developer and information provider. A number of business databases available on CD-ROMs has increased steadily over the past few years. At the same time, most major public libraries, colleges, and *university libraries* have made available at no cost numerous CD-ROM databases for user and customer use.

CD-ROMs Into the Future

Beiser stresses that the emergence of a high-density CD (HiCD) technology opens exciting new possibilities for all sectors of our society—not the least of which are *libraries.* CD-ROMs was a distribution and publishing medium, and not a competitor to hard disk drives. Meanwhile, HiCD can deliver text, graphics and multimedia content as well or better than a high-speed link. It is the stuff of memory cells, the repository of incredible amounts of otherwise evanescent data, a resource without which libraries will be unable to perform their designated role in an information intensive universe.

Online Databases

It offers full texts of journal and magazine articles. Tenopir claimed that academic librarians are actively looking for alternatives to print journal collections:

- As serials budgets stagnate,
- Print journals take up as much space.
- Patrons want to locate and access everything from a single workstation.

Some examples of online databases are EBSCO Elite Periodical Database, FirstSearch Online Databases, INFOTRAC Periodical and Newspaper Databases, etc.

Electronic Journals

Researcher claimed that electronic journals are mushrooming online, on the Web and in CD-ROM format. This phenomenon is due to the rapid advancement of information technologies including the Internet and digitising techniques. The quantity of e-journals is growing larger although no exact number is available.

In recent years, many more journals have been earmarked for digitising, a necessary process for turning a paper journal into an electronic one. In addition, a considerable number of journals are now published only electronically, which significantly enlarges the size of the e-journal pool. Among all the users of e-journals, academic libraries especially, are the major subscribers of e-journals.

LIBRARY INFORMATION SYSTEM AND INFORMATION TECHNOLOGY

In library information system, information technology has had a clear and persuasive impact in almost every area of the library. The most significant development in information technology over the last few years or so is digital technology. Digital technology is revolutionizing the traditional concepts of preservation and access in library and archive communities. The applications of digital system and computing system in the libraries have been a subject of interest to present day professional librarians.

More recently the libraries have sought to implement increasingly complex solution that involved distributed networking and access to remote information resources. During the eighties, the whole focus of the librarians shifted towards library automation but in the nineties it has shifted towards digitization. The phrase library automation has been generally accepted within the profession to encompass early automation activities, yet it does not do justice to the current state of affaires as libraries have move well beyond the automation of internal procedures. In Manipur, however, applications of technologies in libraries are lagging far behind.

There are two university libraries, 74 affiliated colleges, nine public libraries, one state central library at Imphal and others at different districts of Manipur and many high and higher secondary schools libraries. But most of the libraries function in the traditional way with conventional printed shelf collection except some libraries like Manipur University library, Central Agricultural Library, RIMS Library, DOEACC Library etc. These libraries have initiated automation. Manipur University Library started automation since 1989 in the areas such as cataloguing, serial control, information retrieval and circulation recently.

This library provides internet facility, OPAC and has become one of the important nodes in the academic libraries system. As far as college libraries are concerned collections of information resources which support the faculty and students are not up to the mark because of lack planned systematic approach to the development of resources. Many of college libraries built up their collection of printed materials as activities and services are yet to be automated. Only one college library *i.e.* Modern College library has started Data entry using

CDS/ISIS. Books are still the only important channel for dissemi-nation of information. The librarian and other supporting professional staff are not well qualified and trained with the new modern technology. As far as infrastructures are concern a large majority of libraries have not yet automated their activities as they are handicapped to switch over to computeri-zation and modernization because of lack of infrastructural facilities like computer hardware, software, and human-ware.

And most of the libraries are not provided internet facility.Regarding school and higher secondary school libraries, majority of school libraries are not able to provide even the facilities of a traditional library. From the discussion it is evident that the libraries in Manipur, except some, automation of the operations and services progressing very slowly. Automation as well as conversion of digital library will not be possible within five year though plan for automation exist. In Manipur it is not an easy task to develop digital library system as automation in the library is totally absent. Keeping in views of the reasons, authority should take initiative for promoting library automation by implementing new IT in the libraries of Manipur so that users from different communities can get the universe of knowledge available in the digital format.

PROBLEMS OF DIGITAL LIBRARIES SYSTEMS

Problems faced while entering into a digital libraries systems in Manipur can be summarized as:

- Libraries exist only in the traditional form and there is no electronic library/digital resource;
- Most of the libraries function with inadequate number professional staff required for smooth functioning and there is a general unwillingness to develop digital library system;
- Even if the librarian and some professionals are qualified they certainly lag behind because of lack of awareness about value of information, cooperation and coordination in the resource building and sharing of information and poor communication skill;
- Total absence of hardware, software and trained human power is another reason;
- A highly irregular and unpredictable power supply; and
- Libraries lack standardization of methods due to unwillingness to adapt to new requirements;
- Presently large majority of library have no computer and no internet facility and other infrastructural facilities required to exploit the opportunities provided by electronic media. Therefore, the best use of electronic publication on-line and network access are not possible;
- Lack of financial support due to the acute financial problem the state is facing.

In fact, the main problems faced seem to be lack of financial resources and lack of computer education without which automation in the libraries are not possible.

The dawn of information revolution is considered to be one of the marvelous achievements of the 20th century. The rapid growth and development of IT has resulted in the development of digital library, tools and skill relating to encoding information objects in digital format. The application of digital technologies within the library comes along with the development of computer technology. Keeping the points in view it is necessary to consider some perspective of digital library. Digital library not only creates and develops modern libraries but also transforms many existing libraries.

Digital Library introduced the concept of hypertext, facilitates networking in order to communicate and exchange digital information from source location to destination. It also facilitates preservation, storage, and communication of diverse multimedia objects but also provides intensive access from multiple locations and enrich teaching and learning environment which is not possible with the traditional library.

Due to information explosion and existence of information society, everybody is aware of the newly developed technologies. This new developments are reflected in LIS education and in those libraries with existing infrastructure, services and network. In fact, there is a complete change in activities, role of library, librarians and other professionals (staff).

Most of the librarians in Manipur have now entered in the technological era of communication dominated by film and electronic media. The libraries are expected to be an automated information system having pervasive impact in almost every areas of library-be it the online catalogue, online database, online searching, document delivery, inter library loan, circulation etc. Clearly, the impact of automated system in libraries has been pervasive and significant.

STRUCTURE OF INFORMATION SCIENCE IN LIBRARY

Any field is structured along some distinct, larger areas or subdisciplines of enquiry or practice. Think of a number of areas of medicine, computer science, librarianship, and so forth. Information science is not an exception. It has a distinct, two-partite structure. A number of authors observed that the work in information science falls in two large areas or subdisciplines, each, of course, with further subareas or specialties. White and McCain conducted a monumental bibliometric study of the domain of information science by providing extensive analysis of co-citation patterns for 120 authors over a period of 23 years. Borrowing from White and McCain, visualize a map of information science as an ellipse with authors inside, distributed or clustered according to their connections. There are two large clusters at each end of the ellipse, with only a few authors spanning both. In other words, there are two major areas or subdisciplines.

I liked their metaphor:

- *As Things Turn Out, Information Science Looks Rather like Australia*: Heavily coastal in its development, with a sparsely settled interior.

In one of the coastal sections, fall authors that worked on analytical study of literatures; their structures; studies of texts as content-bearing objects; communication in various populations, particularly scientific communication; social context of information; information uses; information seeking and behaviour; various theories of information and related topics. As yet, there is no good label for that cluster. Some call it "information analysis." For simplicity, lets call this the *domain cluster,* as did White and McCain, although "basic" may be a good label. In the other coastal section are authors who concentrated on IR theory and retrieval algorithms; practical IR processes and systems; human-computer interaction; user studies; library systems; OPACs; and related topics.

Let's call this cluster the *retrieval cluster,* although "applied" may also be a good label. Basically, most of the areas in the domain cluster are about study of fundamental manifes-tations and behaviour of phenomena and objects that information science is all about. They are centered on the phenomenon of information and its manifestations in literature. The retrieval cluster deals, by and large, with a variety of implementations, on both practical and theoretical levels. It is about implementation, behaviour, and effects of the interface between literatures and people, including, of course, all kinds of retrieval aspects. Unfortunately, these two main clusters are largely unconnected.

Only a very small number of authors spanned the two clusters. In other words, there are very few integrating works. The last text that undertook an integrative approach encom-passing both clusters. A rare example of such an effort in research is the last work by Tague-Sutcliffe, where she related the notion of informative-ness with evaluation of IR systems.

Several modern texts are specifically aimed at IR but none on information science as a whole. I dare to venture a prediction: fame awaits the researcher who devise a formal theoretical work, bolstered by experimental evidence, that connects the two largely separated clusters, *i.e.*, connecting basic phenomena with their realization in the retrieval world. And a bestseller is awaiting an author that produces an integrative text in information science. Information science will become a full-fledged discipline when the two ends are connected successfully. The two clusters are not equally popu-lated.

The retrieval cluster has significantly more authors, not to mention total number of works. As in many other fields, more effort is expanded on the applied side than on the basic side.In part, this is due to availability of funds for given topics—not surprisingly, research goes after moneyed topics. By and large, over the last decade or so, major granting agencies funded only applied research in information science. For instance, I have been unable to identify a single grant addressing any of the topics in the domain or basic cluster from NSF Division of Information and Intelligent Systems since its preceding Division of Information Science and Technology was reorganized and included in the Directorate for *Computer and Information Science and Engineering* (CISE) in 1985. In de Solla Price's concepts and words, the domain cluster is "little science", while the retrieval cluster is "big science," and the connection between the two has presently no science.

PROBLEMS ADDRESSED

General

Webster routinely defines information science as "the science dealing with the efficient collection, storage, and retrieval of information." It is a general definition of problems addressed by information science. The definition follows pretty much an early and popular one given by Borko as a part of a wide discussion and controversy about the nature of the field in the 1960s.

More specifically, information science is a field of professional practice and scientific enquiry addressing the problem of effective communication of knowledge records—"literature"—among humans in the context of social, organizational, and individual need for and use of information.

The key orientation here is the problem of need for and use of information, as involving knowledge records.To provide for that need, information science deals with specifically, oriented information techniques, procedures, and systems. To elaborate, the specific concentration of information science is on human knowledge records as *content-bearing objects*, in all forms, shapes, and media.

The primary emphasis is on content of these objects, in terms of their potential for conveying information. "Literature" may be used as a generic term for these knowledge records, but "literature" has many other connotations, thus requiring a careful restriction in its use in information science. Because of these connotations, "literature" will not become popular in information science.

Realizing this, I am using the term here only as a shorthand, as did White and McCain, when they elegantly stated:

- "The proper study of information science is the interface between people and literature... modeling the world of publications with a practical goal of being able to deliver their content to enquirers on demand... While many scientists seek to understand communication between persons, information scientists seek to understand communication between persons and certain valued surrogates for persons that literature comprises.

In all of this there is a technological imperative, reflected in efforts to take advantage of modern information technology. While information science is not about technology, the problem of providing effective computer applications pervades the field. Following is a word on the extent and borders of infor-mation science. Focusing information science on the content-bearing properties of literature, and on associated techniques and systems dealing with providing effective access to and use of literature, provides a restriction for information science.

Thus, the field does *not* deal with great many other information systems, such as payroll, inventory, decision support systems, data processing, airline schedules, and a zillion others, nor does it deal with direct communication among and between persons. Information science is about a specific manifestation or type of information that defines its scope and its systems. Information science, as many other fields, also involves a professional component. Starting in 1950s, the profession of information science grew from research and applications in IR, to become a powerful component of the field, and in many ways a leading one in respect to innovation.

As in many other fields, there is an uneasy relation between the scientific or research-oriented component and the professional or practice-oriented one. The profession is responding in its own way to needs of its users and organizations, and chartering its own technological applications, many times independently of research advances, and even in different directions. At present, the connection and feedback between profession and research in information science is not as well established as it is in older fields, such as engineering or medicine. This is a serious inhibitor for progress of both.

More Specific

A number of authors suggested a breakdown of specific areas of information science, beyond the structural analysis offered above. The breakdown among different authors is in significant agreement, although the labels differ somewhat. I will take the breakdown and labels provided by White and McCain. They provided a factor analysis of co-cited authors and extracted 12 factors as specialties.

In descending order of how authors loaded, they labelled the specialties as:

- Experimental *information retrieval* (IR);
- Citation analysis;
- Practical retrieval;
- Bibliometrics;
- General library systems theory;
- Science communication;
- User studies and theory;
- OPACs;
- General imported ideas—other disciplines;
- Indexing theory;

- Citation theory; and
- Communication theory.

While one may quibble with some of the classes and labels, these specialties provide a fairly accurate picture of problem areas in which information scientists worked over the past quarter of a century.

Over time, there were shifts in emphasis and there were movements between specialties. Nothing is permanent. But these are the specialties of information science. New areas are clearly on the horizon. For the 1990s, I would suggest that the major new areas include interaction studies; searching of the Internet; multimedia IR; multilanguage IR; and digital libraries.

These are prime examples of the new significant areas of concentration, not yet evident in the historical record. At the same time, the old area of experimental retrieval is blossoming like never before, courtesy of the *Text Retrieval Conference* (TREC), a government-sponsored mechanism for comparative evaluation of a variety of IR techniques and approaches that involves large test beds. IR was, and still is, the major and most populated area of information science. Thus, a separate discussion of IR follows.

INFORMATION RETRIEVAL

In the early and mid-1950s, a critical mass of scientists, engineers, librarians, and entrepreneurs started working enthusiastically on the problem and solution defined by Bush. By 1960s this became a large and relatively well-funded effort and organized activity. Often, there were heated arguments and controversies about the "best" solution, technique, or system.

These arguments brought on the tradition of evaluation, a major staple of IR research and development. What is now TREC started with Cranfield evaluations in the late 1950s and early 1960s. Remarkably, the basic evaluation principles developed then are still the underpinning of TREC today. Calvin Mooers, an active and highly visible pioneer of information science, coined the term *information retrieval* in 1951. The term took hold, and today is a part of the English language.

At that time, Mooers not only coined the term, but also defined the problems to be addressed:

- "Information retrieval embraces the intellectual aspects of the description of information and its specification for search, and also whatever systems, techniques or machines that are employed to carry out the operation.

Today, we would add that IR also and particularly involves interaction in all of these, with all the contextual-cognitive, affective, situational—aspects that interaction embraces. An expanded Mooers' conception is still valid. As it advanced, IR produced a number of theoretical, empirical, and pragmatic concepts and constructs. Numerous IR systems were developed and successfully deployed. A great many historical examples can be given to illustrate the remarkable evolution of IR systems and techniques, adapting the ever-evolving information technology, from punch cards in the midcentury to the Internet at its close.

Based on IR, an online information industry emerged in the 1970s, and grew through its own version of information explosion, as chronicled by Hahn. IR is one of the most widely spread applications of any information system worldwide. It has a proud history. Surely, information science is more than IR, but many of the problems raised by IR or derived from objects and phenomena involved in IR, are at its core.

Approaches and Paradigm Split

The approach taken by Mooers was to concentrate on the building of systems. This systems emphasis which was formulated early in the 1950s, was the sole approach to IR for some decades. It still predominates in a good part of IR research to this day.

Consequently, most of the IR research and practice concentrated on retrieval systems and processes. However, starting in the late 1970s and gaining steam in the 1980s, a different line of reasoning and research evolved-one that concentrates on the cognitive, interactive, and contextual end of the process. It addressed users, use, situations, context, and interaction with systems, rather than IR systems alone as a primary focus.

The retrieval cluster started splitting into subclusters, as noted by White and McCain, and before by others such as Saracevic and Harter. We now have two distinct communities and approaches to research in the retrieval cluster. They became commonly known as *systems-centred* and *user-centred.* Both address retrieval, but from very different ends and perspectives. The split is not only conceptual, looking very differently at the same process, but also organizational. The systemscentered side is now mostly concentrated in the *Special Interest Group on Information Retrieval* (SIGIR) of the *Association for Computing Machinery* (ACM), while the user-centered cluster congregates around the *American Society for Information Science* (ASIS).

Each has its own communication outlets-journals, proceedings, and conferences. There is less and less overlap of authors and works between the two outlets. We have two camps, two islands, with, unfortunately, relatively little traffic in-between. The systems-centered approach is exemplified by work on algorithms and evaluation based on the traditional IR model, a model that does not consider the users or interaction. The massive research that evaluates a variety of IR algorithms and approaches within TREC is a culmination of this approach.

In contrast, cognitive, situational, and interactive studies and models, involving the use of retrieval systems exemplify the human-centered approach.

Following that approach, interactive models, differing significantly from the traditional IR model, started to emerge. Even in TREC, a group of researchers started an interaction track, but so far have a hard time conceptually and methodologically, thus demonstrating the difficulty in merging the traditional and interactive models and approaches. Let me characterize, in a simplified way, the relationship between the two approaches or subclusters addressing different sides of retrieval.

On the one hand, the human-centred side was often highly critical of the systems side for ignoring users and use, and tried valiantly to establish humans as the proper center of IR work. The mantra of human-centred research is that the results have implications for systems design and practice. Unfortunately, in most human-centred research, beyond suggestions, concrete design solutions were not delivered. On the other hand, the systems side, by and large, ignores the human side and user studies, and is even often completely ignorant of them. As to design, the stance is "tell us what to do and as suggested, do it." But nobody is really telling, or if telling, nobody is listening.

As a rule, in systems-oriented projects, people and users are absent. Thus, there are not many interactions between the two camps. Let me provide some examples. A rough analysis of the 1997 SIGIR proceedings found only 3 papers of some 34 that dealt in some way with people and users; in the ACM's Digital Libraries 1997 conference proceedings, of 25 papers only 3 mentioned people and users. If one reads authors such as Dervin and Nilan, and many of their successors, who champion the human centered approach, one gets the impression that there is a real conflict between the two sides and approaches, and that there is an alternative way to the "dreadful" systems approach.

In a way, this stance is a backlash caused by the excesses, failures, and blind spots of systems-centered approaches not only in IR, but also in great many other technological applica-tions. Unfortunately, sometimes the backlash is justified. All of us who work on the humancentered side are not that dismissive of the systems side. But the issue is not whether we should have systems-*or* humancentered approaches. The issue is even less of human*versus* systems-centered. *The issue is how to make human*and *systems-centered approaches work together.* In this sense, a number of works have addressed integrating usercentered and systems-centered approaches in IR, but this has been discussed mostly by researchers from the usercentered side.

Examples are works by:

- Bates,
- Belkin,
- Cool,
- Stein,
- Thiel,
- Fidel

- Efthimidiadis,
- Robertson and
- Beaulieu.

To reiterate, it is not one camp against the other but how can we incorporate the best features of both approaches and make them work jointly. The issue is how to deliver and incorporate the desired design features that will improve systems orientations towards users, integrate them with systems features, and use advantages provided by both, humans and technology. In other words, the issue is *putting the human in the loop* to build better algorithms and to exploit computational advantages. Real progress in information science, and by extension in IR, will come when we achieve this. Lately, the NSF has championed human-centered design involving an interdisciplinary approach to information systems. Hopefully, this will go beyond rhetoric. It is not easy to do. But, that is what research is for—to address difficult, not only easy problems.

Proprietary IR

By the 1980s, the commercial information industry based on IR became successful and profitable. Out of academe, grants, and government, IR became a money-making propo-sition. This, of course, is another and important sign of success. Not surprisingly, a number of former IR researchers, practitioners, and graduates of IR programmes ventured out to become IR entrepreneurs.

Sure enough, throughout information science history there were many entrepreneurs, and they were highly significant in development of the field. But this generation of entrepre-neurs was different. They ventured to develop and market a variety of IR procedures based on algorithms, applicable and scalable to large files, multiple applications, and/or various advanced technologies. It was knowledge industry at its purest. But, as in all commercial knowledge industries, the product was proprietary. While it was not that hard to guess the base of these various proprietary algorithms and how they worked—after all they were derived from publicly available knowledge and experiences, such as those that came from SMART experi-ments—they remain unpublished and "secret."

A new kind of IR evolved, separate from the rest, not communicating as to intellectual advances with the rest. None of these ventures became a high commercial success, as measured by Silicon Valley standards. But the World Wide Web, emerging in the first half of the 1990s, changed all this. The acceleration of the growth of the Web is an information explosion of the like never before seen in history. Not surprisingly then, the Web is a mess. No wonder that everybody is interested in some form of IR as a solution to fix it.

A number of academic-based efforts were initiated to develop mechanisms, search engines, "intelligent" agents, crawlers, and so forth, to help control the Web. Some of these were IR scaled, and adapted to the problem; others were a variety of extensions of IR. Many had few, if any original, developments, besides new packaging or labeling; and a good number were just the usual hype. The wheel was reinvented a number of times. But out of this, and fast, came commercial ventures, such as the pioneering Yahoo!, whose basic objective is to provide search mechanisms for finding something of relevance for users on demand.

And to make a lot of money. These enterprises pride themselves on having proprietary methods by which they are accomplishing the retrieval tasks. The connection to the information science community is tenuous, and almost Non-existent. The flow of knowledge, if any, is onesided, from IR research results into proprietary engines. The reverse contribution to public knowledge is zero. A number of evaluations of these search engines have been undertaken simply by comparing some results between them or comparing of their retrieval against some benchmarks.

Some evaluations were done within, others outside of information science. Results were not complimentary. The Web-based proprietary IR is expanding and flourishing outside of the field. It is addressing a vexing problem, the like we have not seen before. But as yet, the success is elusive and questionable.

RELEVANCE

As information science pioneers developed IR processes and systems in the 1950s, they defined as the main objective retrieval of *relevant* information. Effectiveness was expressed in terms of relevance. From then to now, IR is explicitly geared not towards any old kind of information, but towards *relevant information*. Various IR approaches, algorithms, and practices were, and still are, evaluated in relation to relevance. Thus, relevance became a key notion in information science. It is also a complex phenomenon with a long and turbulent history in information science transcending IR, going back to early 1950s. Of course, there was a choice.

Relevance did not have to emerge as the key notion. Uncertainty was one choice suggested by a number of theorists to be the base of IR, and thus to reflect effectiveness. But it did not take. In contrast, uncertainty is the basic notion underlying expert systems. If the pioneers had not embraced relevance, but instead, let's say, uncertainty, as the base for IR, we would have today a very different IR, and probably not that successful. In general, relevance, according to *Webster*, means having significant bearing on matter at hand. As with many other concepts, relevance assumes related but more specific meaning in more specific contexts and applications.

In the context of information science, relevance is the attribute or criterion reflecting the effectiveness of exchange of information between people and IR systems in communi-cation contacts based on valuation by people. With relevance as the criterion, and human Judgements of relevance of retrieved objects as the measuring instrument, the measures of precision and recall are widely used in evaluation of IR systems. The strength of these measures is that they involve people—users—as judges of effectiveness of performance. The weakness is the same: it involves Judgement by people, with all the perils of subjectivity and variability. Relevance indicates a relation. For relevance, many relations have been investigated.

An consensus has emerged in information science that we can distinguish between several differing relations that account for different manifestations or types of relevance:

- *System or Algorithmic Relevance:* Relation between a query and information objects in the file of a system as retrieved, or as failed to be retrieved, by a given procedure or algorithm. Comparative effectiveness in inferring relevance is the criterion for system relevance.
- *Topical or Subject Relevance:* Relation between the subject or topic expressed in a query and topic or subject covered by retrieved texts, or, more broadly, by texts in the system file, or even in existence. Aboutness is the criterion by which topicality is inferred.
- *Cognitive Relevance or Pertinence:* Relation between the state of knowledge and cognitive information need of a user and texts retrieved, or in the file of a system, or even in existence. Cognitive correspondence, infor-mativeness, novelty, information quality, and the like are criteria by which cognitive relevance is inferred.
- *Situational Relevance or Utility:* Relation between the situation, task or problem at hand and texts retrieved by a system, or in the file of a system, or even in existence. Usefulness in decision making, appropriateness of information in resolution of a problem, reduction of uncertainty, and the like are criteria by which situational relevance is inferred.
- *Motivational or Affective Relevance:* Relation between the intents, goals, and motivations of a user and texts retrieved by a system, or in the file of a system, or even in existence. Satisfaction, success, accomplish-ment, and the like are the criteria for inferring motivational relevance.

Practically, IR systems assess systems relevance only-that is, they respond to queries-hoping that the objects retrieved may also be of cognitive relevance, and even more so of utility. However, a user may judge an object by any or all types of relevance-for a user they may interact dynamically. Difficulties arise when an object is of system relevance but not of cognitive relevance or utility, or conversely.

If items are of cognitive relevance or utility, but were not reflected in the query, they are not and cannot be retrieved. At the bottom of IR research is a quest to align systems with other types of relevance.

People all over have a strong intuitive understanding of relevance, thus, they intuitively understand, without manuals, what IR is all about. This makes IR systems generally understandable and acceptable-a critical attribute in their widespread application.

DISCIPLINARY RELATIONS

Two things introduced interdisciplinarity in information science. First and foremost, the problems addressed cannot be resolved with approaches and constructs from any single discipline-thus, intedisciplinarity is predetermined, as it is in many modern fields. Second, interdisciplinarity in information science was introduced and is being perpetuated to the present by the very differences in backgrounds of people addressing the described problems. Differences in background are many; they make for richness of the field and difficulties in communication and education. Clearly not every discipline in the background of people working on the problem made an equally relevant contri-bution, but the assortment was responsible for sustaining a strong interdisciplinary characteristic of information science. I will concentrate on interdisciplinary relations with two fields: librarianship and computer science. Obviously, other fields, most notably cognitive science and communication, have also interdisciplinary relations, but these are the most significant and developed ones.

Librarianship

Librarianship has a long and proud history devoted to organization, preservation, and use of graphic records and records in other media. This is done through libraries not only as a particular organization or type of information system, but even more so as an indispensable social, cultural, and educational institution whose value has been proven manifold throughout human history, and across all geographic and cultural boundaries.

Researcher defines the library as:

- ...Contributing to the total communication system in society... Though the library is an instrumentality created to maximize the utility of graphic records for the benefits of society, it achieves that goal by working with the individual and through the individual it reaches society.

The common ground between library science and information science, which is a strong one, is in sharing of their social role and in their general concern with effective utilization of graphic and other records, particularly by individuals.

But there are also very significant differences in several critical respects, among them:

- *Selection of Problems Addressed and the Way they were Defined*: A majority of the problems were not and are not addressed in library science;

- *Theoretical Questions Asked and Frameworks Established*: The theories and conceptual frameworks in librarian-ship have no counterpart in information science, and *vice versa*;
- *The Nature and Degree of Experimentation and Empirical Development and the Resulting Practical Knowledge and Competencies Dderived*: There is very little overlap in experimentation and development between the two, and professional requirements differ as well to a significant degree;
- *Tools and Approaches Used:* A most telling example is the very different approach undertaken in relation to utilization of technology in IR and in library automation; and
- *The Nature and Strength of Interdisciplinary Relations Established and the Dependence of Progress on Inter-disciplinary Approaches*: Librarianship is much more selfcontained.

All of these differences warrant a conclusion that librarian-ship and information science are two different fields in strong interdisciplinary relations, rather than one and the same field, or one being a special case of the other. This is not a matter of turf battles, or of one being better or worse than the other. Such arguments, while common between many fields, matter little to progress of either field. But differences in selection and/or definition of problems addressed, agenda, paradigms, theoretical base, and practical solutions *do* matter. Thus the conclusion that librarianship and information science, while related, are different fields. The differences are most pronounced in the research agenda and directions.

Interestingly, research on OPACs, now that they are incorporating more and more IR features, is bringing the two fields in closer relation. Probably, so will the research in digital libraries, but at this time, it is too early to tell. The conclusion is not without heated controversy.

Among other authors, Vakkari contends on information science and librarianship being one and the same field, with the now commonly used name of "library and information science." Does it matter? Administratively yes, very much so, particularly in universities and professional societies. Otherwise, no. The issue is, and always will be, in the problems addressed and solutions undertaken. I contend that they differ significantly.

Computer Science

The basis of relation between information science and computer science lies in the application of computers and computing in IR, and the associated products, services, and networks. In the last few years, this relation also involves research on the evolving digital libraries, with their strong technological base.

To illustrate the connection, we use a definition by Denning:

- "The discipline of computing is the systematic study of algorithmic processes that describe and transfer information: their theory, analysis, design, efficiency, implementation, and application. The fundamental question underlying all of the computing is: "What can be automated?"

Computer science is about algorithms related to infor-mation interpreted in the first, whereas information science is about the very nature of information and its use by humans, interpreted in the third or broadest sense. Computer science is about symbol manipulation, whereas information science is about content manipulation, where symbol manipulation is the indispensable infrastructure. The two concerns are not in competition, they are complementary—they lead to different basic and applied agendas. Computer science is also many times larger than information science.

A number of computer scientists have been involved in research and development on information and its many spin-offs, to the point of being recognized leaders in information science. Gerard Salton is a prime example. In addition, there are several streams of research and development in computer science that had no connection with the early evolution of information science, but have addressed information problems similar to those in information science. Among others, these include works on expert systems, knowledge bases, hypertext, and human-computer interaction.

More recently, this involves research and development on digital libraries, a "hot", financially heavily supported area by a host of government agencies in the U.S. and many other countries. Bolstered by heavy support, interest in digital library research exploded on the scene in 1990s, attracting the attention of computer scientists from a wide variety of streams, as well as people from many other disciplines. These areas have a significant informational component that is associated with information representation, its intellectual organization, and linkages; meta-information, information seeking, searching, retrieving, and filtering; use, quality, value, and impact of information; evaluation of information systems from user and use perspective; and the like-all traditionally addressed in information science.Conversely, these streams of computer science research and development provide a different outlook, framework, and approach, and even a different paradigm, not only for information science research and development, but also for its academic and continuing education. Again, as with librarianship, the issue is not about turf. It is about paradigms, theoretical foundations, and pragmatic solutions; and ultimately, it is about their appropriateness to human information problems.

EDUCATION

That education is critical for any field is a truism that hardly needs to be stated. In particular, research lives by education, it cannot be better than the education that researchers receive and then extend and plow back into education. Unfortunately, education in information science has not received the attention that it deserves. This may explain the many difficulties in the field that I have discussed. Educational models that evolved differed to a degree or even substantially from country to country. I am concentrating here on the U.S. models only.

In the United States, two educational models evolved over time. I call them the Shera and Salton models, after those that pioneered them. Both have strengths and weaknesses. Jesse H. Shera was a legendary library school dean from the 1950s until the 1970s at Western Reserve University. Among others, he was instrumental in starting the Center for Documentation and Communication Research in 1955. Shortly thereafter, the library school curriculum started to include courses such as "Machine Literature Searching" and several other more advanced courses and laboratories on the topics of research in the Centre.

The basic approach was to append those courses, mostly as electives, to the existing library school curriculum, without modifications of the curriculum as a whole, and particularly not the required core courses. Information science became one of the specialty areas of library science. The base or core courses that students were taking rested in the traditional library curriculum. Information science education was an appendage to library science. A few attempts to spin off information science as an independent degree and curriculum were not followed widely. But Shera's model was. Library schools in the U.S. and in many other countries imitated Shera's model.

They used the same approach and started incorporating information science courses in their existing curriculum as a specialty. Out of this was borne the current designation "library and information science." Shera's model is still the prevalent approach in schools of library and information science. The strength of the Shera model is that it posits education within a service framework, connects the education to professional practice and to a broader and user-oriented frame of a number of other information services, and relates it to a great diversity of information resources.

The weakness is a lack of a broader theoretical frame-work and a total lack of teaching of any formalism related to systems, such as development and understanding of algori-thms. The majority of researchers in the human-centered side, as I described earlier, came from or are associated with this educa-tional environment. Gerard Salton was first and foremost a scientist, a computer scientist, and the father of modern IR.

As such, he pioneered the incorporation into IR research a whole array of formal and experimental methods from science, as modified for algorithmic and other approaches used so successfully in computer science. His primary orientation was research. For education, he took the time-honoured approach of a close involvement with research. Salton's model was a laboratory and research approach to education.

As Shera's model resulted in information science educa-tion being an appendage to library science education, Salton's model of IR education resulted in it being a specialty of and an appendage to computer science education. Computer science students that were already well-grounded in the discipline, got involved in SMART and other projects directed by Salton, worked and did research in the laboratory, completed their theses in areas related to IR, and participated in the legendary IR seminars.

They also published widely with Salton and with each other, and participated with high visibility in national and international conferences. From Harvard and Cornell, his students went to a number of computer science departments where they replicated Salton's model. Many other computer science departments in the U.S. and abroad took the same approach.

The strength of Salton's model is that it:

- "Starts from a base of a firm grounding in formal mathematical and other methods, and in algorithms, and
- Relates directly to research.

The weakness is in that it:

- Ignores the broader aspects of information science, as well as any other disciplines and approaches dealing with the human aspects that have great relevance to both the outcomes of IR research and the research itself, and
- Does not incorporate professional practice where these systems are realised and used. It loses users.

Consequently, this is a successful, but narrowly concen-trated education in IR as a specialty of computer science, rather then in information science. Not surprisingly, the researchers in the systems-centred approach came out of this tradition. The two educational approaches are completely independent of each other. Neither is connected to the other. Neither reflects fully what is going on in the field. While in each model there is an increase in cognizance of the other, there is no educational integration of the systems-and usercentered approaches.

APPLICATION IN INFORMATION SYSTEM

Internet is a global information system, consisting of billions of web pages from which we can get information. The major activity on the Internet, that is electronic publishing and information uploading, are being done in quiet an unorganized way.

The lack of proper organizing huge quantities of information has not retrieve from the Internet. In any information system, we have followed certain tools and techniques to tell us which document contains what information. These tools and techniques can be classification, cataloguing, indexing, etc., in the case of traditional information systems.

As Internet is a distributed information system with disjoint information sources spread across the globe, we cannot bring the related documents together in the retrieval process. Hence the tools and techniques meant for pinpointing information on the Internet need to be more accurate. XML is significant because it makes it much easier to share and search resources that are in different formats. Until fairly recently, this wasn't much of an issue for libraries. Historically, libraries have served as centralized repositories of information. They purchased books, journals, films, and other information resources on physical media, and patrons found what the library owned by consulting a catalogue that listed holdings. Most catalogs are designed with the assumption that once a library records some descriptive information about each resource it has purchased, this information won't have to be radically altered. For physical resources, this works pretty well, since the authors, titles, subjects, and physical characteristics of a book don't change. Once access to the Internet became widespread, it became clear that providing access to remote electronic resources could be very problematic. Catalogs are designed to provide access to physical resources that are under direct control of the library. However, people want to read journal articles, books, and useful Web pages stored in dynamically updated databases that are maintained and owned by other organizations that might be thousands of miles away. Online library catalogs are poorly suited for providing access to these works; so many libraries do not include these types of resources in the catalogue. As a result, it is often very difficult for patrons to know what electronic resources they can get t1hrough their libraries.

This is where XML comes into the picture. It is impossible to search or display information unless it is structured in a meaningful way. In plain English, this means that information providers need to agree on standards for encoding electronic documents so they can be retrieved in a uniform way. Libraries have encoded bibliographic records in MARC for many years, and that has allowed them to easily share catalogue records, which reduces costs while improving services. For a variety of reasons, it is not feasible to encode the new types of resources patrons want access to in MARC. However, when the information is stored in XML, it is possible to share and combine that data in ways that would not otherwise be possible.

INTERNET AND ITS' SEARCH ENGINES, SEARCH DIRECTORY AND META SEARCH ENGINES

There are many 'search engines'; 'meta search engines' and 'search directory' are available in the Internet. This is obvious from the two following important observations:

- The result of aparticular search is so high in recall and low in precision.
- The output of the search result has no standard of 2any kind.

The search tools on the Internet use robots to collect information about the documents to generate keyword indexes. Generally, these tools use different algorithms to assign keywords to the document. Some of the robots collect keywords from the title whereas some collect from the first few lines of the document. But the very pre-assumption of the search robots, that the titles are expressive and the beginning few lines of a document focuses the content, do not hold good for maximum documents. To give an example, if we search the Internet for term 'data', we should be sure to get results at least regarding 'database', 'data center', 'data warehouse', etc. Certainly the recall will be very high. The retrieval of irrelevant result can be reduced by subject gateway approach, but cannot be eliminated. The main cause of the problem in *Hyper Text Markup Language* (HTML), the standard for web publication is system-defined tag. This *'tag set'* is mainly for display of the content and HTML provides no tag to address the content precisely. *eXtensible Markup Language* (XML) designed by *World Wide Web Consortium* (W3C) promises a possible solution to this problem. The major advantage of XML over HTML is its extensibility, *i.e.*, provision of user defined tags and attributes to identify the structural elements of a document. XML also provides structural complexity to define document structure that can be nested at any level of complexity.

WHAT IS XML?

XML is a extensible markup language for documents containing structured information. Structured information contains both content and some indication of what role that content plays. Almost all documents have some structure. A markup language is a mechanism to identify structures in a document. The XML specification defines a standard way to add markup to documents.

XML IS JUST LIKE HTML

No. In HTML, both the tag semantics and the tag set are fixed. An <h1> is always a first level heading and the tag <ati.product.code> is meaningless. The W3C, in conjunction with browser vendors and the WWW community, is constantly working to extend the definition of HTML to allow new tags to keep pace with changing technology and to bring variations in presentation to the Web. However, these changes are always rigidly confined by what the browser vendors have implemented and by the fact that backward compatibility is paramount. And for people who want to disseminate information widely, features supported by only the latest releases of Netscape and Internet Explorer are not useful.

XML IS JUST LIKE SGML

No. Well, yes, sort of. XML is defined as an application profile of SGML. SGML is the Standard Generalized Markup Language defined by ISO 8879.

SGML has been the standard, vendor-independent way to maintain repositories of structured documentation for more than a decade, but it is not well suited to serving documents over the web. Defining XML as an application profile of SGML means that any fully conformant SGML system will be able to read XML documents. However, using and understanding XML documents *does not* require a system that is capable of understanding the full generality of SGML. XML is, roughly speaking, a restricted form of SGML.

WHY XML

It is important to understand why it was created. XML was created so that richly structured documents could be used over the web. The only viable alternatives, HTML and SGML, are not practical for this purpose. HTML comes bound with a set of semantics and does not provide arbitrary structure. SGML provides arbitrary structure, but is too difficult to implement just for a web browser.

Full SGML systems solve large, complex problems that justify their expense. Viewing structured documents sent over the web rarely carries such justification. This is not to say that XML can be expected to completely replace SGML.

While XML is being designed to deliver structured content over the web, some of the very features it lacks to make this practical, make SGML a more satisfactory solution for the creation and long-time storage of complex documents. In many organizations, filtering SGML to XML will be the standard procedure for web delivery.

ORIGIN AND GOALS

XML was developed by an XML Working Group formed under the auspices of the *World Wide Web Consortium* (W3C) in 1996. It was chaired by Jon Bosak of Sun Microsystems with the active participation of an XML Special Interest Group also organized by the W3C. Dan Connolly served as the Working Group's contact with the W3C. The design goals for XML are:

- XML shall be straightforwardly usable over the Internet.
- XML shall support a wide variety of applications.
- XML shall be compatible with SGML.
- It shall be easy to write programmes which process XML documents.
- The number of optional features in XML is to be kept to the absolute minimum, ideally zero.
- XML documents should be human-legible and reasonably clear.
- The XML design should be prepared quickly.
- The design of XML shall be formal and concise.
- XML documents shall be easy to create.
- Terseness in XML markup is of minimal importance.

HOW XML WORKS

In XML, *Document Type Definitions* (DTDs) may accompany a document, essentially defining the rules of the document, such as which elements are present and the structural relationship between the elements. DTDs help to validate the data when the receiving application does not have a built-in description of the incoming data. With XML, however, DTDs are optional. Data sent along with a DTD is known as 'valid' XML. In this case, an XML parser could check incoming data against the rules defined in the DTD to make sure data was structured correctly.

Data sent without a DTD is known as 'well-formed ' XML. With both valid and well-formed XML, XML encoded data is self-describing. The open and flexible format used by XML allows it to be employed anywhere a need exists for the exchange and transfer of information. This makes it powerful. For instance, XML can be used to describe information about HTML pages, or it can be used to describe data contained in business rules or objects in an electronic - commerce transaction, such as invoices, purchase orders and order forms.

XML is separate from HTML, but XML could also be added inside HTML documents. By embedding XML data inside an HTML page, multiple views could be generated from the delivered data, using the semantic information contained in the XML. Moreover, XML can be used for such compelling applications as distributed printing, database searches, and others. When most people think of the things that can be done with XML, they are actually thinking about a family of related technologies rather than a single markup language. On a related note, it is better to think of XML as a grammar than as a language. XML establishes rules for defining new formats. In regular markup languages such as the *HyperText Markup Language* (HTML), authors must use certain tags that make the text bold, create clickable links, draw tables, apply style sheets, etc. With XML, authors are free to make up their own tags and attributes if they don't feel that those that have been created by others meet their needs.

XML AND LIBRARIES

For years, libraries have been quietly using XML to perform functions such as improving access to archival materials, simplifying interlibrary loan processing, and enhancing digital collections, but increased reliance on the Internet for delivering information resources has brought XML into the mainstream, where its impact is starting to be felt by libraries of all sizes. As early as 1993, the library at the University of California- Berkeley started developing a method for encoding archival materials in XML. The outcome of this project was the development of the *Encoded Archival Description* (EAD) standard, which is now maintained by the Library of Congress. Use of EAD has been increasing steadily over the years as a growing number of archival finding aids have been moved to the Web. For the past several years, individual libraries have been improving their services and saving money by developing their own XML applications. Since 1998, Oregon State University has been using an application called *InterLibrary Loan Automated Search And Print* (ILL ASAP) to automatically search interlibrary loan requests and print request forms sorted by location and call number, complete with availability information, scannable Ariel addresses, shipping labels and billing data customized to the borrowing library or consortium involved. This free application has been adopted by dozens of libraries around the country. More-ambitious XML projects have also been successfully implemented.

The Washington Research Library Consortium uses XML to provide access to subscription databases, digital collections, materials requested via interlibrary loan, and library catalogs that run on a combination of commercial, open source, and locally developed platforms. This system, known as *Access to Library And Database Information Network* (ALADIN) not only delivers content to seven academic research libraries, but also performs critical related tasks such as patron authentication using XML messages transmitted between applications over the Web. In the spring of 2002, the Library of Congress announced an official specification for representing MARC data in an XML environment, MARC XML.

Even though sharing data between catalogs is relatively easy because of widespread support for the MARC format, the ability to express MARC data in XML is useful for any library trying to develop tools or access mechanisms that combine MARC data with non-MARC resources. Now that a standard has emerged for representing MARC, it is reasonable to assume that vendors and others will develop tools that take advantage of the huge amount of data already stored in MARC format.

As a matter of fact, within a few weeks of the announcement of LC's specification, well-known tools used for manipulating MARC records such as *Java MARC Events* (JAMES) and MarcEdit already contained support for the new standard.

As more libraries use XML, they are finding more uses for it. The eScholarship initiative at the California Digital Library not only uses XML to store books in a standardized format, but it also uses XML technologies to allow users to define their own displays. The *Open Archives Initiative* (OAI), an effort supported by OCLC, has developed a protocol that makes it easy to send a query to a database over the Web and receive the results in XML. OAI effectively makes it possible to perform searches of multiple databases simultaneously without the need for proprietary hooks into local databases. While this functionality is very similar to what was promised with Z39.50, OAI is much easier to implement, so the hope is that it will be widely used for many kinds of databases.

INFORMATION TECHNOLOGY-BASED LIBRARY SERVICES

New information technology can potentially support a range of traditional and Non-traditional library services. Most of the library services generated using information technology resemble closely to those generated manually with improvements and modifications to suit the requirements of automated services.

OPAC AND WEBPAC

Remote access to the Library catalogues (OPAC) was possible only through a telnet connection before the Web was launched. The web-based interfaces are now available for most of the integrated library software packages including Libsys. Web sites are increasingly providing links to their webPAC instead of telnet links to their Library OPAC.

Exploiting the provisions of hyperlinking that the web provides, various searchable elements of a bibliographic record in a webPAC are hyperlinks to other records in the database. For example, an author is a hyperlink to all records in the database for that author, a series is an hyperlink to all serial title under that series; a keyword for a record is a link to all records in database having that keyword,,etc. In effect, a web PAC adds softwarebased functionality to a conventional OPAC. A user has additional incentives to visit the library web page hosting webPAC.

With web-based resources and services in place, many libraries are phasing out their dumb terminals. The library web sites are increasingly becoming a more logical gateway to the catalogue and other web-based library resources. The acceptability of web-based interfaces to the Library OPAC is much greater because web interfaces are familiar to the users with its graphical and navigational interfaces. The users can click complex subjects instead of typing them or remembering complex commands.

INFORMATION ALERTING SERVICES

As the name implies, information alerting services or Current Awareness Services (CAS) are produced by the libraries for their users to alert them about new developments in a given field of study. Information alerting services are issues periodically by the libraries either for internal distribution amongst staff and employees or externally to other users.

The alerting service may be issued as a newsletter reporting new developments, programmes, forthcoming seminars and conferences, events, training programmes,,etc. It may also consist of recent additions of books and other documents in the library for a specified time period. Most library integrated system facilitate generation of such a service organised according to subject category for a given time period.

Alerting service may also consist of an indexing service issued by a library or a commercial publisher or a society that regularly indexes the contents of periodicals and some other publications systematically in a specified subject field. Such indexing services are issued at a regular interval. Abstracting services are essentially indexing services wherein an abstract of articles are included in addition to its bibliographic details. Index India and Reader's Guide to Periodical Literature are examples of indexing services. Biological Abstracts, Chemical Abstracts and Index Medicus are example of abstracting services. Most indexing and abstracting services are now available as web-based databases with sophisticated search interface.

Selective dissemination of information (SDI) is a personal form of Current Awareness Service (CAS). It refers to the mechanism of selectively directing new items of information from primary or secondary sources to individuals based on their current interests in a particular subject. SDI is delivered based on a user interest profile which is matched with updates on databases for finding the items of interest for a given user. Push technology or personalisation are more recent terms that are used in place of SDI.

DIGITAL REFERENCE SERVICE

Reference service and imparting instructional training to the library users are key areas of activities for any library. The technology now allows reference librarians to reach out to the users using the network instead of waiting at the reference desk for users to come by. Besides, imparting instructions on mechanisms of using a library, a reference librarian is also involved in delivering reference service that require deep intellectual understanding of subject.

Although automated libraries are not yet sufficiently advanced to offer interactive reference services, electronically-mediated reference services are increasingly available through libraries and information centres. Digital reference service, also called 'Ask-An-Expert' or 'Ask-A-Librarian' services are Internet-based question and answer service that connect users with individuals who possess specialised subject knowledge and skill in conducting precision searches. As opposed to static web pages, digital reference services use the Internet to place people in contact with people who can answer specific question and instruct users on developing certain skills. The people who serve as digital reference experts (also called volunteers or mentors) are most of the time information specialists, affiliated to various libraries.

LIBRARY CHAT ROOMS

Several libraries have started experimenting with offering real time digital reference service, using chat software, live interactive communication activities, call counter management software, web contact software, bulletin board services, interactive customer assistance system or related technologies. Many libraries are experimenting with Internet chat technology as an innovative method to extend and enhance traditional and remote reference service. While digital reference service is asynchronous method of information delivery, the

Internet chat providing the benefit of synchronous communication between a user and a reference librarian (or mentor). Interactive reference services facilitate a user to talk to a real, live reference librarian at any time of day or night from anywhere in the world. Unlike with e-mail reference, the librarian can perform a reference interview of a sort by seeking clarifications from the user. The librarian can conduct Internet searches and push Web sites onto the patron's browser, and can receive immediate feedback from the patron as to whether his or her question has been answered to his satisfaction. Most libraries currently involved in real-time reference service are part of a collaborative network so that they can share staffing and work around the clock to truly provide reference service any time. Library of Congress Collaborative Digital Reference Service is one of such services.

Several institutions including Cornell University, Internet Public Library, Michigan State University and North Carolina University are offering Internet chat-based services using software like LivePerson, AOL Instant Messenger, Conference Room and Netscape Chat. The librarians have observed that their relatively new chat-based service logged significantly more questions in a relatively short time than their well-established e-mail digital reference service. LiveRef(sm) maintains an online registry of real-time digital reference services.

ELECTRONIC DOCUMENT DELIVERY SERVICES

The term 'electronic document delivery systems' implies delivery of electronic version of a document that might involve reproduction of an electronic copy of a document if it is not available in electronic format. The libraries had been using fax machines for immediate delivery of photocopies of articles via telephone lines.

The first use of electronic document delivery was based on scanning technology. With maturity of scanning equipment and technology, document supply services started scanning the documents as bitmap page images. Applications are built in such a way so as to automatically produce a hard copy together with a header page containing the address of the applicant which can again be send by snail mail or facsimile. A software package known as 'Ariel' is used in several libraries in developed countries for delivery of scanned articles via Internet.

The Ariel software is loaded on an Internet-enabled computer, can receive and send electronic information to other libraries which have installed Ariel. Availability of most of the peer reviewed research journals in electronic format, inexpensive technology to scan articles and improved electronic delivery mechanisms are some of the enabling factors that have contributed to well-established electronic document delivery system now available commercially. More recently most of the secondary services that were available on CD ROM or through online search services are now available on the Internet where the bibliographic references are linked to their full-text on the publisher's site. The technology has now been perfected and there are several electronic document delivery services that allow a user to download an article in full-text from their site or deliver them electronically as attachment to e-mails. Most electronic publishers and aggregators like OCLC, OVID,etc., are offering full-text of articles through their web sites. Different vendors have various payment options; some charge each time the journal is used, whereas others provide open access for a set annual fee. A user who wishes to have the item delivered can enter a credit card number and specify a delivery method (postal, UPS, fax, e mail,,etc.,) and indicate whether it is a rush item (with a rush order fee attached.) The ADONIS (Article Delivery Over Network information Systems) can be considered as a landmark development in electronic document delivery system. The project was launched by a consortium of five major publishers - Academic Press, Blackwell's Scientific Publications (merged with Wiley InterScience), Elsevier Science Publications, and Springer Verlag.

The project uses combination of laser scanning, printing and digital optical storage technology for storage and retrieval of complete pages of over 650 scientific, technical and medical journal articles. The issues of journals are available on CD ROM with weekly updates for distribution to each centre in various countries licensed to use the system for document delivery.

LIBRARY WEB SITES

Libraries are using web technology to create home pages as starting points or as gateways for searching information about the library. A home page reflects characteristics of an academic institution.

It provides an opportunity to the library to propagate its services and facilities to the academic community worldwide. The home pages of libraries are increasingly used as an integrated interface designed to deliver detailed information about a library as well as to provide access to all computer-based services offered by a library.

Several library web sites facilitate virtual guide to the physical facilities including collections, services and infrastructure available in the library through their web sites. Most library web sites provide library layouts and floor plans to guide users to physical location of facilities and services along with link to relevant information. Besides offering information, the library web sites of academic institutions invariably hosts subject gateways or subject portals that contains links to web resources for subjects of interest to the institution. Most of the IT-based library services mentioned in this article are offered through the web sites of libraries. The library web sites can have features like have Frequently Asked Questions (FAQ) along with their answers, library calendar listing events or show information for forthcoming events, Web forms for inviting feedback. Moreover, libraries may also use bulletin boards, threaded discussion forum and listservs to help promote and evolve web-based library services.

WEB-BASED USER EDUCATION

The www provides a dynamic environment for distributing information over a large network and web-based instructions is a suitable tool to do so. Web-based guides and teaching tools can be easily updated, accessed, and printed on demand. They may include colour graphics and screenshots. The web-based user education provides a high degree of interactivity and flexibility to the users offering them the benefit of self-pace, graduated to teach from basic to highly advanced levels and designed in a wide range of formats that accommodate diverse learning styles.

The proliferation of digital resources will generate greater demands on reference and instructional services. With availability of digital resources that can be used anywhere at any time, requirement for instructional and reference services would also grow. Failure to develop both the technological aspects and required service components would lead to under utilisation of digital resources. The library web sites can use web-based user education for imparting training to users in the following areas:

- Basic library skills along with glossary of library terms;
- Using Library OPAC/ webPAC, locating books, magazines and other library materials;
- Instructions for searching CD ROM and web-based databases and other electronic resources; and
- Instructions on subject searching training, using Boolean operators and searching Internet resources through search engines.

The web technology provides for incorporating both synchronous and asynchronous interactivity in the web-based user education.

INFORMATION EXPLOSION AND THE DIRECT RELATION OF INFORMATION TO DEVELOPMENTS

The present information explosion and the direct relation of information to developments in all walks of life emphasizes the need to give greater priority to the planning of systems which give library and information services to the people. Such systems can only be planned at national levels, if the total information resources of the nation is to be pooled together in a federal country like India, and shared between the cons-tituent states to make it available to all the users who require it in an equally and unbiased way at optimal cost.

Such library and information systems are to be founded upon sound legislation, if they are to attain their objectives the Society's information need has become so imperative that, many of the national and international library organizations has started to stress the urgent need for national library systems working together and sharing their services and materials at international level to provide better services to the people. Better can be defined here in quantitative and qualitative terms. Such national level and international level networking and resource sharing between library systems make possible service at lower cost, convenience of access, access to more materials and more rapid availability of materials.

PREAMBLE OF STATE ACTS

The preamble of a Library Act should summarise and state the aims and objectives of that Library Act. Even though the preamble of KPLA went on to explain the existing situations and the intentions with which the Act was initiated in an elaborate and vague form, it has given what is to be in preamble just before the preamble in precise and clear words as a long title ofthe Act. This summary or long title of the Act which we have to consider as preamble contains the basic concept of modern public library service which the actual preamble failed to state and the KPLA in its totality failed to support.

Like the Model Act, this summary provides for the establishment and maintenance of a system of public libraries and for the comprehensive development and organisation of all kinds of library and information services required for the people. The long title that follows the title of the Act in KPLA states, it is: An Act to consolidate and unify the library laws in the State and to provide for the reorganisation of the entire library system in the State of Kerala with a view to the develop-ment and maintenance of a comprehensive rural and urban library service and for matters connected therewith or incidental thereto.

Ranganathan has laid clear emphasis on legislation for public library service and for the organisation of a comprehensive library system. But all other Acts except KPLA provides for establishment and maintenance of public libraries only. They all cling to the obsolete concept of treating public libraries as independent units in their collection and services. So in this statement of the purpose of the Act, KPLA has accepted the most modern concept of Public Library legislation and the statement is a distinct improvement over those in all other existing State Acts.

THE MODEL ACT OF S.R. RANGANATHAN

To attain these objectives Dr. S.R. Ranganathan had framed the first model public libraries Act in 1930 which he placed for discussion at the Educational Conference at Banaras. Before framing the Act, this internationally reputed library scientist had travelled through most countries of the world where library legislation existed and had evaluated them and in many countries his ideas helped them to improve the systems.

In his Library Development Plan which he submitted in 1947 to Government of India he had included a union library bill and a revised state library bill also which envisaged the national public library and information system according to the most modern principles. Another model library Act was drafted in 1963 by a committee under the chairmanship of D.M. Sen on behalf of the Ministry of Education, Government of India. In 1966 the Library Legislation Sub Committee of the Planning Commission also prepared a model bill. The library Acts that came into existence in Madras, Hyderabad, Andhra, Karnataka and Maharastra totally or partially accept the ideas of Rang ana than as reflected in his Model Acts and bills. These States became the laboratories where the ideas evolved by Ranganathan were experimented and observed.

In the light of these observations and suggestions contained in the other model bills and Acts, Ranganathan has improved his model Act by rectifying the clauses found to be defective in working and by adding new provisions that seemed essential. This model libraries Act was published in 1972. This is the latest and most advanced Model Act. Ten States out of the 25 States and 7 union territories have enacted library legislation. They are Madras 1948, Andhra 1960, Karnataka 1965, Maharastra 1967, West Bengal 1979, Manipur 1985, Kerala 1989 and Haryana 1989.

Others are Goa and Mizoram. But none of them are considered perfect or efficient. So in this comparative analysis of the essential aspects of State Public Library Acts, the Model Public Library Act, 1972 of Dr. S.R. Ranganathan is taken as the measuring rod or ideal situation with which the State Act is compared. Whenever some notable additional provisions or improvements are found in other existing Acts the same is discussed at the concerned contexts. The Kerala Act to which stress is given in this study and Ranganathan's Model Act of 1972 will be referred herein after as KPLA and Model Act respectively.

PURPOSE AND ADVISING OF STATE LIBRARY COMMITTEE

The Model Act provides for a *State Library Committee* (SLC) for the purpose of advising the SLA on all matters arising under the Act. All existing State Acts and Model Bills enacted or drafted in India provide for appointment of such a Committee or Council. KPLA names it as Kerala State Library Council. All Acts of the states except Kerala's have prescribed its membership on somewhat similar lines. All Acts provides that this body will be headed by Minister for Education. Despite differences in nomenclature and composition the function of this committee or council envisaged everywhere is basically the same *i.e.,* to advise the SLA or State Government in all matters arising out of the Act.

Kerala State Library Council (KSLC)

A careful analysis of the Kerala State Library Council (KSLC) in comparison with the SLC as provided in the Model Act or other State Acts will reveal that it is not a councilor committee of advisory nature as SLCs are. KSLC is an

SLC and at the same time an SLA by itself. Naming it as a council is a difference in terminology only. Instead of appointing a Minister as SLA as in Mysore it appoints a body as SLA. But the Act fails to name it as SLA. The duties, powers and functions assigned to KSLC is inclusive of all those assigned to SLA and SLC in Model Act.

Sub-section 1 of the Section 3 of KPLA dealing with the constitution and composition of KSLC states9; KSLC shall be a body corporate having perpetual succession and a common seal with power, to acquire hold and dispose of property, both movable and immovable and to enter into contracts and shall by its name sue and be sued. This is an adaptation of the class related to Karnataka State Library Authority of Karnataka Act. No other Act including Model Act has so clearly defined the nature of this body and assigned so much powers as this like the Acts of Kerala and Karnataka. The powers and functions assigned to KSLC includes both the advisory functions of the committees and councils provided by Model Act and other Acts and the duties assigned to SLA by Model Act and Karnataka Act.

Sub-sections of section 8 of KPLA provides that the KSLC may:

- Advise the government of all matters connected with the administration of that Act and... the overall library policy of the State.
- Co-ordinate the working of the District Library Councils and Taluk Library Unions and...supervise and direct all matters relating to library service in the state.
- Establish one or more State Libraries... at such place or places in the State as may be considered necessary.
- Appoint and control such officers and servants as may be necessary for the efficient performance of its duties and functions under this Act and the rules made there under.
- Give to the District Library Councils and Taluk Library unions directions in the performance of their functions under this Act and... they shall not in-the discharge of their functions under this Act depart from directions given by the KSLC.

While we consider these classes and compare them with the parellel sections of the Model Act or other Acts it becomes clear that the classes which assigns the duties, powers and functions of KSLC is a distinct improvement from all others. KPLA has identified most of the functions and duties expected from such a body and very clearly assigned them to it without giving space for doubt and vagueness.

Composition of KSLC

If KSLC is to become able to fulfil such duties and functions expected from it, the composition of the body should be done accordingly. Membership of such a body should include persons who have contributed to the growth of knowledge, who has evolved or developed methods and techniques for collecting, organising and disseminating information and who have wide experience in related fields of activity. It is not the method of representation but the quality of representation that will make possible the efficient functioning of the system.

The sections which prescribe the membership of SLA in Karnataka Act and SLC in Model Act and other State Acts prescribe their membership on somewhat similar lines. Prof. P.B. Mangla in his study of library legislation opines that it should be a body having representatives from various institutions, organisations, government etc. interested in and connected with the growth and development of library and information services in the State.

The Model Act, the opinion of experts and recommen-dations of committees set for studying library legislation agrees that such a body should include among its members; the Minister for Libraries if there is one, otherwise Minister for Education, then Minister in charge of Local-Self-Government, Director of Libraries, State Librarian, sufficient number of representatives from State Legislative Assembly by election from among themselves, Secretary to Government for Education, representatives elected from Local Library Authorities by rotation to limit size of the body, representatives of associations of library profession and experts with specialization in library and information services and represen-tatives of Universities of the State. It would be essential that the Minister in charge of Libraries should act as *ex-officio* chairman and the Director of Public Libraries or State Librarian should act as ex-officio secretary of the committee.

The rationale behind such a composition of this body is that it is a body which is to advise the government and discuss continuously on a most important responsibility of the government, that is organisation and dissemination of information required by the society. But disregarding all these principles KPLA provides for constituting a body of members who were not suitable to undertake this work. The section 3 sub-section (2) related to the composition of the KSLC in KPLA provides: The KSLC shall consist of one member each from Taluks, elected by the general body of the District Library councils, and five members of whom one shall be a librarian, another a person belonging to the scheduled caste or scheduled tribe and another a woman nominated by the government. Library and information service is an intellectual service. It goes without saying that this body as provided in KPLA will not be able to fulfil satisfactorily the purpose for which it is intended.

In these days of information explosion and flooding of vast and varied types of books and other printed materials that originates every minute without wide familiarity of all spheres of knowledge and expertise in handling their information in most effective way at minimum cost the body which heads such a system will be having a mere formal and useless existence. As we have seen in section 8 of KPLA the most important function of KSLC is to advise the government on all matters connected with the administration of this Act and overall library policy ofthe State. It is not clear how this committee will be competent to render such expert technical advise when it has only persons as members, who has come through election without expertise or knowledge about information work and without even any educational qualifications. Library and information service to the peopleif provided efficiently will be the continuously active service of government and will require expert advise everyday on many matters. The KSLC's inability to provide such expert advise will make government's efforts futile and to overcome this, govern-ment will be forced to create a continuous chain of Advisory Committees which is also not very practicable. While no hard and fast rule can be laid down about the size of this body it is generally felt that it should not have more than twenty members.

The KSLC may remain a supreme body in name only for real powers of the council have been passed over to a smaller body which is the executive committee. But it also becomes an unwieldy body with membership of 25 persons. Thus KSLC has acquired all the defects existing in SLAs and SLCs into one body. This Executive Committee is a new addition in our library Acts. But the findings of Ashok Mehta Committee and various committees appointed by many State Governments to study Panchayat Raj Institutions advise us against such an elected body like KSLC for organising important service as library and information service to the people. Instead of adopting the constitution and composition of SLA and SLC provided by the Model Act or followed by the other State Acts KPLA gave legal sanction to the organi-zational set up of an association that was already existing there, that is Kerala Granthasala Sangham.

The constitution and composition of KSLC and its Executive Committee is the same followed by Sangham for its general body and Bharanasamithi. In all other provisions KPLA follows the same pattern of Sangham with some minor alterations. For more than half a century Sangham was pressurizing the Government to give legal sanction to Sangham to be the SLA and to accept its system as it is,as State's Library System. But experts have continuously pointed out during this period the futility of such a system for library and information service. But Sangham objected government's all other attempts to enact a modern library system legislation and at last come out successful in legalizing its own system. But this in fact totally prevents the State from having an advanced library legislation and developing its library and information services in conformity with the requirements of the time.

CONCEPT OF THE STATE LIBRARY AUTHORITY

The concept of the *State Library Authority* (SLA) underwent an evolution from State Library Committee to Minister of Education or Libraries; everywhere in the world. The Model Act recommends that for the purpose of promoting and organising a library system in the State the Ministry for

Education of the State shall be the SLA. It shall be the duty of the SLA to provide; for an adequate library and information service in the State and, for the progressive development of the institutions devoted to the purpose and to secure the effective execution by *Local Library Authorities* (LLA) of the national policy for providing adequate library service to the people in every locality. In the existing' State Acts only Karnataka Public Library Act, 1965 provides and clearly names SLA.

The Act provides for the constitution and composition of the SLA.6 SLA shall be a body corporate having perpetual succession and a common seal with power, to acquire, hold and dispose of property and to contract and may by the same time sue and be sued. It consists of twenty members from the fields concerned with information creation, organisation and services, with Minister for Education who shall ex officio be the President and State Librarian who shall ex officio be the Secretary of SLA. But it is desirable to make only one person, instead of a corporate body to be the supreme authority for providing this very important service, for that gives a unified command from administrative points of view. And this person should not be any person less than the Minister for Education, because he is directly responsible to the legislature and his term of office being limited to a period of five years he is ultimately responsible to the people. Hewit who made a study of the library legislation in India; it will be observed that two kinds of supreme authority are favoured in existing legislation and in the drafts of the model bills framed in India. One is a body of persons *i.e.,*

State Library Councilor Committee and second is a Minister of State. He suggests the second as the better of the two, mainly because a Minister is responsible to his legislature, and through it, to the electors and many be called to account therein. A body of persons even though a Minister may be President or Chairman thereof is not so easily questioned.

In any case; so important an activity as the provision for public library and information service to the people fully justifies direct representation in State Legislature. So all the studies on library legislations and the evaluation of existing legislations throughout the world and especially in third world counties, like that of Gardners's study comes to the conclusion that providing up of a body or a person as SLA and clearly naming and defining its powers and functions is certainly essential for the successful working of library Acts. But KPLA is very vague in this aspect and it fails to name a person or body as SLA.

DEPARTMENT OF PUBLIC LIBRARIES AND OFFICIALS

It is generally emphasized that in order to develop a system of public libraries in a State or country on proper lines, it is essential that a separate department of public libraries be created at par with the department of education and that the former should not be a part of the later or any other' department.

The Acts of Andhra, Maharashtra, West Bengal and Karnataka prescribe for the creation of separate department of Public Libraries.

Director of Public Libraries

Most of the recommendations related to public library system legislation emphasizes that the department of Public Libraries should be headed by a Director of Public Libraries (DPL), whose rank must be equivalent to that of Director of Education. He must be a person with qualification and experience in Library and Information Science. Emphasis on his being a professional is laid because it is he to whom the whole public library system in the State would look for guidance and inspiration and his professional outlook would normally greatly help the development of the system on desired lines.

The first public library Act in this country; the Madras Public Library Act, 1948 provided for the appointment of DPL. Andhra, Maharastra and West Bengal also prescribes for the creation of DPL. In Madras and Andhra the Director of Public Instruction is made the ex-officio Director of Public Libraries also.

The disadvantages of such an administrative set-up are quite obvious. The Department of Public Libraries becomes an additional burden to the Director of Public Instruction. This new department will be looked upon as an uninvited guest. A. R. Hewit has rightly pointed out that many of the duties of Director of Public Libraries would require technical knowledge and skill in librarianship. So professional experts only can undertake this responsibility efficiently.

State Library

All the Acts except KPLA which is not providing for these offices, combines the responsibilities of developing and managing the State Central Library Superintending and directing all matters related to the State library system in a single person called State Librarian or DPL. The Model Act also recommends this pattern. But the Sinha Committee report suggested the creation of two separate posts for this purpose when it said "The DPL may have the overall responsibility to organize develop and supervise the public library system as the Head of the Department of Public Libraries. The State Librarian should have the responsibility to manage supervise and develop State Central Library and should be the Chief Technical Advisor of the DPL, with no responsibility for the administration of the service in the State. This responsibility should be entirely that of DPL. But in KPLA there is no provision for appointing a Director of Libraries or State Librarian. While the class by class discussion of the Bill was going on in Assembly Mr. V.M. Sudheeran; member presented an amendment to add a new clause in the Act providing for appointment of a Director of Libraries. But was not considered.

Administration

For the administration of public libraries all the State Acts have created a department or directorate of public libraries. It is put under the charge of Director of Libraries or State Librarian who is to be the *ex-officio* Secretary of SLA. The functions of these posts as prescribed by all Acts including the Model Act are: to supervise and direct all matters relating to public libraries, to direct and control the working of LLAs, submit reports to Government and deal with schemes and plans relating to libraries. Many of the highly technical and specialized works of State Central Library also is to be supervised by them.

So it is clear that these posts which are carrying heavy responsibility concerning various matters-financial, advisory, administrative, technical, supervisory and so on-under the Act would require technical knowledge and skill in library and information service. So the Secretary or High Officer of this body should be a whole time officer having the prescribed qualifications to practice the library profession. Disregarding all the facts KPLA assigns all these duties and powers to a Secretary elected by members of the Executive Committee ofKSLC. Section 3 sub-section (5) of KPLA provides that the elected members of the Executive Committee shall elect a President, Vice-President, Secretary and Joint Secretary from among themselves to be the President, Vice-President, Secretary and Joint Secretary respectively of the State Library Council and of the Executive Committee. Their term of office will be for three years.

KPLA assigns to the Secretary of KSLC the duties and powers which other State Acts assign to State Librarian or Director of Libraries. Section 9 Sub-section (1) States: the Secretary of the State Library Council shall be Chief Executive Authority of KSLC.

The nature of the office of Secretary of KSLC requires professional knowledge and experience as well as continuity of office for the successful operation of the Act, so it is inevitable that this provision will prevent KPLA from fulfilling the objectives for which a modern library legislation should exist. This serious defect of the Act has been pointed out by many members during the discussion of the bill. Dr. M.Kuttappan has brought to the notice of the Assembly that such an important system like that for library and information service requires qualified government officials as their secretaries at State, District and Taluk levels. The period of an elected Non-official member may be over by three years and if he misappropriates government fund allotted for library development it will not be possible for the government to take action on him. Sri Ishac Kurikkal suggested an amend-ment to the Bill to provide that the Secretary of the SLC shall be appointed by the Government on the advice of the Kerala Public Service Commission. Another member Sri Kodiyeri Balakrishnan opined that the Secretary of KSLC should be appointed by Government and the Act should specify the qualifications and method of appointment for this post. Sri Ramesh Chennitthala presented an amendment to add the following sub-clause in KPLA namely: The Secretary shall be a person not below the rank of a Joint Secretary to Government appointed by Government from among persons qualified and competent to hold such post. But all these suggestions were rejected and principles were disregarded to maintain a democratic system for constituting the SLA.

Library Co-operation

To make the best possible use of the document resources not only in the public library system but also in other types of libraries in the State such as universities, special libraries etc, a system of inter library co-operation needs to be developed in the state as a whole. It would also be useful and economical if centralization of different aspects such as acquisition programme, technical processing etc. of documents should be introduced at State level or at different levels of the system. The KPLA gives no such provision for co-operation or centralized processing and the institution which is to give leadership in such activities that is SCL is absent in KPLA.

State Central Library

The existing State legislations and the Model Act provide for a State Central Library (SCL) as an integral part of the Public Library Service. The SCL is normally the copy right collection. It should collect as far as its resources allow, expensive work and literature published abroad, material for which the local public library would have little need and could not afford. All the countries of the world possessing adequate library systems, have national library systems and all have national central library as distinct from the other libraries in the system, but is accessible to all through any library of the system.

The same role of National Central Library to the National system is done by SCL to the State system. Usually the library legislations designate the biggest collection available in the State as SCL and makes its resources and services available to the system. Even though various Acts and Model Act give different names to SCL like State Service Library, etc. in a public library system only one such library will be maintained and its resources will be shared by all participating units. Maintaining more than one SCL is unnecessary duplication of work and waste of resources.

Most of the State Acts and Model bills drafted, designate the biggest public library existing in the State as SCL and adopts it to the system and shares its resources among participating units. But instead of designating Trivandrum Public Library, the oldest and biggest collection in the State as SCL, the KPLA deems it to be one of the many State libraries it will establish.

The Act provides for no SCL in its system. Instead it provides that KSLC shall establish one or more state libraries at such place or places in the State as may be considered necessary. The relation of State libraries with other state libraries and different level service units and the purpose of more than one such institution is not defined in the Act.

Bibliography

A.A.N. Raju: *Facets of Library and Information Science*, Ess Ess Publications, Delhi, 2012.

Ajit Singh: *Siwatch Encyclopedic Dictionary of Library and Information Science, Vols. I to III*, Shree Publishers, Delhi, 2010.

Amjad Ali: *Ane's Encyclopedic Dictionary of Library and Information Science*, Ane Books India, Delhi, 2006.

B S Aggarwal: *An Introduction to Library and Information Science*, ABD Publication, Delhi, 2005.

B. Rajasree and P. Aravinda: *Glossary of Library and Information Science*, Anmol Publication, Delhi, 2010.

C Lal and K Kumar: *Descriptive Questions in Library and Information Science,* Ess Ess Publication, Delhi, 2010.

C.R. Karisiddappa: *Current Studies in Library and Information Science*, Manak Publication, Delhi, 1994.

G. Devarajan: *Applied Research in Library and Information Science*, Ess Ess Publication, Delhi, 2005.

H.K. Srivastava: *Foundation of Library and Information Science*, Mohit Publication, Delhi, 2011.

I.M. Goswami: *Encyclopaedia of Library and Information Science (5 Vols-Set)*, Commonwealth Publication, New Delhi, 1997.

Jogender Singh Burman: *Encyclopaedic Survey of Library and Information Science : Principles and Practices (5 Vols-Set)*, Rajat Publication, Delhi, 2006.

K.A. Isaac: *Glimpses of Library and Information Science*, Ess Ess Publication, Delhi, 2001.

Krishan Kumar And Jaideep Sharma: *Library And Information Science Education In India*, Har-anand Publications, Delhi, 2009.

Kundan Godia: *Electronic Services in Library and Information Science*, Adhyayan Publication, Delhi, 2007.

L.S. Ramaiah: *Images and Perceptions in Library and Information Science*, Ess Ess Publication, Delhi, 1998.

Mahendra Kumar Seth: *A Guide to Library and Information Science Jobs*, Abhijeet Publications, Delhi, 2006.

Mahendra Singh Sodhi: *Advancement in Library and Information Science*, Adhyayan Publication, Delhi, 2006.

P.S.G. Kumar: *Foundations of Library and Information Science: Paper 1 of UGC Model Curriculum,* B.R. Publishing Corporation, 2012.

Poonam: *HRD in Library and Information Science*, ACE Books, Delhi, 2010.

Punit Ralhan: *Advancement in Library and Information Science*, Oxford Book Company, Delhi, 2009.

Raghunath Pandey and M.N. Velayudhan Pillai: *History of Library and Information Science*, Jnanada Prakashan, Delhi, 2011.

Shiv Ram Verma: *Foundations of Library and Information Science*, Shree Publication, Delhi, 2005.

T. Nasirudheen: *A Comprehensive Course in Library and Information Science*, Ess Ess Publications, Delhi, 2012.

Tariq Ashraf and Sanjay Kumar Jha: *Handbook of UGC Net for Library and Information Science*, Bookwell, 2008.

Vaishali Khaparde: *Advancement in Library and Information Science*, Ess Ess Publications, Delhi, 2012.

Y.L. Chopra and Mamta Chopra: *Challenges Before Library and Information Science in New Millennium*, Ess Ess Publication, Delhi, 2001.

Index